contenders

Spring/Summer 2006

Cover image and incidental drawings by John Pham

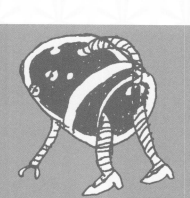
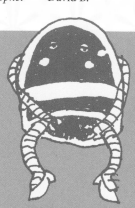
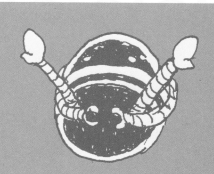

MOME 4: SPRING/SUMMER 2006
Published by Fantagraphics Books, 7563 Lake City Way NE, Seattle,
Washington, 98115. MOME is copyright © 2006 Fantagraphics Books.
Individual stories are copyright © 2006 the respective artists. All
rights reserved. Permission to reproduce material from the book,
except for purposes of review and/or notice, must be obtained from
the publisher. Edited by Eric Reynolds and Gary Groth. Designed
by Jordan Crane and Adam Grano. Production assistance by Paul
Baresh. Promoted by Eric Reynolds. Published by Gary Groth and
Kim Thompson.

First edition: June 2006. ISBN 10: 1-56097-726-4.
ISBN 13: 978-1-56097-726-1. Printed in Singapore.

SUBSCRIBE TO MOME:
Save 10 dollars per year off the cover price.
Rates for a four-issue subscription are as follows:
$49.95 U.S. & Canada only
$54.95 for global surface mail
$69.95 for global air mail

Each issue is carefully boxed prior to being shipped. To subscribe
using your Visa or MasterCard, call us toll-free at 1-800-657-1100 or
visit our website: WWW.FANTAGRAPHICS.COM. Otherwise, send U.S.
check or money order to: MOME SUBSCRIPTIONS, c/o Fantagraphics
Books, 7563 Lake City Way NE, Seattle, WA 98115 USA.

For a free catalog of comics and cartooning, please telephone at
1-800-657-1100 or consult WWW.FANTAGRAPHICS.COM.

STILL AVAILABLE:
MOME SUMMER 2005 (VOL. 1)
MOME FALL 2005 (VOL. 2)
MOME WINTER 2006 (VOL. 3)

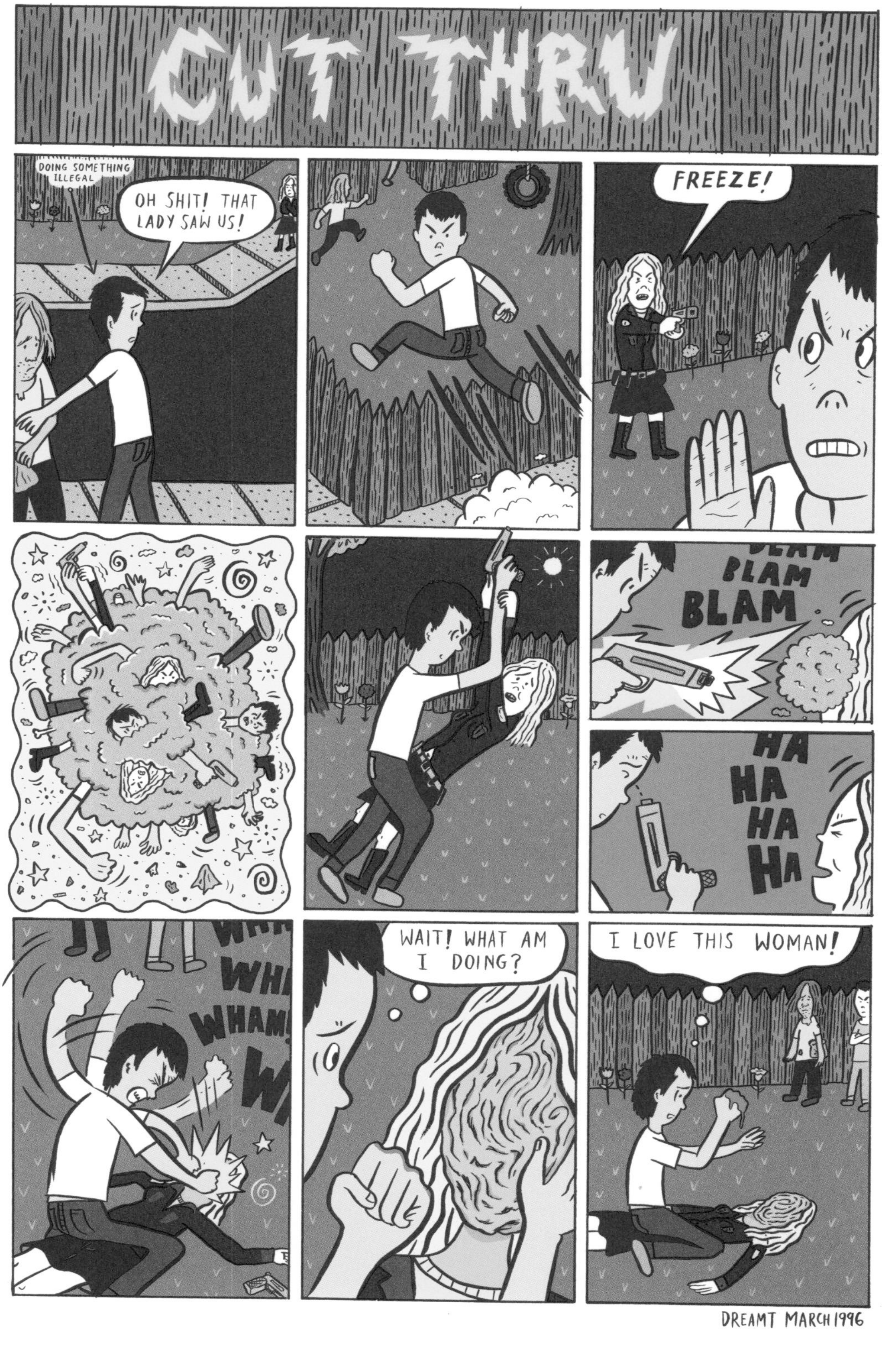
CUT THRU
DOING SOMETHING ILLEGAL
OH SHIT! THAT LADY SAW US!
FREEZE!
BLAM BLAM
HA HA HA HA HA
WHAM
WAIT! WHAT AM I DOING?
I LOVE THIS WOMAN!

DREAMT MARCH 1996

EDITORS' NOTES:

a. Welcome to the fourth issue of MOME (following MOME WINTER 2006). The next volume will be titled FALL 2006 and appear in August or so. Please stick around.

b. This issue features the last MOME installment of John Pham's *221 Sycamore Street*. Future *221* stories will appear in Pham's upcoming comic book series for Fantagraphics, SUBLIFE.

c. David Heatley's *Overpeck* will conclude in MOME WINTER 2007 (Vol. 6).

d. *The Veiled Prophet* originally appeared in the French anthology, LAPIN, published by L'Association, and is published here in English for the first time, with a translation by Kim Thompson.

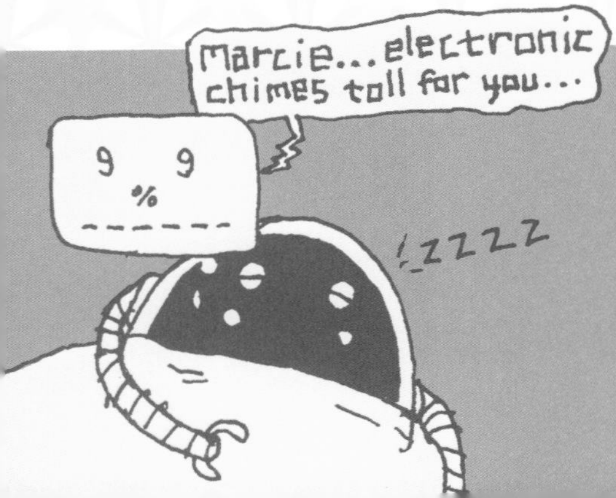
marcie... electronic chimes toll for you...
9 9
%
ZZZZ

[redacted]

THE FOLLOWING IS A [redacted] STORY I DID SEVERAL YEARS AGO, AFTER FINISHING SCHOOL AND MOVING TO SAN FRANCISCO AND WONDERING WHAT THE HELL I WAS DOING. AS AN ARTIST OR A CARTOONIST OR WHATEVER I WAS. I EVENTUALLY WENT BACK TO IT AS A STARTING POINT FOR WHAT BECAME DOGS AND WATER. IT'S A TRANSITIONAL PIECE BETWEEN THE INSTALLATION WORK I WAS (MOSTLY) DOING IN SCHOOL, AND THE CARTOONING I EVENTUALLY COMMITTED TO. A COUPLE OF YEARS AFTER THAT I STARTED GRAD SCHOOL IN CHICAGO AND MET THIS CUTE GIRL ACCROSS THE HALL WHO WAS STARTING A SMALL ART PRESS. WE STARTED WORKING ON DOING THIS PIECE AS A BOOK... BUT THEN WE GOT ROMANTICALLY INVOLVED AND THE BOOK SOMEHOW GOT SIDETRACKED. THE STORY IS CALLED 'NOTHING SO FAR'. IT'S APPEARING HERE, IN MOME, FOR CHERYL.

—ANDERS NILSEN 2006

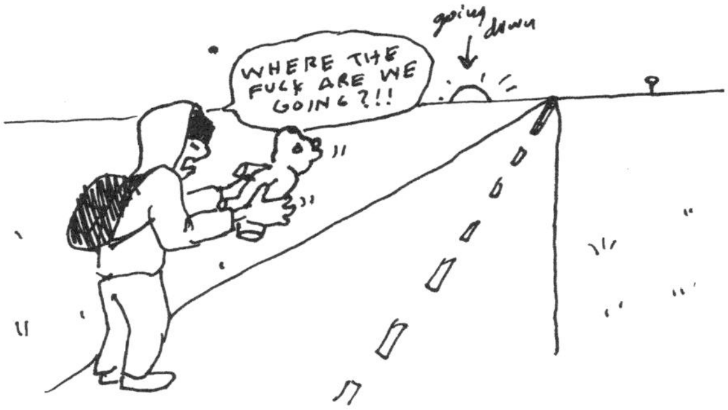
WHERE THE FUCK ARE WE GOING?!!
going down

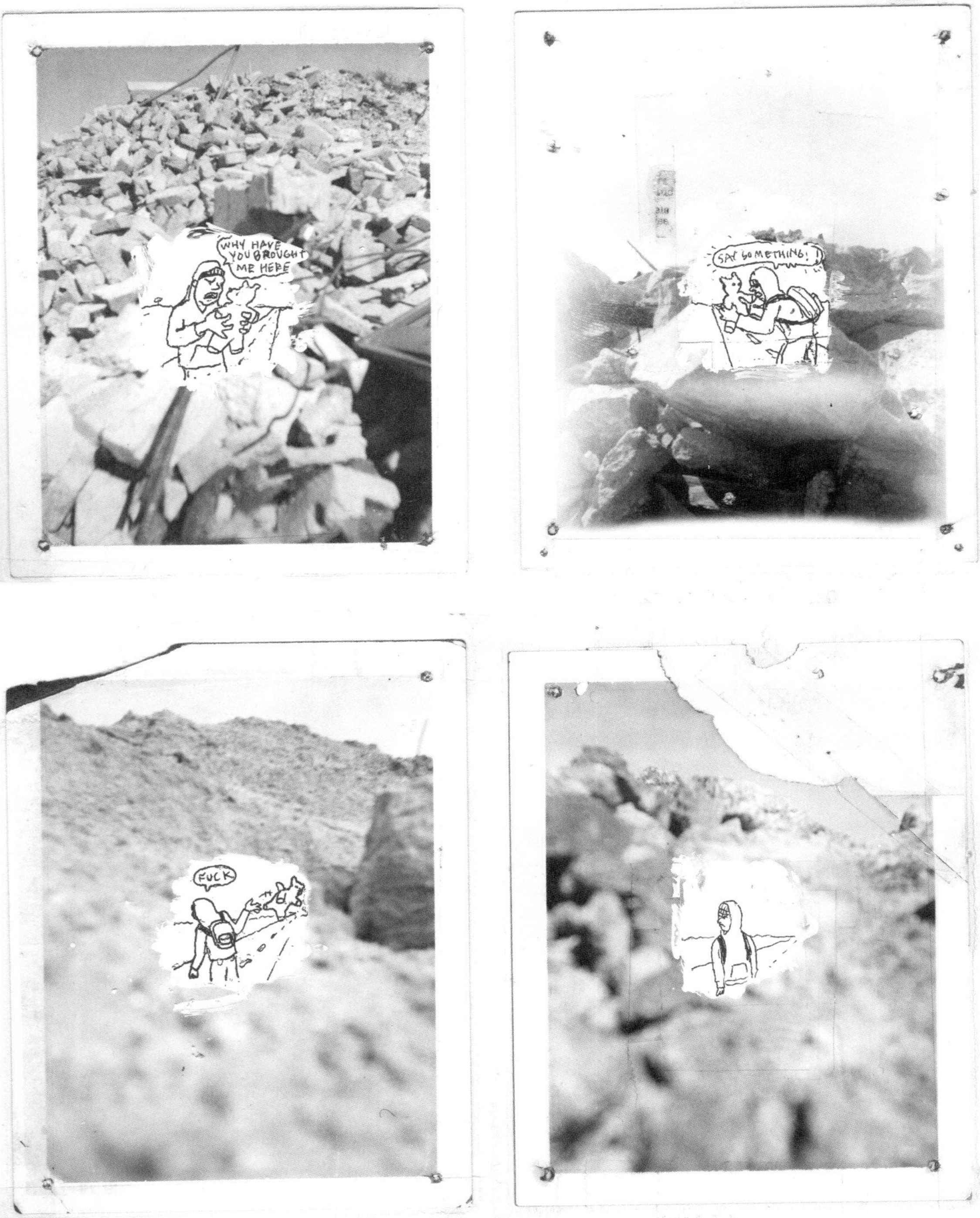
WHY HAVE YOU BROUGHT ME HERE
SAY SOMETHING!
FUCK

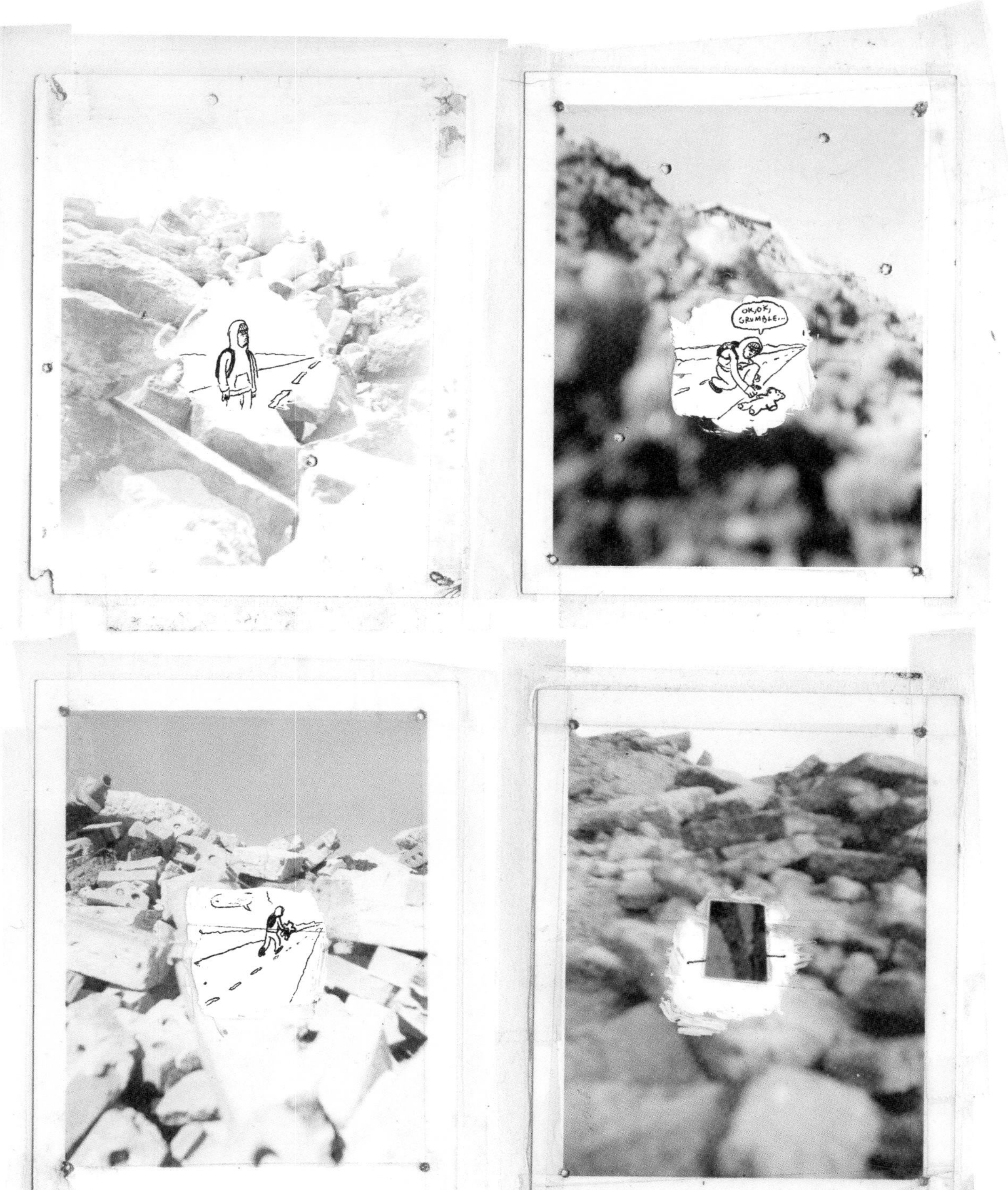
OK, OK, GRUMBLE...

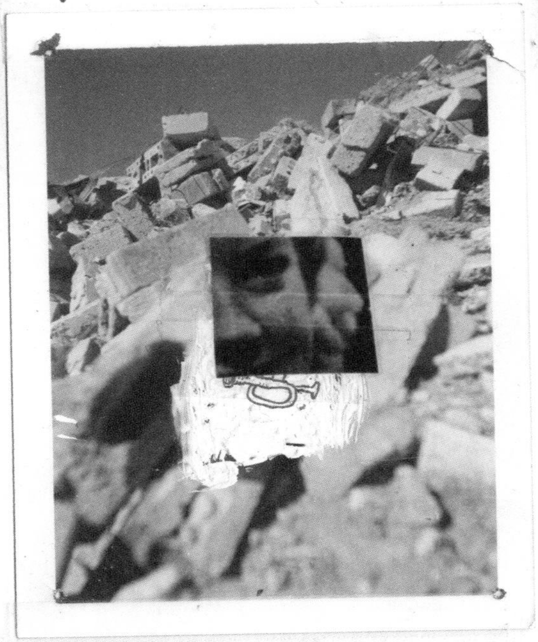

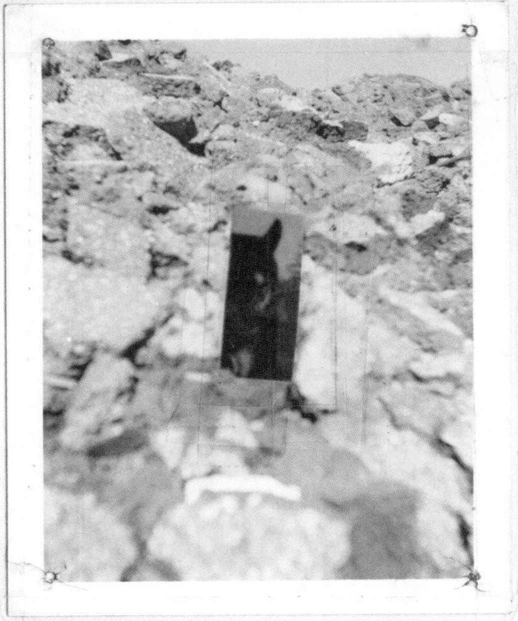

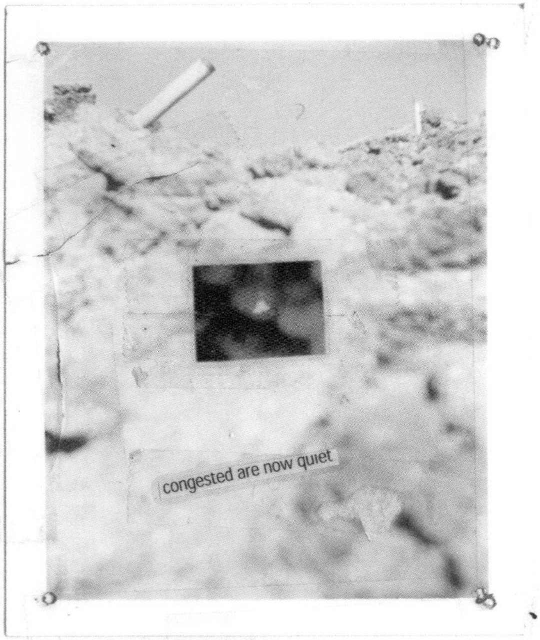
congested are now quiet

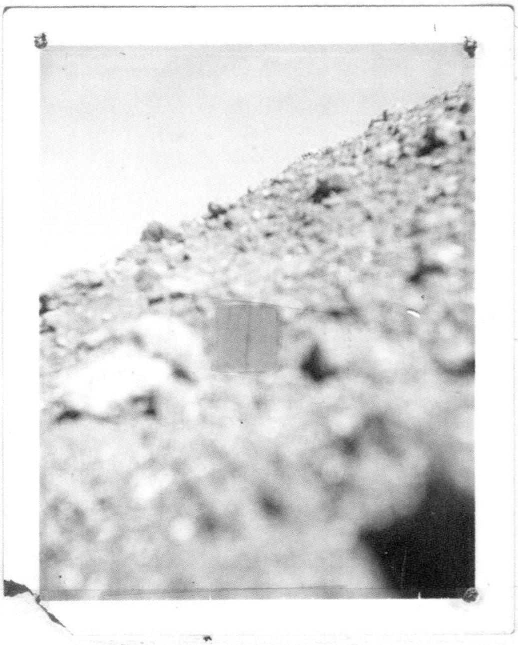

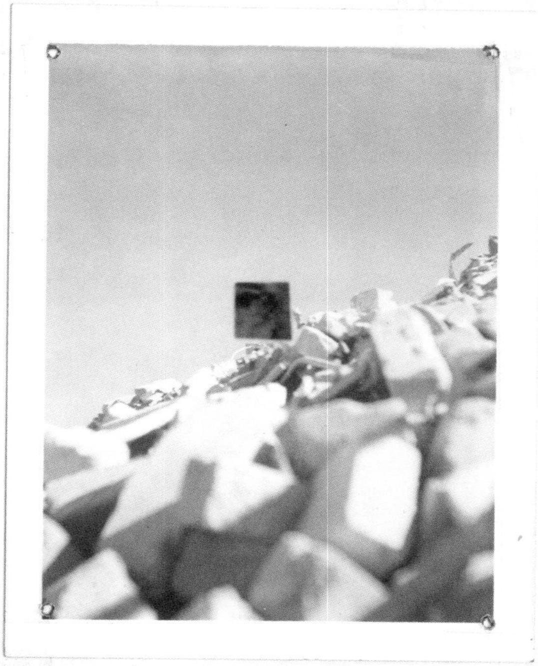
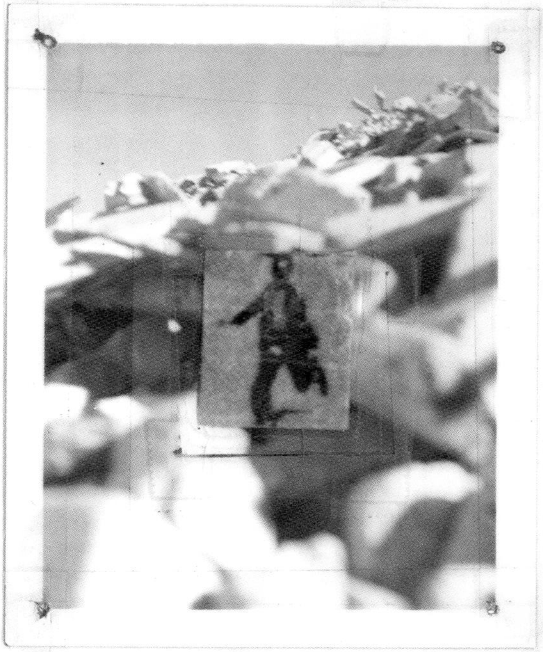
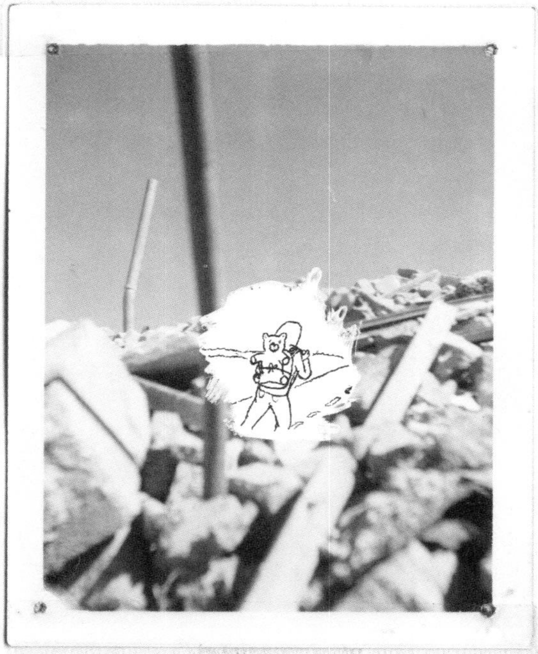
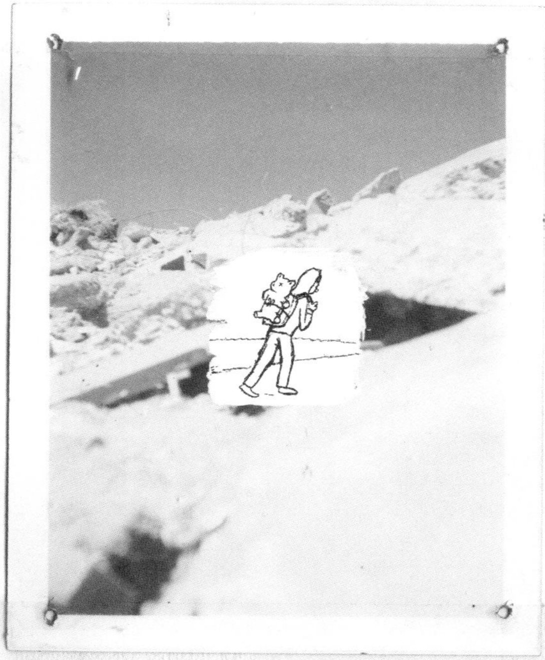

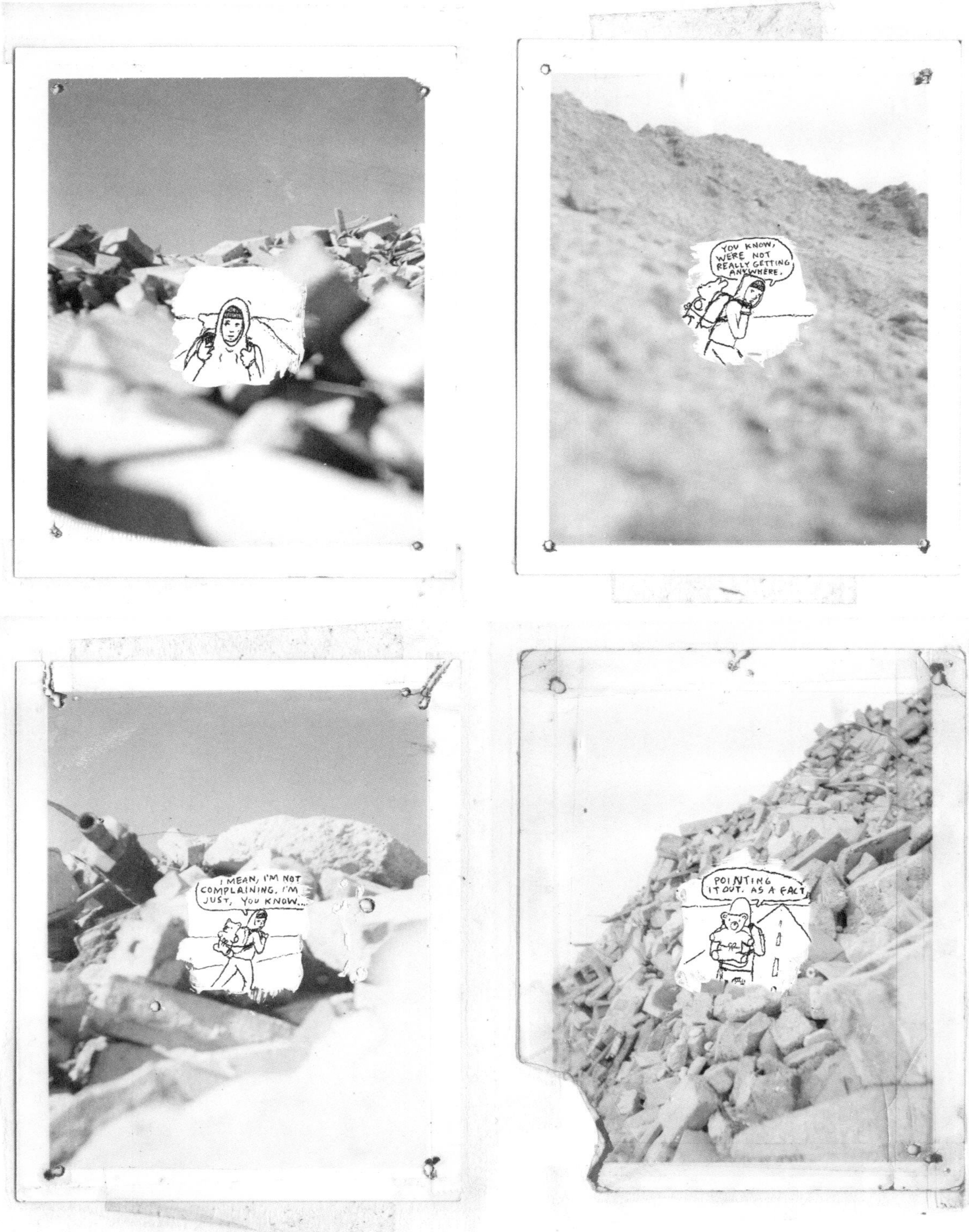
YOU KNOW, WERE NOT REALLY GETTING ANYWHERE.
I MEAN, I'M NOT COMPLAINING. I'M JUST, YOU KNOW...
POINTING IT OUT. AS A FACT

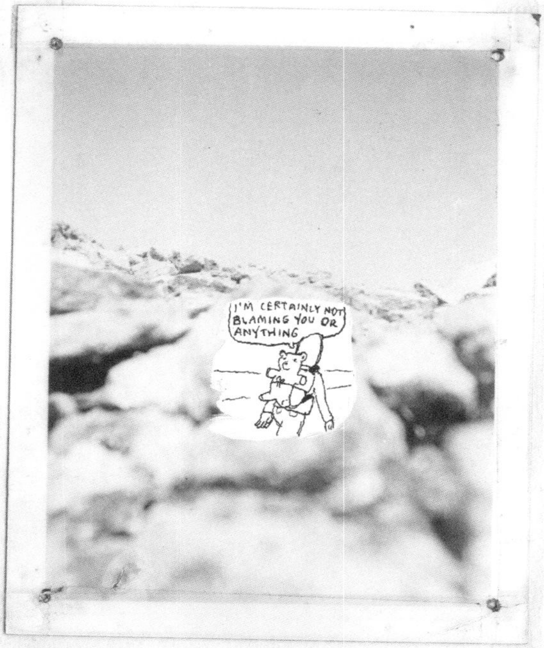
I'M CERTAINLY NOT BLAMING YOU OR ANYTHING

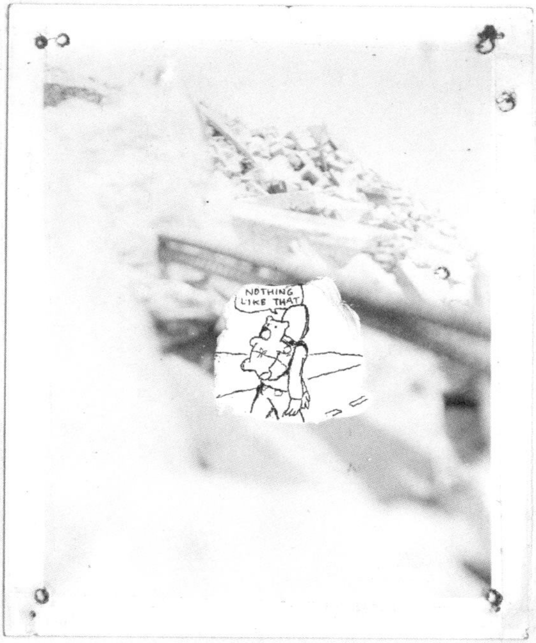
NOTHING LIKE THAT

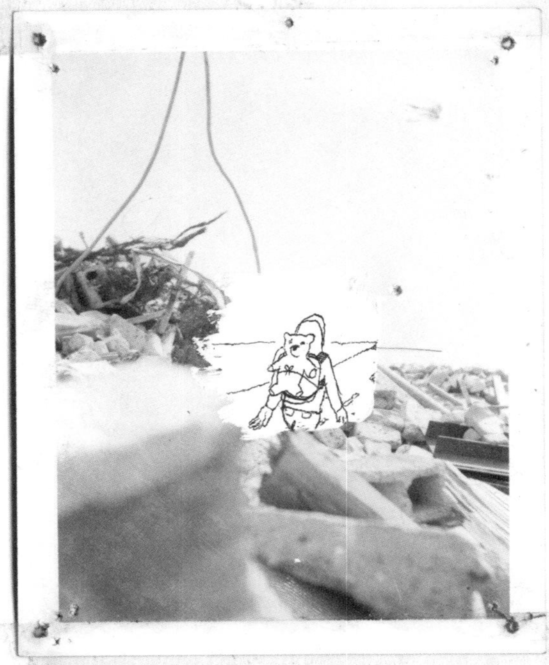

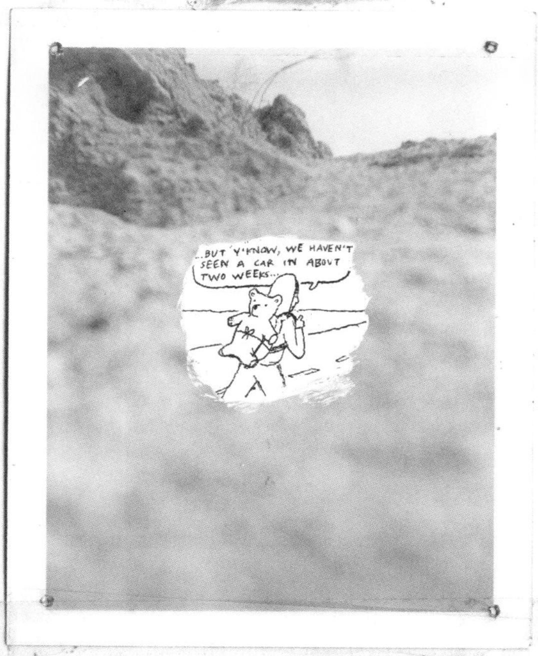
..BUT Y'KNOW, WE HAVEN'T SEEN A CAR IN ABOUT TWO WEEKS...

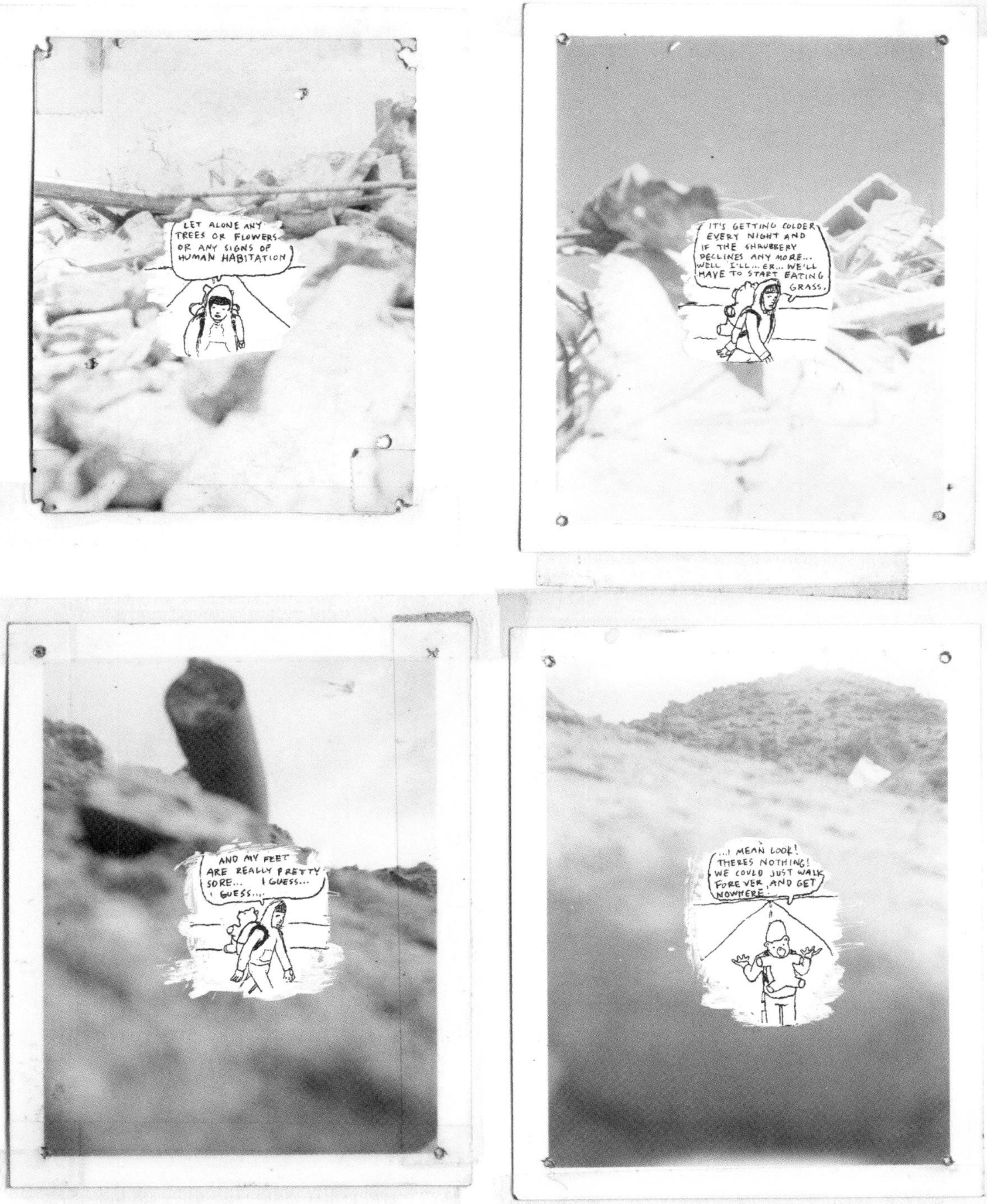
LET ALONE ANY TREES OR FLOWERS OR ANY SIGNS OF HUMAN HABITATION
IT'S GETTING COLDER EVERY NIGHT AND IF THE SHRUBBERY DECLINES ANY MORE... WELL I'LL... ER... WE'LL HAVE TO START EATING GRASS.
AND MY FEET ARE REALLY PRETTY SORE... I GUESS... I GUESS....
...I MEAN LOOK! THERES NOTHING! WE COULD JUST WALK FOREVER, AND GET NOWHERE.

I MEAN, MAYBE IF WE WERE TO TURN AROUND NOW...
WE...UH...
NEVERMIND.

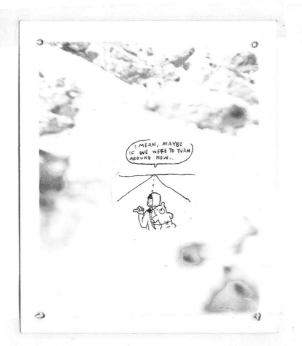

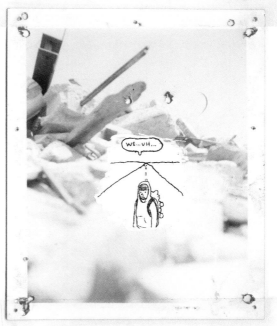

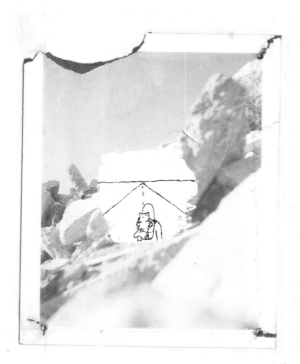

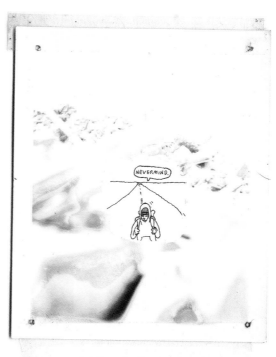

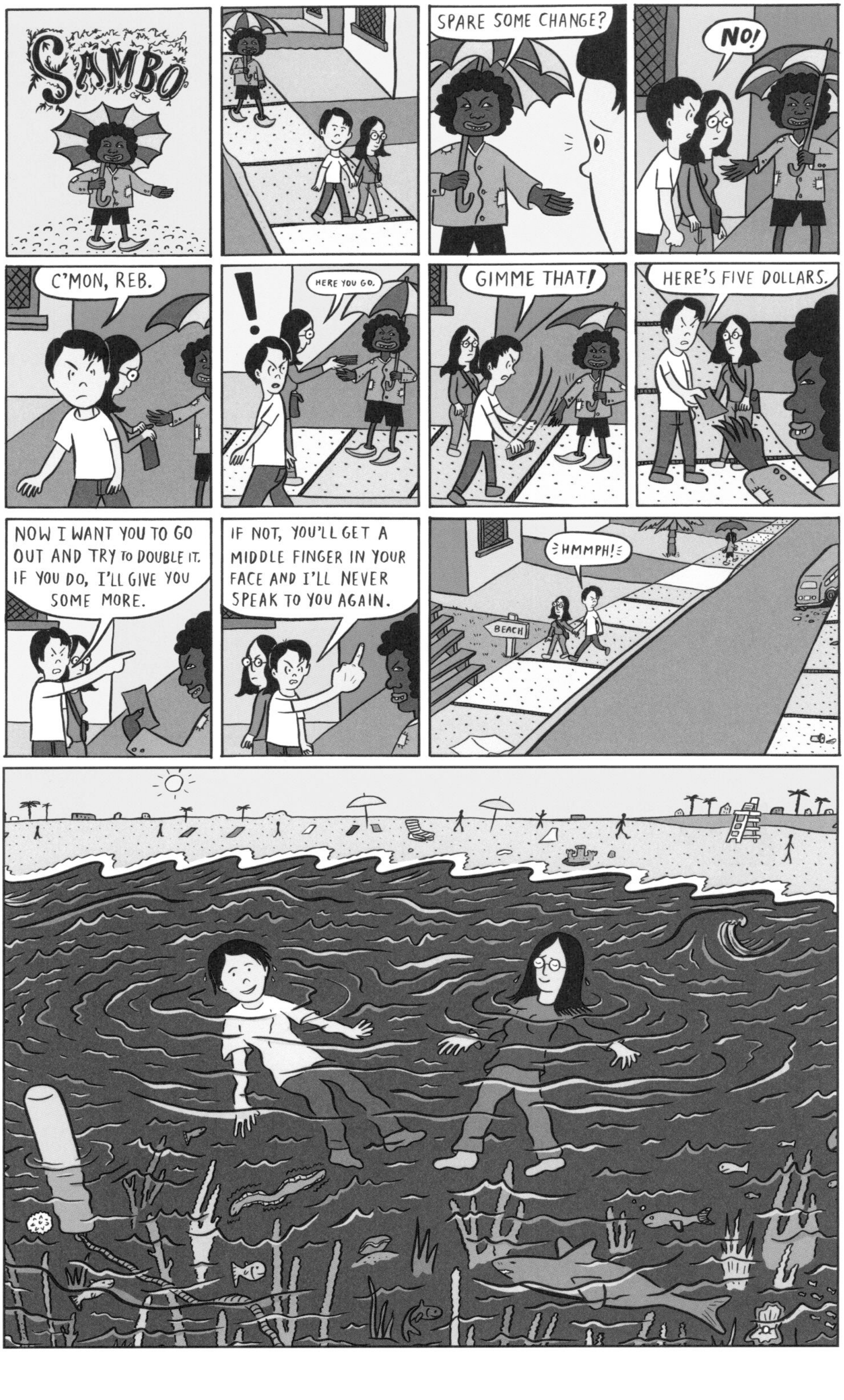
SAMBO
SPARE SOME CHANGE?
NO!
C'MON, REB.
!
HERE YOU GO.
GIMME THAT!
HERE'S FIVE DOLLARS.
NOW I WANT YOU TO GO OUT AND TRY TO DOUBLE IT. IF YOU DO, I'LL GIVE YOU SOME MORE.
IF NOT, YOU'LL GET A MIDDLE FINGER IN YOUR FACE AND I'LL NEVER SPEAK TO YOU AGAIN.
HMMPH!
BEACH

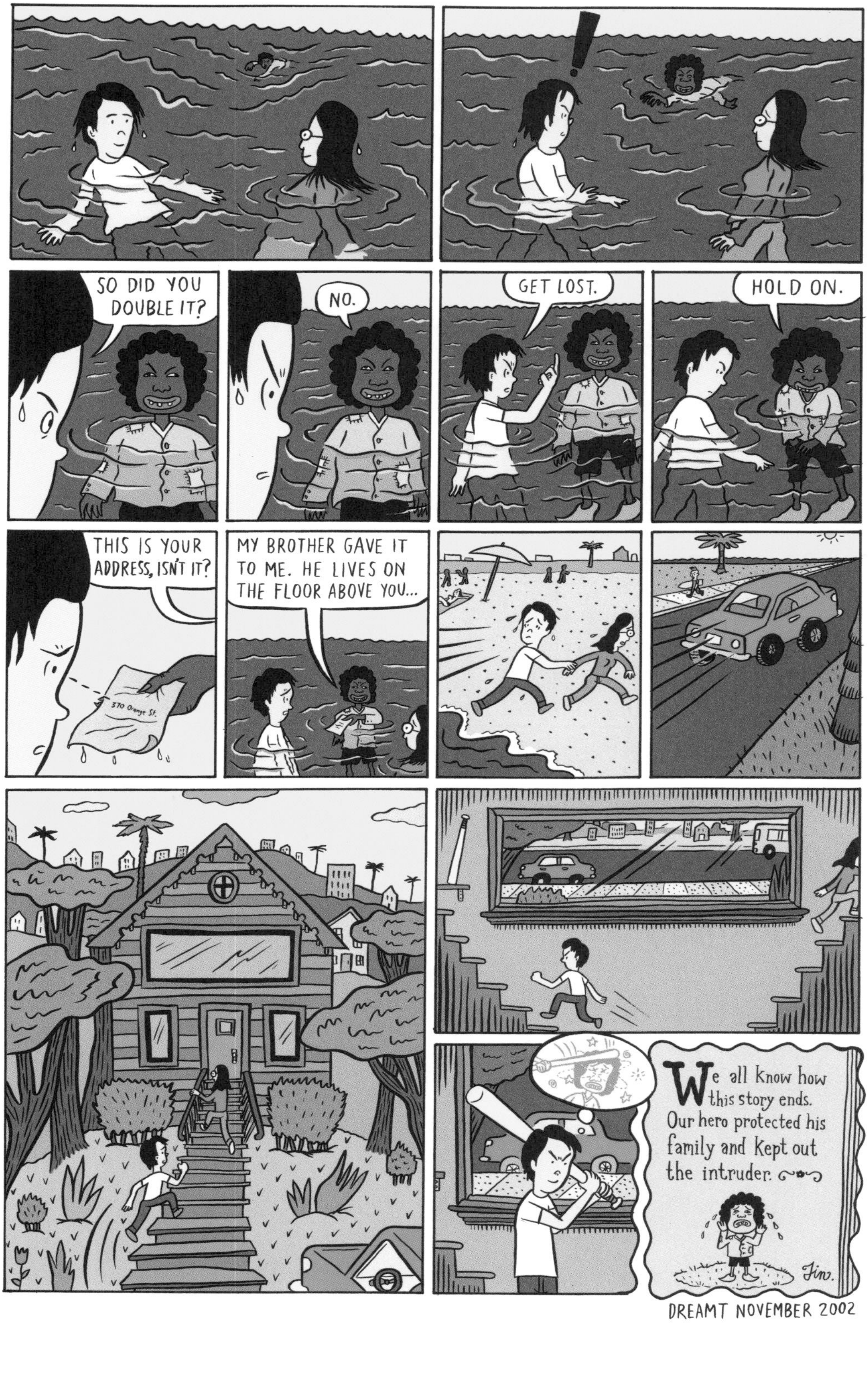
SO DID YOU DOUBLE IT?
NO.
GET LOST.
HOLD ON.
THIS IS YOUR ADDRESS, ISN'T IT?
370 Orange St.
MY BROTHER GAVE IT TO ME. HE LIVES ON THE FLOOR ABOVE YOU...
We all know how this story ends. Our hero protected his family and kept out the intruder.
Jin.
DREAMT NOVEMBER 2002

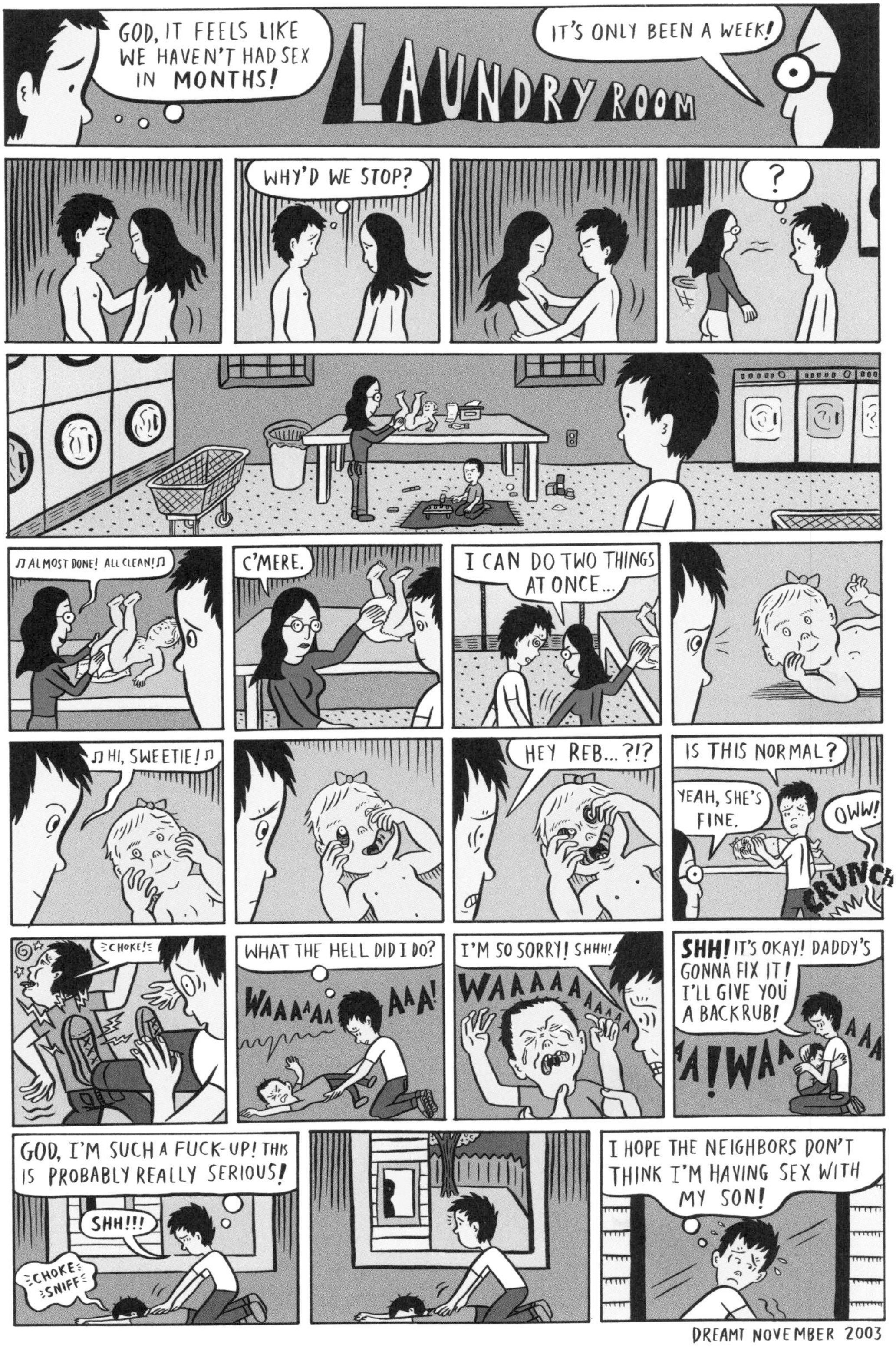
LAUNDRY ROOM
GOD, IT FEELS LIKE WE HAVEN'T HAD SEX IN MONTHS!
IT'S ONLY BEEN A WEEK!
WHY'D WE STOP?
?
♫ ALMOST DONE! ALL CLEAN! ♫
C'MERE.
I CAN DO TWO THINGS AT ONCE...
♫ HI, SWEETIE! ♫
HEY REB...?!?
IS THIS NORMAL?
YEAH, SHE'S FINE.
OWW!
CRUNCH
CHOKE!
WHAT THE HELL DID I DO?
WAAAAAA AAA!
I'M SO SORRY! SHHH!
WAAAAAAAAAA
SHH! IT'S OKAY! DADDY'S GONNA FIX IT! I'LL GIVE YOU A BACKRUB!
AAA
A!WAA
GOD, I'M SUCH A FUCK-UP! THIS IS PROBABLY REALLY SERIOUS!
SHH!!!
CHOKE SNIFF
I HOPE THE NEIGHBORS DON'T THINK I'M HAVING SEX WITH MY SON!
DREAMT NOVEMBER 2003

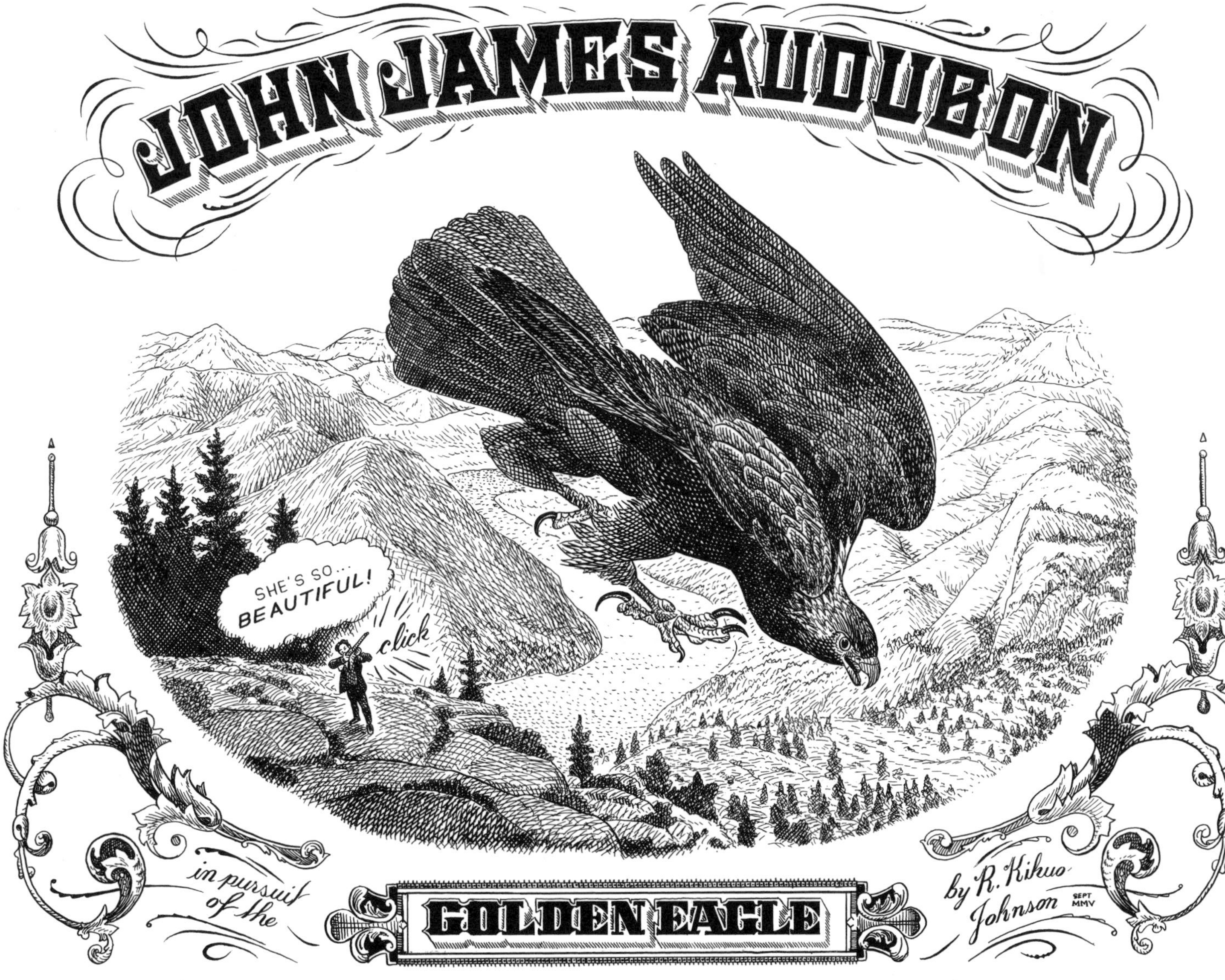

JOHN JAMES AUDUBON
SHE'S SO... BEAUTIFUL!
click
in pursuit of the
GOLDEN EAGLE
by R. Kikuo Johnson
SEPT MMV

England was especially smitten by the flamboyant American frontiersman who emerged at the height of the continent's Romantic Era.

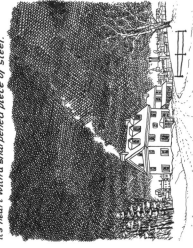

This method, which to Audubon seemed the most humane, afflicted everyone in the house except the bird, and after two unsuccessful days, he reluctantly pierced its heart with a sharpened piece of steel.

In fact, he purchased a live Golden Eagle in Boston in 1833. By then, the first volume of "Birds of America," his mammoth collection of 435 life-size engravings, had been published, and Audubon's fame was gaining momentum.

But, in an age before photography, taking the bird's portrait meant taking its life. In the end, he conceded to asphyxiate his prisoner by enclosing it over a smoldering pot of coal.

We know Audubon (1785–1851) did not obtain his specimen this way, but ever the myth-maker, this is the version his drawing records.

For days, he studied the eagle, agonizing over "how pleasing it would be to see him spread out his broad wings and sail away towards the rocks of his wild haunts."

Shaken but determined, he immediately set to work, arranging the corpse on mounting wires.

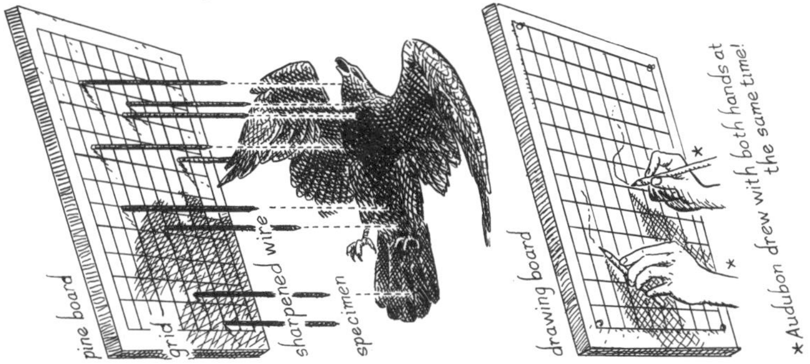
pine board
grid
sharpened wire
specimen
drawing board
*
*
* Audubon drew with both hands at the same time!

Across fourteen days, he worked with such frenzy that he had a seizure.

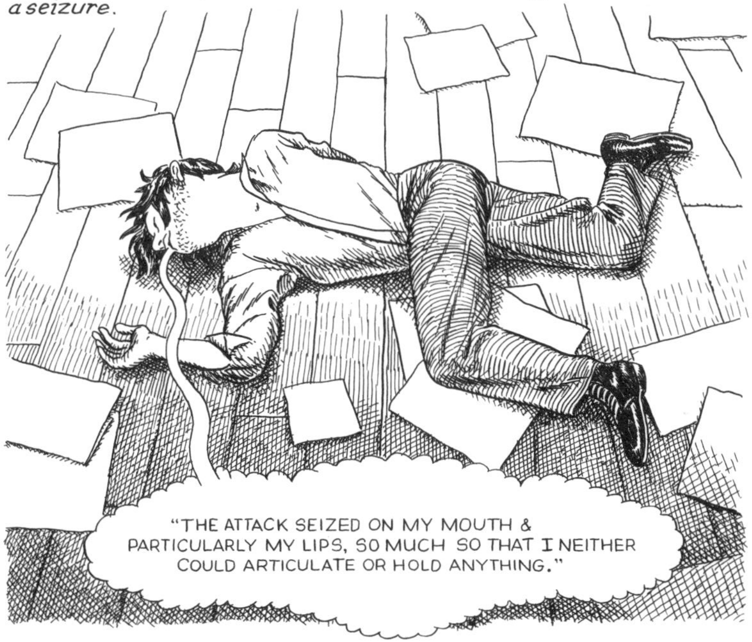
"THE ATTACK SEIZED ON MY MOUTH & PARTICULARLY MY LIPS, SO MUCH SO THAT I NEITHER COULD ARTICULATE OR HOLD ANYTHING."

He would recover, but the finished drawing retains the ferocity with which it was produced. The image is unique in Audubon's catalogue in its inclusion of a tiny self-portrait.

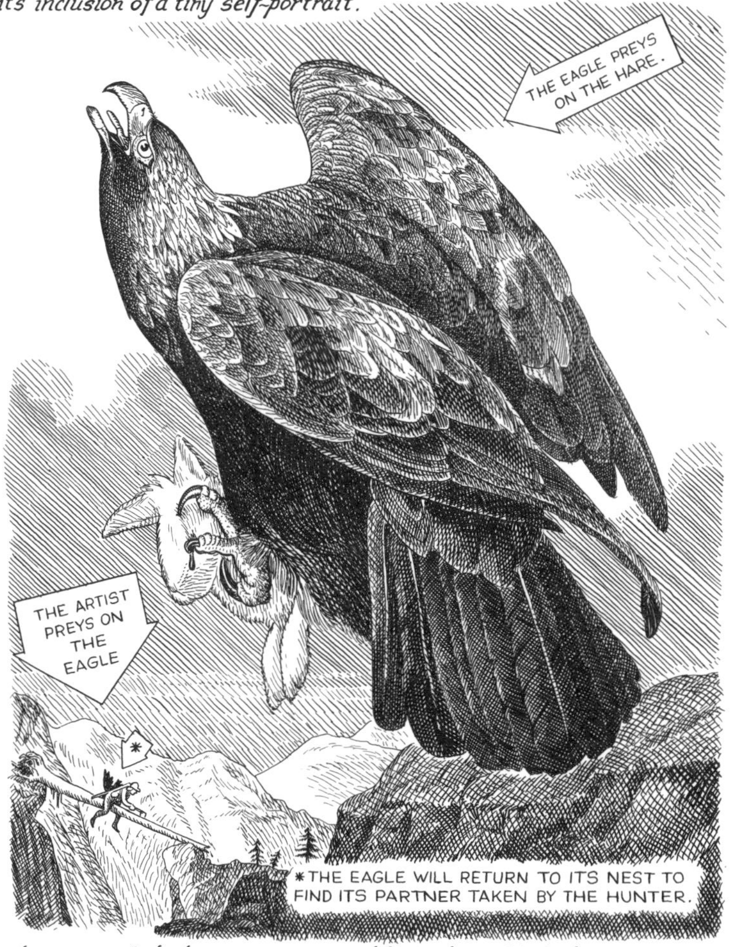
THE EAGLE PREYS ON THE HARE.
THE ARTIST PREYS ON THE EAGLE
*
* THE EAGLE WILL RETURN TO ITS NEST TO FIND ITS PARTNER TAKEN BY THE HUNTER.

The image of the hunter was omitted from the published version, perhaps having been judged too allegorical.

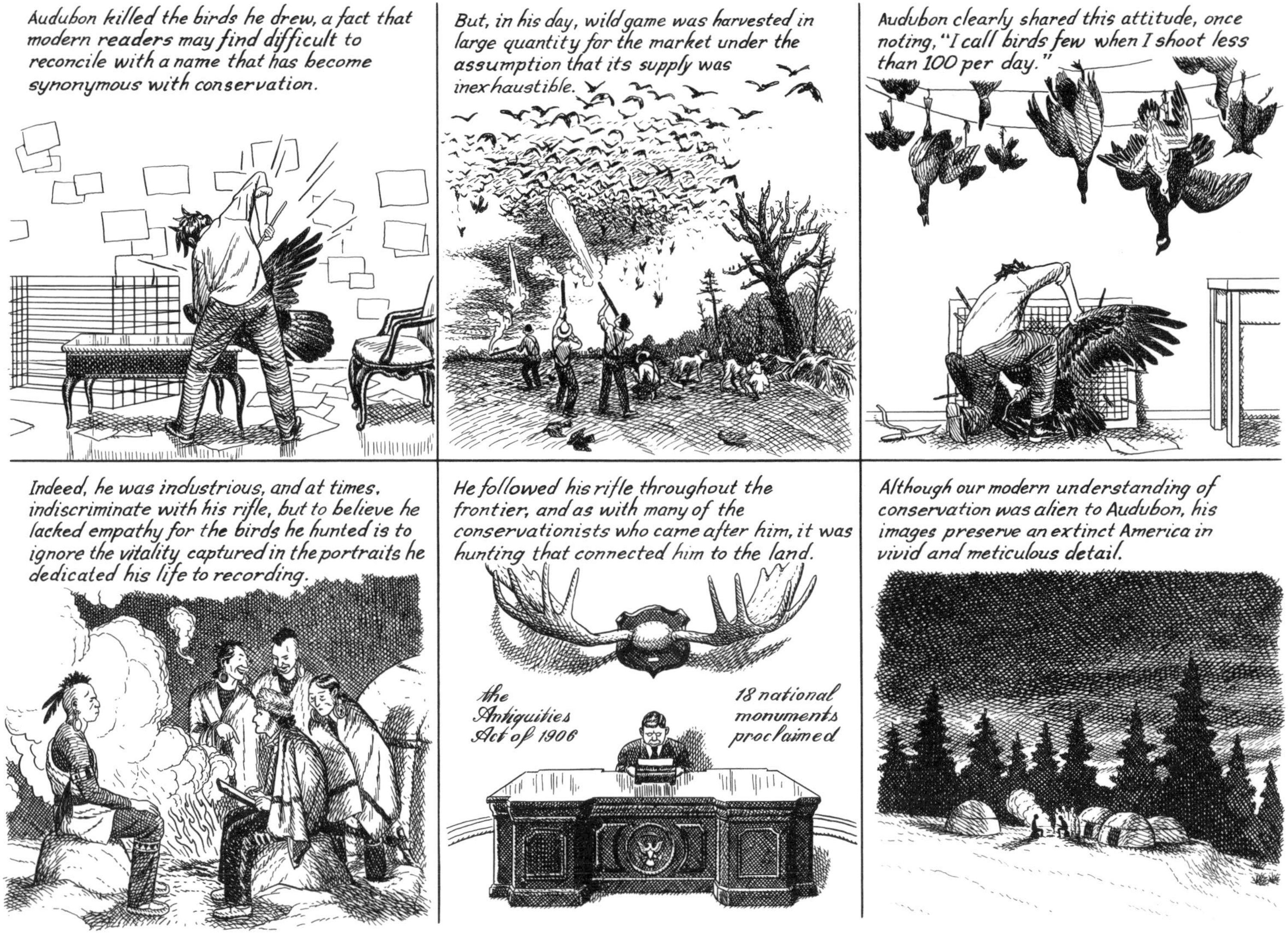
Audubon killed the birds he drew, a fact that modern readers may find difficult to reconcile with a name that has become synonymous with conservation.
But, in his day, wild game was harvested in large quantity for the market under the assumption that its supply was inexhaustible.
Audubon clearly shared this attitude, once noting, "I call birds few when I shoot less than 100 per day."
Indeed, he was industrious, and at times, indiscriminate with his rifle, but to believe he lacked empathy for the birds he hunted is to ignore the vitality captured in the portraits he dedicated his life to recording.
He followed his rifle throughout the frontier, and as with many of the conservationists who came after him, it was hunting that connected him to the land.
the Antiquities Act of 1906
18 national monuments proclaimed
Although our modern understanding of conservation was alien to Audubon, his images preserve an extinct America in vivid and meticulous detail.

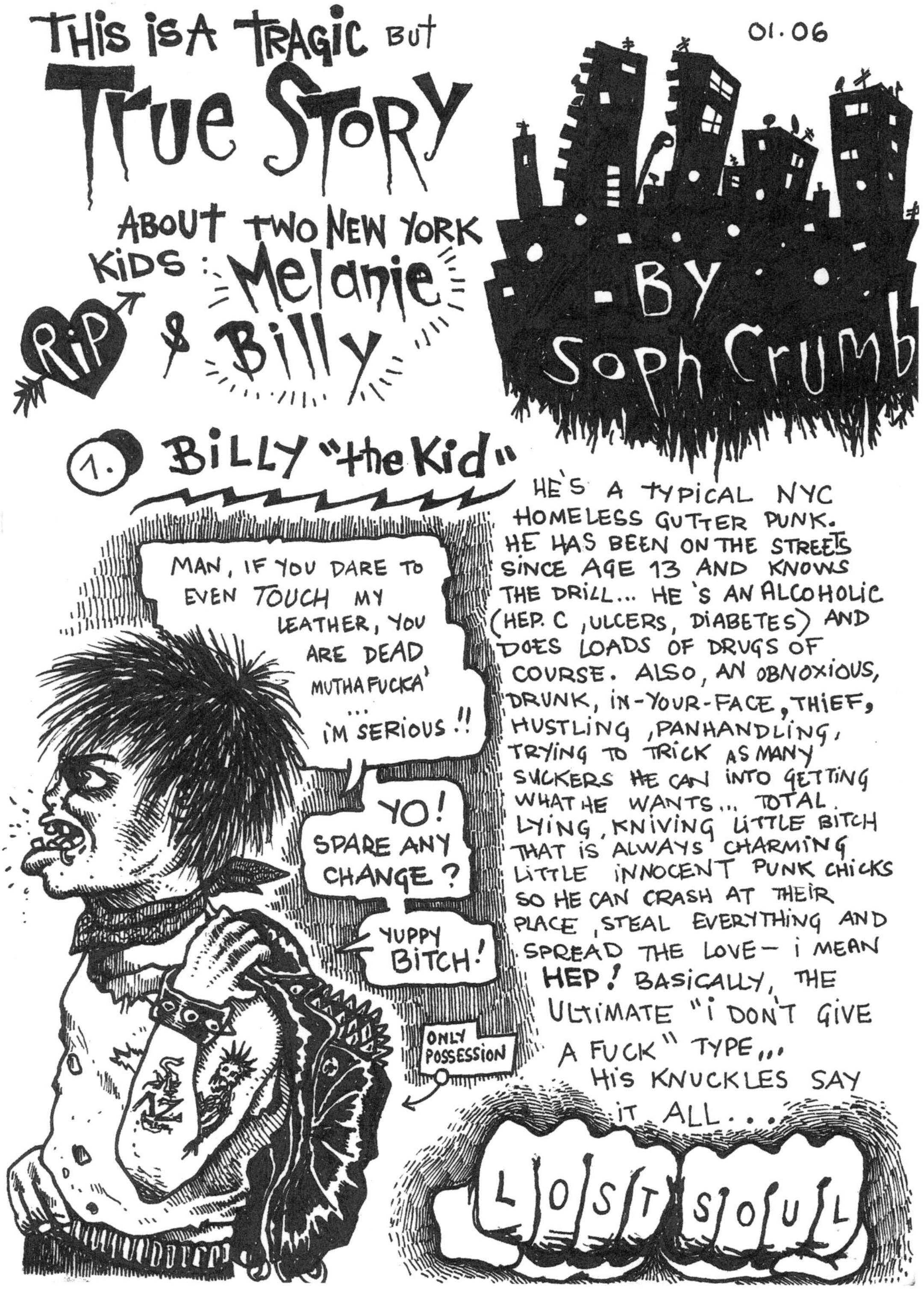
THIS IS A TRAGIC BUT
TRUE STORY
ABOUT TWO NEW YORK KIDS: Melanie & Billy
RIP
01.06
BY Soph Crumb
1. BILLY "the Kid"
HE'S A TYPICAL NYC HOMELESS GUTTER PUNK. HE HAS BEEN ON THE STREETS SINCE AGE 13 AND KNOWS THE DRILL... HE'S AN ALCOHOLIC (HEP. C, ULCERS, DIABETES) AND DOES LOADS OF DRUGS OF COURSE. ALSO, AN OBNOXIOUS, DRUNK, IN-YOUR-FACE, THIEF, HUSTLING, PANHANDLING, TRYING TO TRICK AS MANY SUCKERS HE CAN INTO GETTING WHAT HE WANTS... TOTAL LYING, KNIVING LITTLE BITCH THAT IS ALWAYS CHARMING LITTLE INNOCENT PUNK CHICKS SO HE CAN CRASH AT THEIR PLACE, STEAL EVERYTHING AND SPREAD THE LOVE — I MEAN HEP! BASICALLY, THE ULTIMATE "I DON'T GIVE A FUCK" TYPE... HIS KNUCKLES SAY IT ALL...
MAN, IF YOU DARE TO EVEN TOUCH MY LEATHER, YOU ARE DEAD MUTHAFUCKA' ... I'M SERIOUS!!
YO! SPARE ANY CHANGE?
YUPPY BITCH!
ONLY POSSESSION
LOST SOUL

2. Melanie

SHE WAS A WILD, BEAUTIFUL 19 YEAR OLD. SHE'D HAD A SCREWED UP PAST, FILLED WITH SUICIDE, DRUGS, FOSTER HOMES AND HOMELESSNESS... BUT SHE SEEMED TO ALWAYS BE PUT TOGETHER AND PRETTY, AND APPEARED TO BE HAPPY; BUBBLY, SMILING, GIGGLING... WHEN I MET HER SHE WAS SECRETLY SLEEPING AT THE TATTOO SHOP ON ST. MARKS WHERE SHE WORKED THE FLOOR, AND SHE WOULD LET ALL THE HOMELESS / TRAVELING PUNKS STAY THERE AT NIGHT!

UNLIKE MOST CRUSTIES WHO TAKE PRIDE IN BEING AS FILTHY AND SHOWERLESS AS POSSIBLE, I THINK MEL DIDN'T WANT TO LOOK POOR OR HOMELESS AND WENT TO GREAT LENGTHS TO APPEAR CLEAN + WELL-DRESSED, AND SEEING HER, YOU'D THINK SHE WAS JUST ANOTHER HIP, WILLIAMSBURG-TYPE, WELL-OFF COLLEGE STUDENT...

BUT SHE WASN'T...

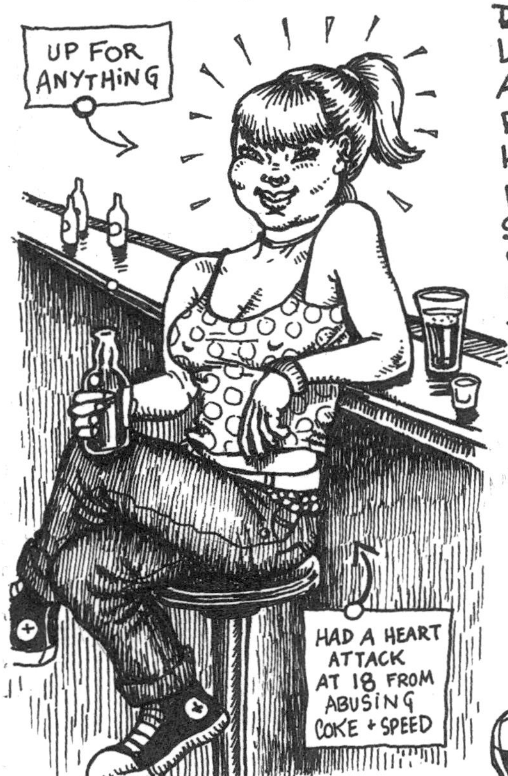
UP FOR ANYTHING
HAD A HEART ATTACK AT 18 FROM ABUSING COKE + SPEED

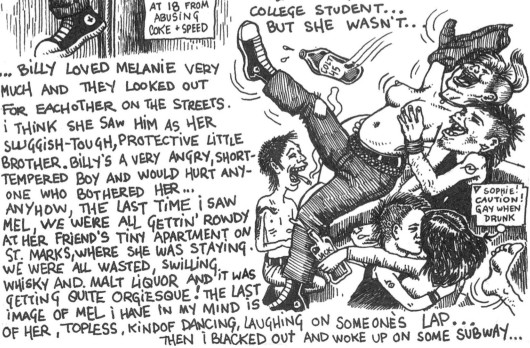

... BILLY LOVED MELANIE VERY MUCH AND THEY LOOKED OUT FOR EACHOTHER ON THE STREETS. I THINK SHE SAW HIM AS HER SLUGGISH-TOUGH, PROTECTIVE LITTLE BROTHER. BILLY'S A VERY ANGRY, SHORT-TEMPERED BOY AND WOULD HURT ANYONE WHO BOTHERED HER...

ANYHOW, THE LAST TIME I SAW MEL, WE WERE ALL GETTIN' ROWDY AT HER FRIEND'S TINY APARTMENT ON ST. MARKS, WHERE SHE WAS STAYING. WE WERE ALL WASTED, SWILLING WHISKY AND MALT LIQUOR AND IT WAS GETTING QUITE ORGIESQUE! THE LAST IMAGE OF MEL I HAVE IN MY MIND IS OF HER, TOPLESS, KINDOF DANCING, LAUGHING ON SOMEONE'S LAP...

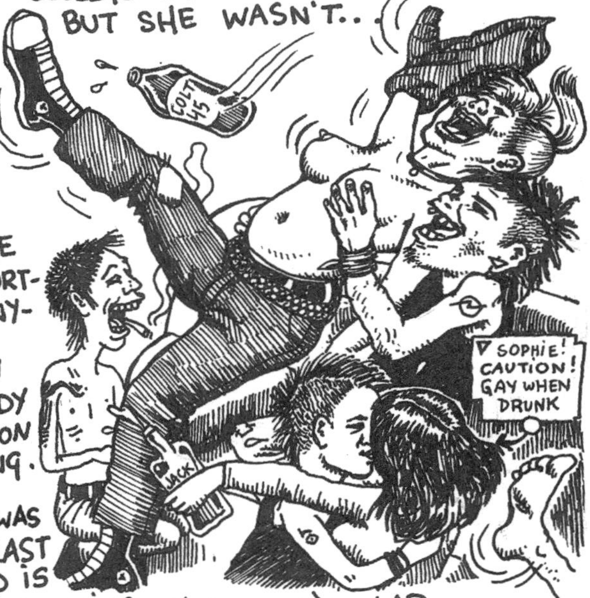
COLT 45
JACK
SOPHIE! CAUTION! GAY WHEN DRUNK

THEN I BLACKED OUT AND WOKE UP ON SOME SUBWAY...

MELANIE WOULD SNORT HEROIN, BUT, TO MY KNOWLEDGE, HAD NEVER SHOT IT. A MONTH OR SO AFTER I LAST SAW HER, SHE WAS AT THAT SAME ROOM ON ST. MARKS, ALONE WITH THIS CREEPY GUY JOE, THAT WASN'T REALLY FRIENDS WITH ANYONE IN THE NEIGHBORHOOD, BUT WE'D SEEN HIM AROUND... THEY WERE DOING DOPE AND JOE, I SUPPOSE, CONVINCED HER TO DO A SHOT... IT WAS TO BE HER FIRST, AND *LAST* SHOT OF HEROIN. HE SHOT HER UP, AND WHEN SHE NODDED OFF AND DIDN'T WAKE UP, WHEN HER LIPS STARTED TO TURN BLUE, HE PANICKED AND RAN, LEAVING HER THERE TO DIE.

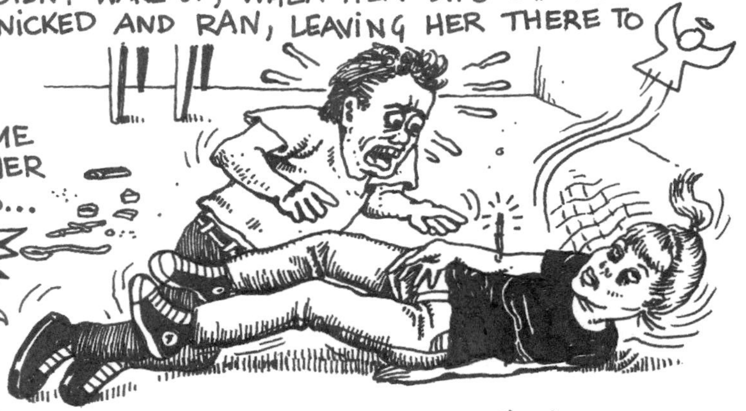

HER ROOM-MATE CAME BACK AND FOUND HER LYING THERE DEAD...

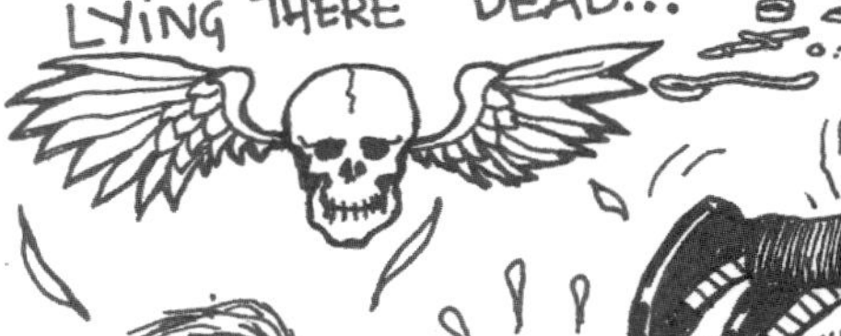

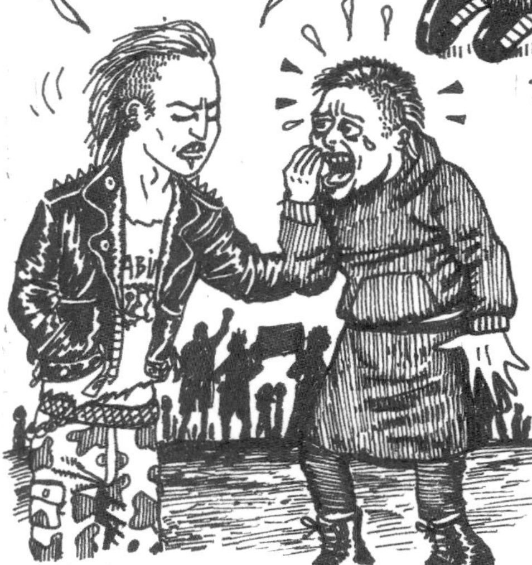

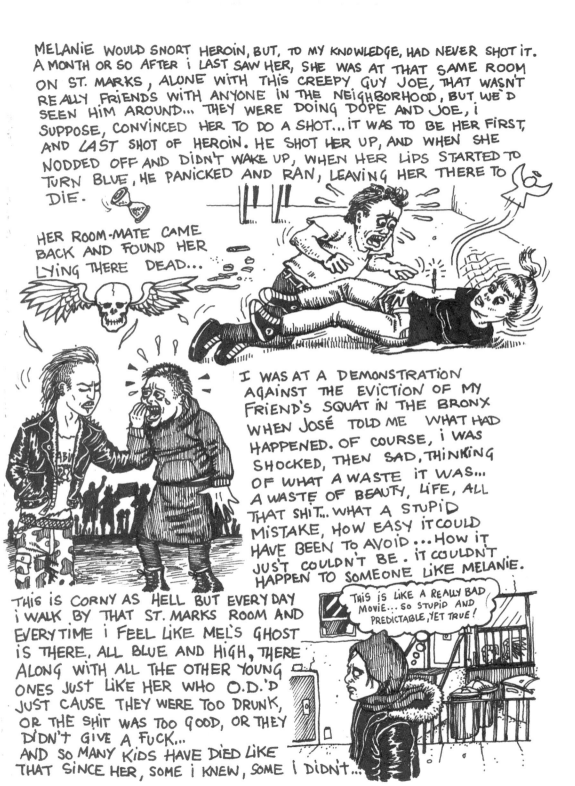

I WAS AT A DEMONSTRATION AGAINST THE EVICTION OF MY FRIEND'S SQUAT IN THE BRONX WHEN JOSÉ TOLD ME WHAT HAD HAPPENED. OF COURSE, I WAS SHOCKED, THEN SAD, THINKING OF WHAT A WASTE IT WAS... A WASTE OF BEAUTY, LIFE, ALL THAT SHIT... WHAT A STUPID MISTAKE, HOW EASY IT COULD HAVE BEEN TO AVOID... HOW IT JUST COULDN'T BE. IT COULDN'T HAPPEN TO SOMEONE LIKE MELANIE.

THIS IS CORNY AS HELL BUT EVERY DAY I WALK BY THAT ST. MARKS ROOM AND EVERYTIME I FEEL LIKE MEL'S GHOST IS THERE, ALL BLUE AND HIGH, THERE ALONG WITH ALL THE OTHER YOUNG ONES JUST LIKE HER WHO O.D.'D JUST CAUSE THEY WERE TOO DRUNK, OR THE SHIT WAS TOO GOOD, OR THEY DIDN'T GIVE A FUCK...
AND SO MANY KIDS HAVE DIED LIKE THAT SINCE HER, SOME I KNEW, SOME I DIDN'T...

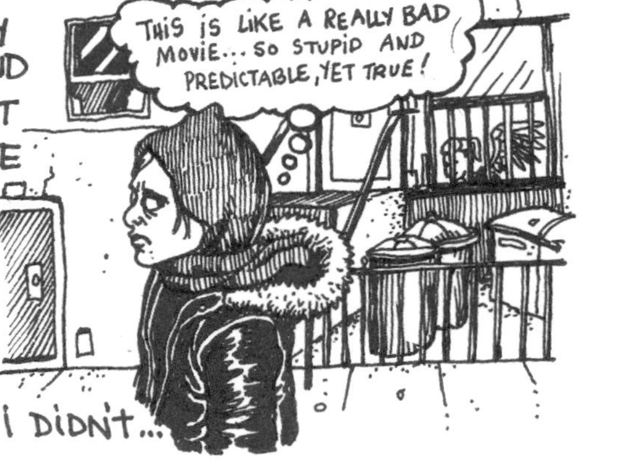
THIS IS LIKE A REALLY BAD MOVIE... SO STUPID AND PREDICTABLE, YET TRUE!

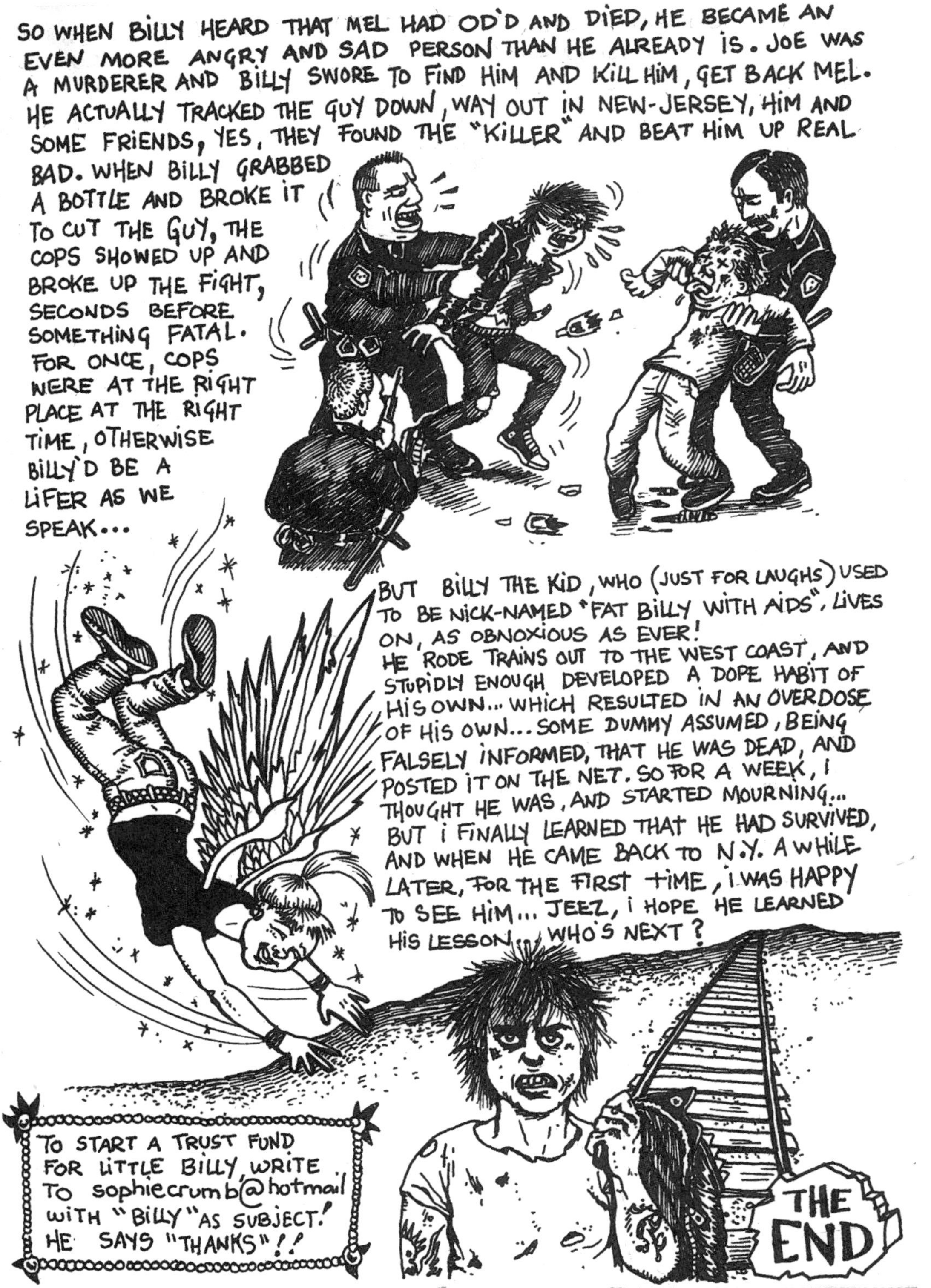
SO WHEN BILLY HEARD THAT MEL HAD OD'D AND DIED, HE BECAME AN EVEN MORE ANGRY AND SAD PERSON THAN HE ALREADY IS. JOE WAS A MURDERER AND BILLY SWORE TO FIND HIM AND KILL HIM, GET BACK MEL. HE ACTUALLY TRACKED THE GUY DOWN, WAY OUT IN NEW-JERSEY, HIM AND SOME FRIENDS, YES, THEY FOUND THE "KILLER" AND BEAT HIM UP REAL BAD. WHEN BILLY GRABBED A BOTTLE AND BROKE IT TO CUT THE GUY, THE COPS SHOWED UP AND BROKE UP THE FIGHT, SECONDS BEFORE SOMETHING FATAL. FOR ONCE, COPS WERE AT THE RIGHT PLACE AT THE RIGHT TIME, OTHERWISE BILLY'D BE A LIFER AS WE SPEAK...
BUT BILLY THE KID, WHO (JUST FOR LAUGHS) USED TO BE NICK-NAMED "FAT BILLY WITH AIDS", LIVES ON, AS OBNOXIOUS AS EVER!
HE RODE TRAINS OUT TO THE WEST COAST, AND STUPIDLY ENOUGH DEVELOPED A DOPE HABIT OF HIS OWN... WHICH RESULTED IN AN OVERDOSE OF HIS OWN... SOME DUMMY ASSUMED, BEING FALSELY INFORMED, THAT HE WAS DEAD, AND POSTED IT ON THE NET. SO FOR A WEEK, I THOUGHT HE WAS, AND STARTED MOURNING... BUT I FINALLY LEARNED THAT HE HAD SURVIVED, AND WHEN HE CAME BACK TO N.Y. A WHILE LATER, FOR THE FIRST TIME, I WAS HAPPY TO SEE HIM... JEEZ, I HOPE HE LEARNED HIS LESSON... WHO'S NEXT?
TO START A TRUST FUND FOR LITTLE BILLY, WRITE TO sophiecrumb@hotmail WITH "BILLY" AS SUBJECT! HE SAYS "THANKS"!!
THE END

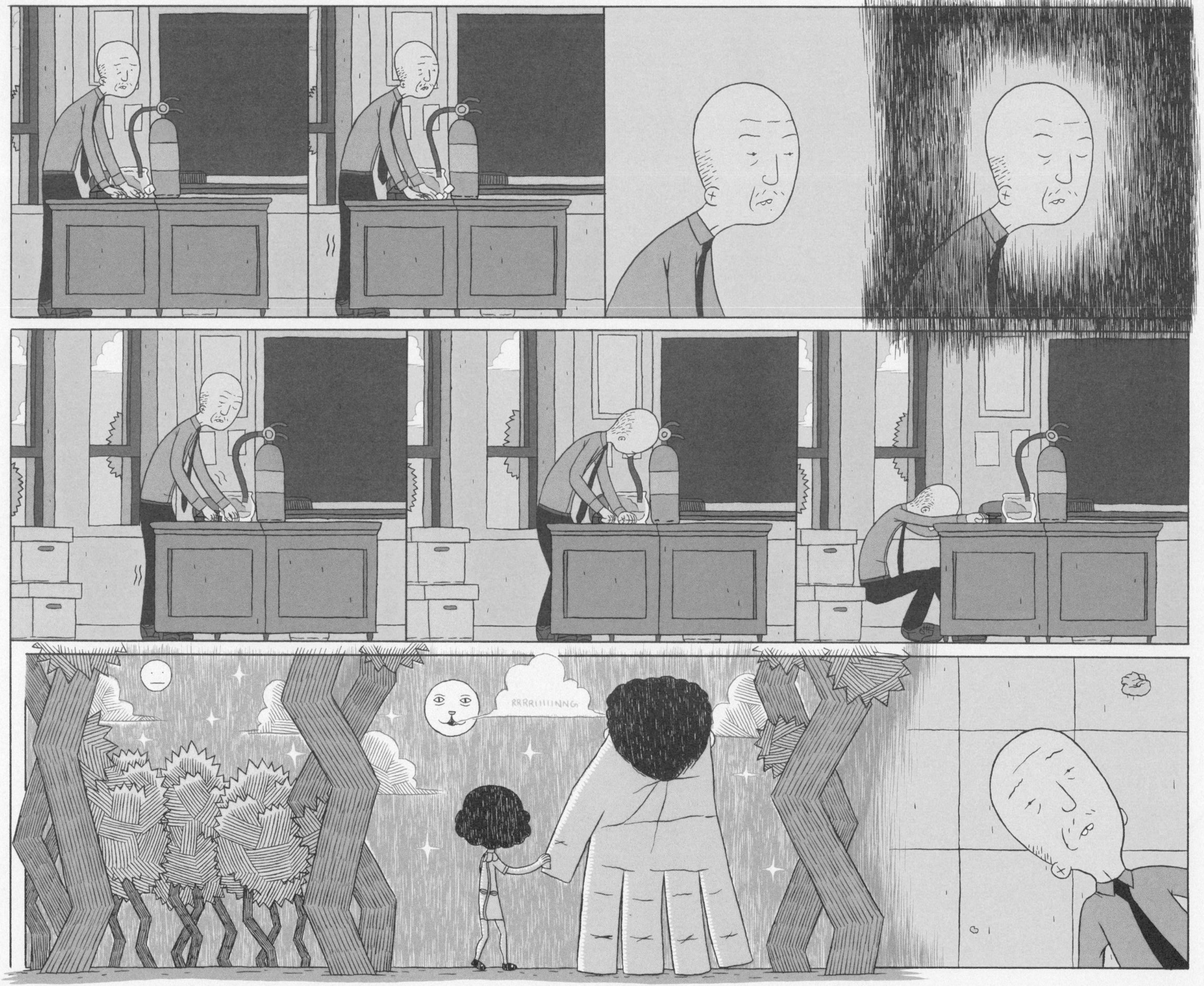
RRRRIIIIIINNG

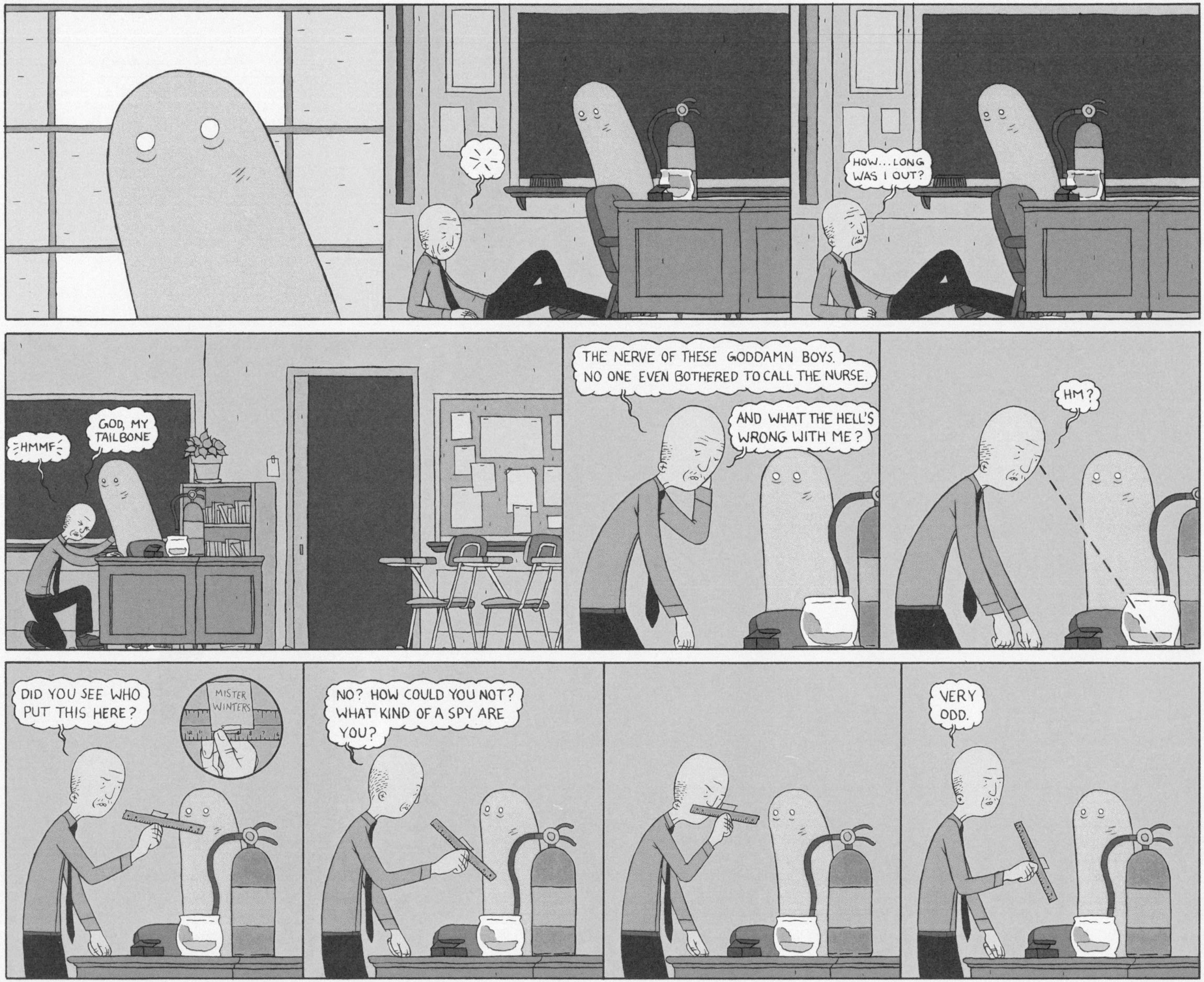

HOW... LONG WAS I OUT?
HMMF
GOD, MY TAILBONE
THE NERVE OF THESE GODDAMN BOYS. NO ONE EVEN BOTHERED TO CALL THE NURSE.
AND WHAT THE HELL'S WRONG WITH ME?
HM?
DID YOU SEE WHO PUT THIS HERE?
MISTER WINTERS
NO? HOW COULD YOU NOT? WHAT KIND OF A SPY ARE YOU?
VERY ODD.

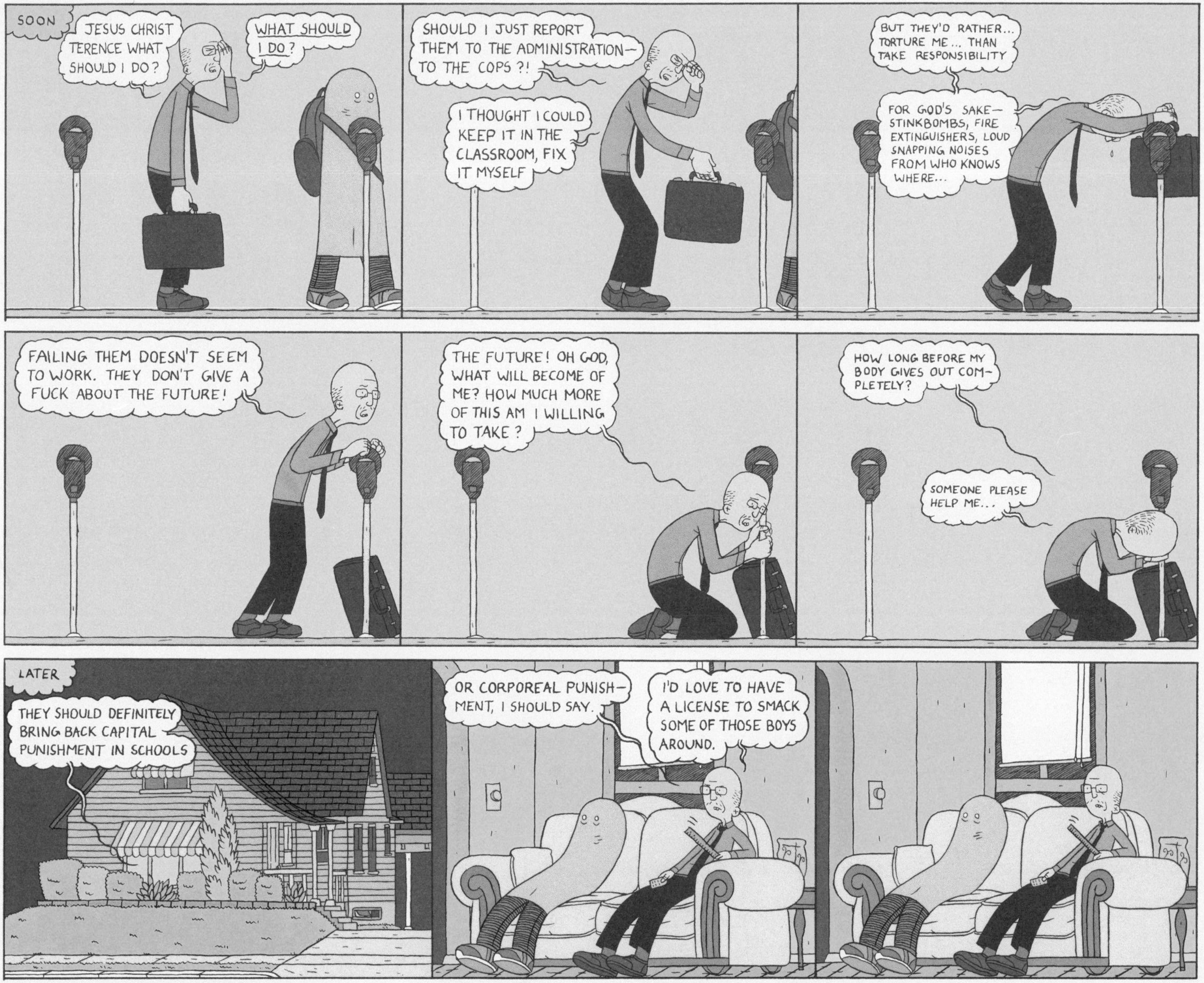
SOON
JESUS CHRIST TERENCE WHAT SHOULD I DO?
WHAT SHOULD I DO?
SHOULD I JUST REPORT THEM TO THE ADMINISTRATION— TO THE COPS?!
I THOUGHT I COULD KEEP IT IN THE CLASSROOM, FIX IT MYSELF
BUT THEY'D RATHER... TORTURE ME... THAN TAKE RESPONSIBILITY
FOR GOD'S SAKE— STINKBOMBS, FIRE EXTINGUISHERS, LOUD SNAPPING NOISES FROM WHO KNOWS WHERE...
FAILING THEM DOESN'T SEEM TO WORK. THEY DON'T GIVE A FUCK ABOUT THE FUTURE!
THE FUTURE! OH GOD, WHAT WILL BECOME OF ME? HOW MUCH MORE OF THIS AM I WILLING TO TAKE?
HOW LONG BEFORE MY BODY GIVES OUT COMPLETELY?
SOMEONE PLEASE HELP ME...
LATER
THEY SHOULD DEFINITELY BRING BACK CAPITAL PUNISHMENT IN SCHOOLS
OR CORPOREAL PUNISHMENT, I SHOULD SAY.
I'D LOVE TO HAVE A LICENSE TO SMACK SOME OF THOSE BOYS AROUND.

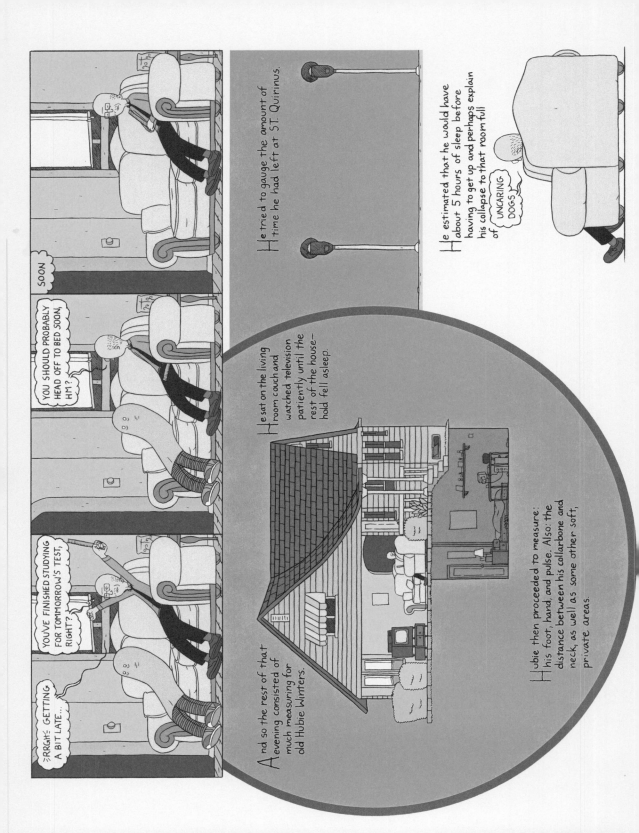

":RRGH: GETTING A BIT LATE..."

"YOU'VE FINISHED STUDYING FOR TOMMORROW'S TEST, RIGHT?"

"YOU SHOULD PROBABLY HEAD OFF TO BED SOON, HM?"

"SOON"

And so the rest of that evening consisted of much measuring for old Hubie Winters.

He sat on the living room couch and watched television patiently until the rest of the house-hold fell asleep.

Hubie then proceeded to measure: his foot, hand, and pulse. Also: the distance between his collarbone and neck, as well as some other soft, private areas.

He tried to gauge the amount of time he had left at ST. Quirinus.

He estimated that he would have had about 5 hours of sleep before having to get up and perhaps explain his collapse to that room full of UNCARING DOGS.

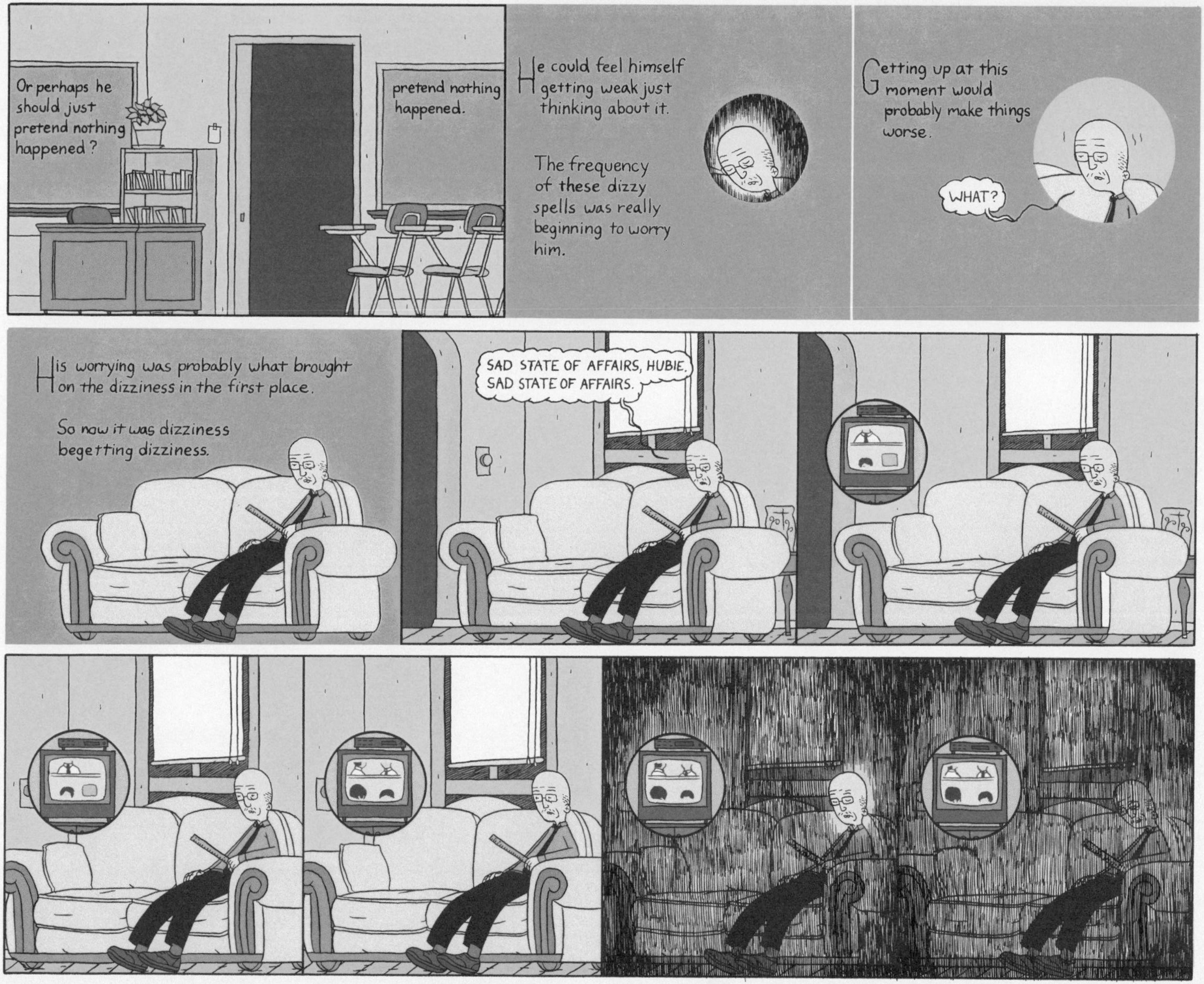
Or perhaps he should just pretend nothing happened?
pretend nothing happened.
He could feel himself getting weak just thinking about it.
The frequency of these dizzy spells was really beginning to worry him.
Getting up at this moment would probably make things worse.
WHAT?
His worrying was probably what brought on the dizziness in the first place.
So now it was dizziness begetting dizziness.
SAD STATE OF AFFAIRS, HUBIE.
SAD STATE OF AFFAIRS.

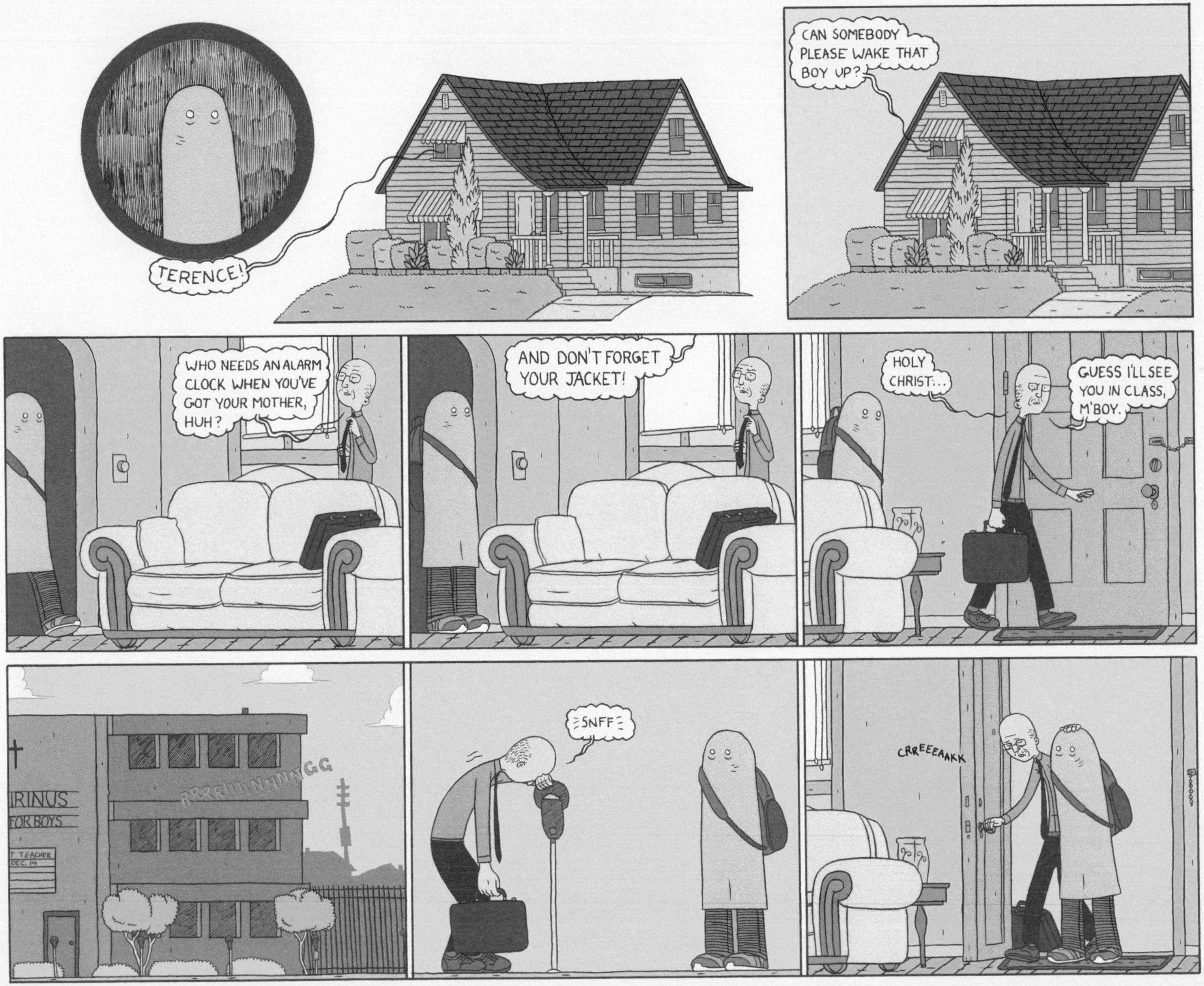
TERENCE!
CAN SOMEBODY PLEASE WAKE THAT BOY UP?
WHO NEEDS AN ALARM CLOCK WHEN YOU'VE GOT YOUR MOTHER, HUH?
AND DON'T FORGET YOUR JACKET!
HOLY CHRIST...
GUESS I'LL SEE YOU IN CLASS, M'BOY.
IRINUS
FOR BOYS
T TEACHER
DEC. 14
RRRRIIINNNNGG
SNFF
CRREEEAAKK

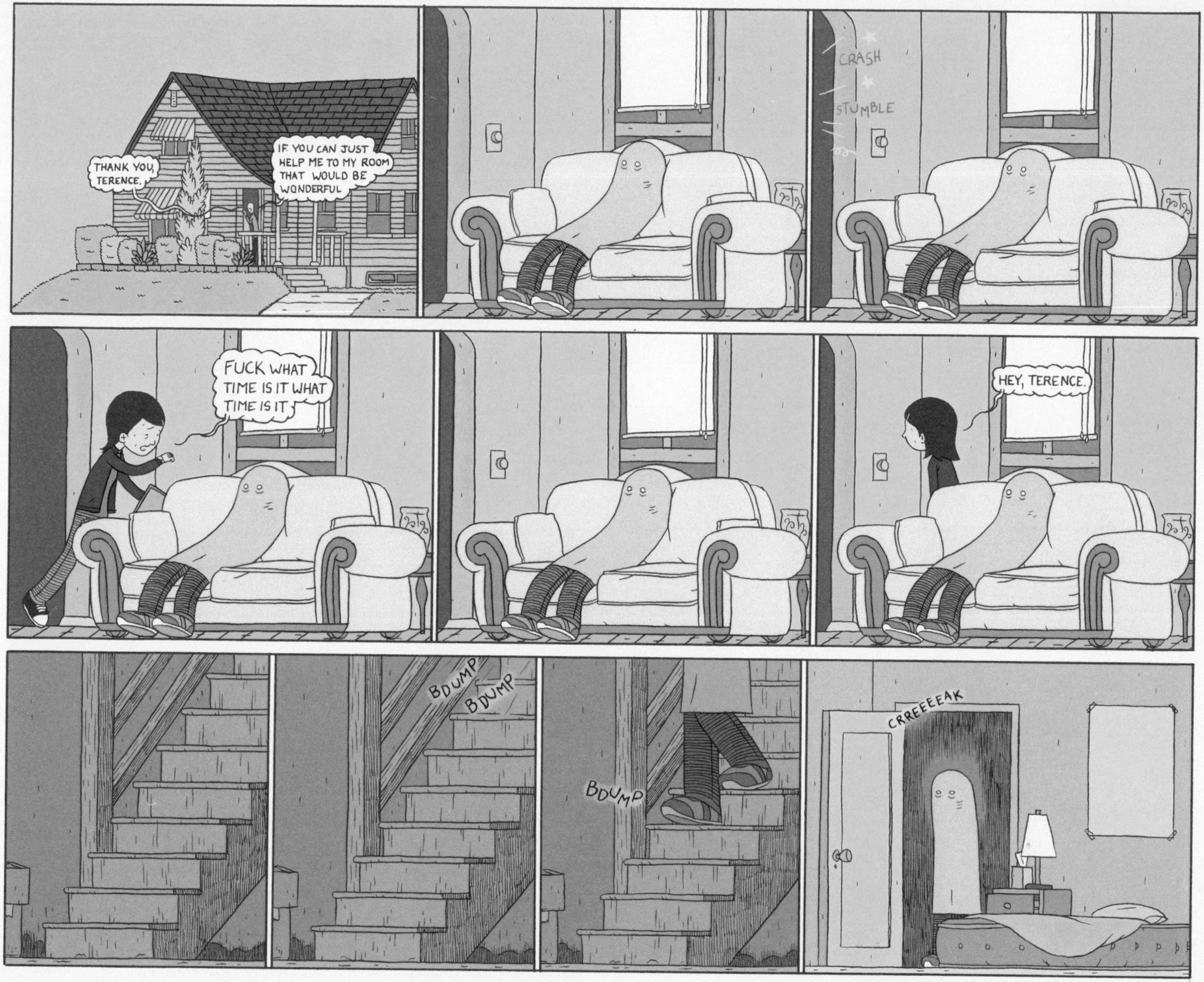
THANK YOU, TERENCE.
IF YOU CAN JUST HELP ME TO MY ROOM THAT WOULD BE WONDERFUL
CRASH
STUMBLE
FUCK WHAT TIME IS IT WHAT TIME IS IT
HEY, TERENCE.
BDUMP
BDUMP
BDUMP
CRREEEEAK

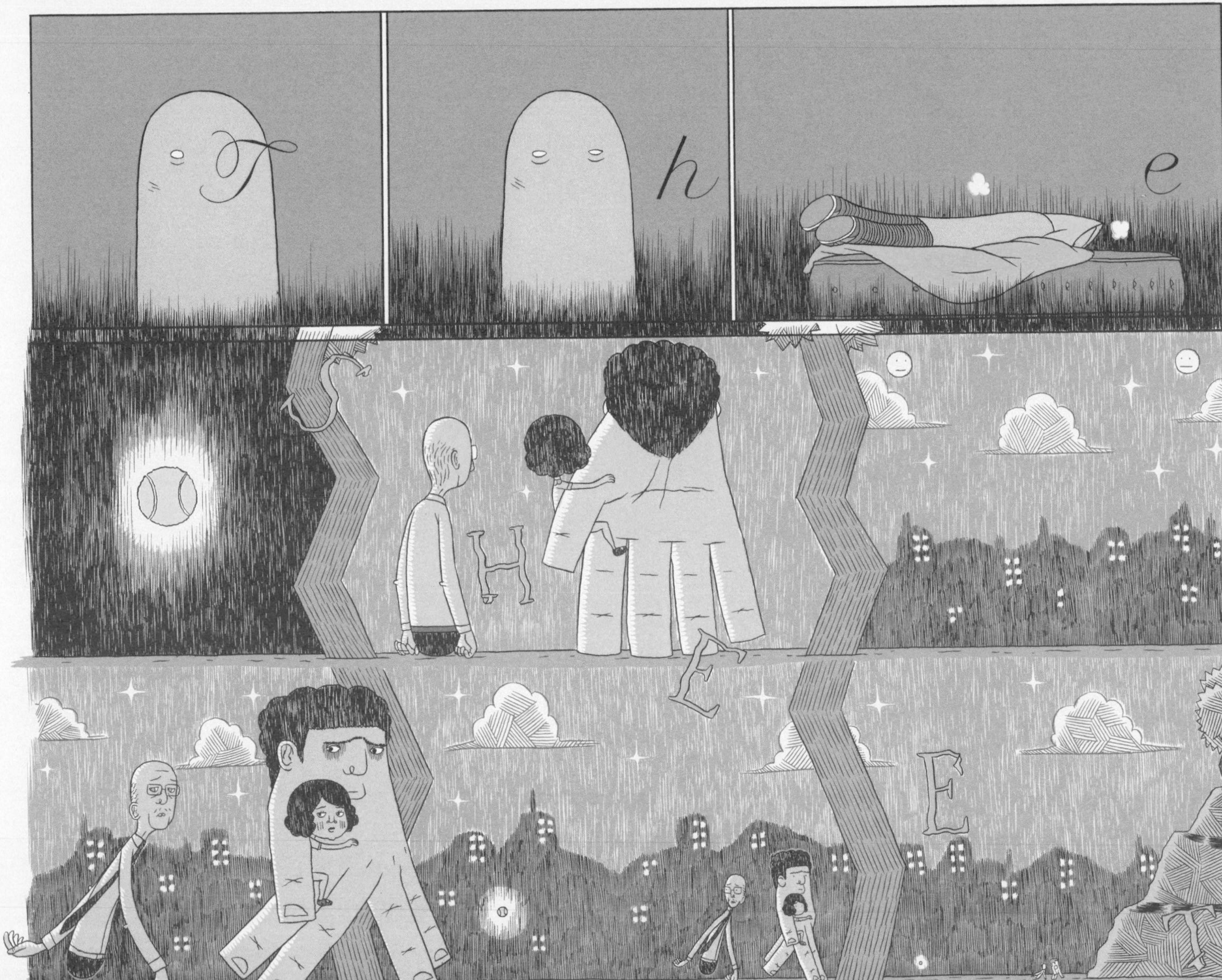
T
h
e
H
E
E

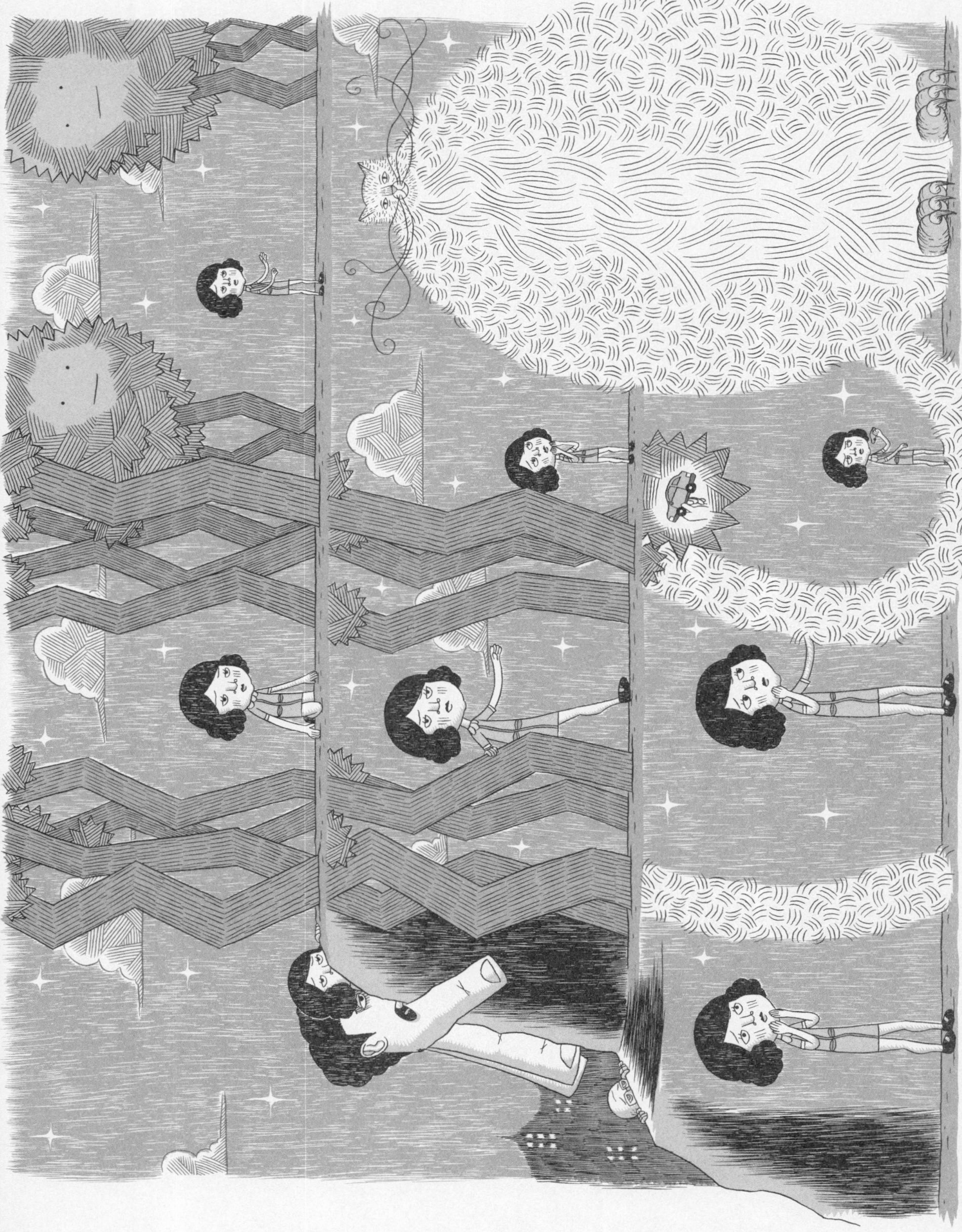

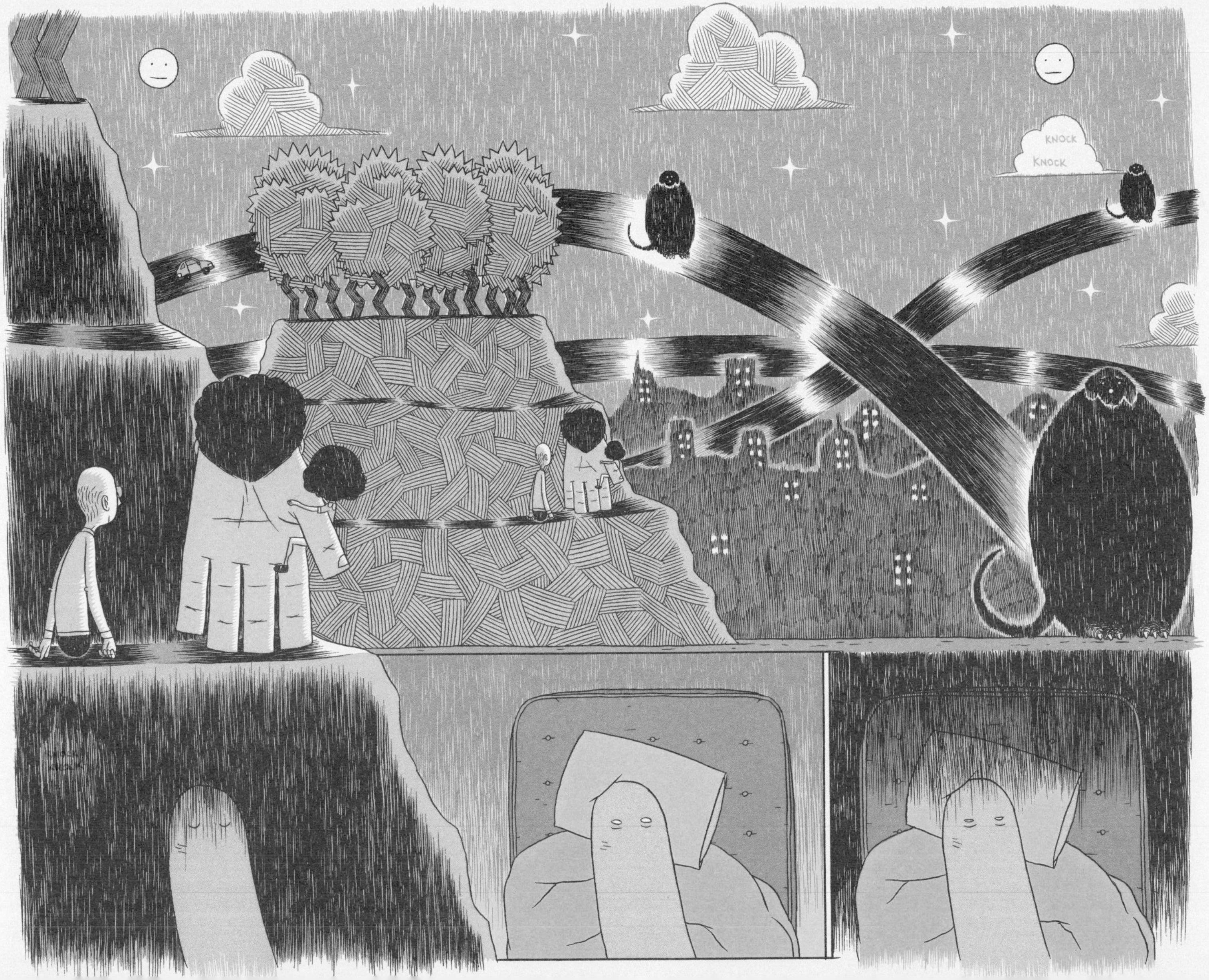
KNOCK
KNOCK

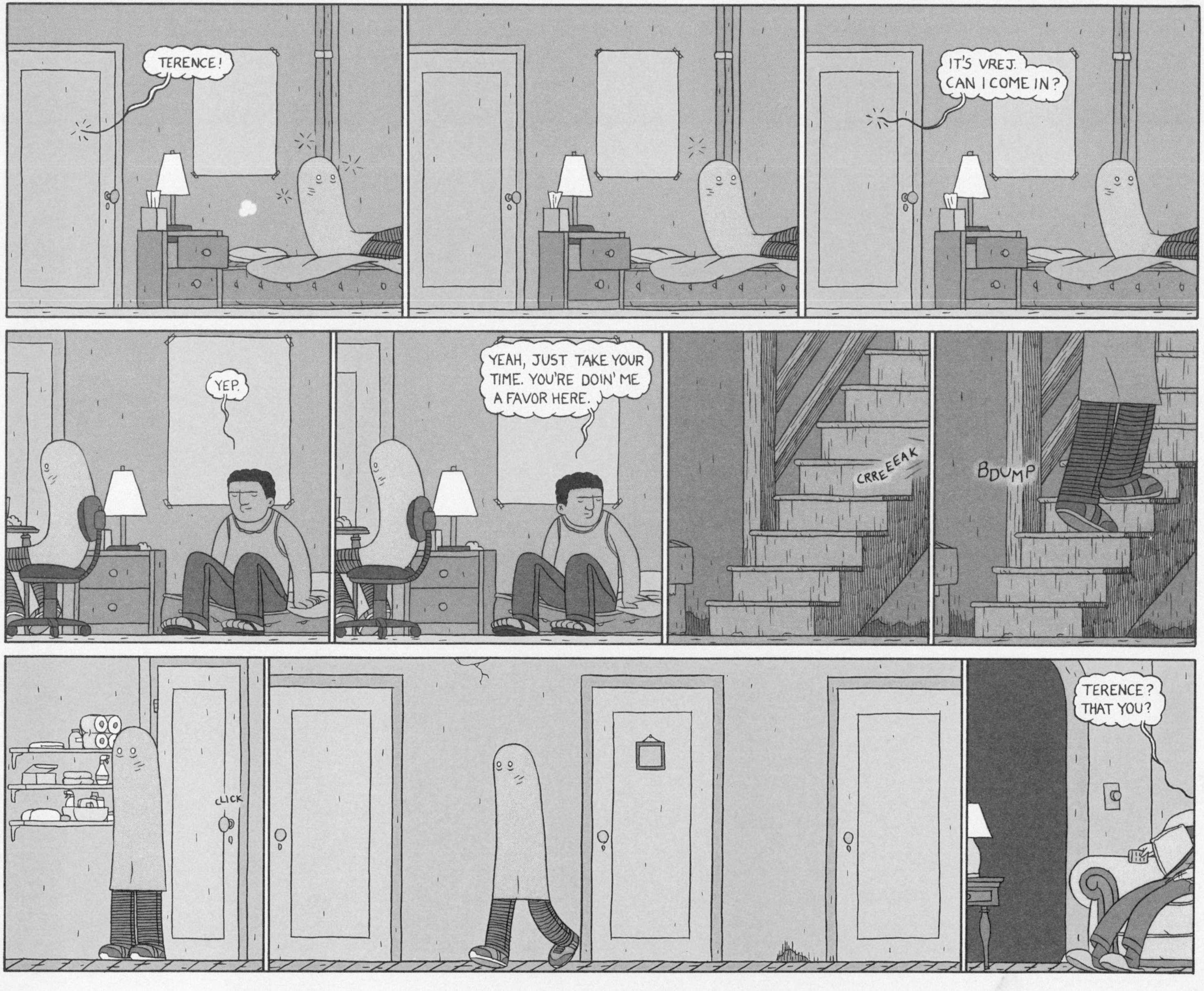
TERENCE!
IT'S VREJ. CAN I COME IN?
YEP.
YEAH, JUST TAKE YOUR TIME. YOU'RE DOIN' ME A FAVOR HERE.
CRREEEAK
BDUMP
CLICK
TERENCE? THAT YOU?

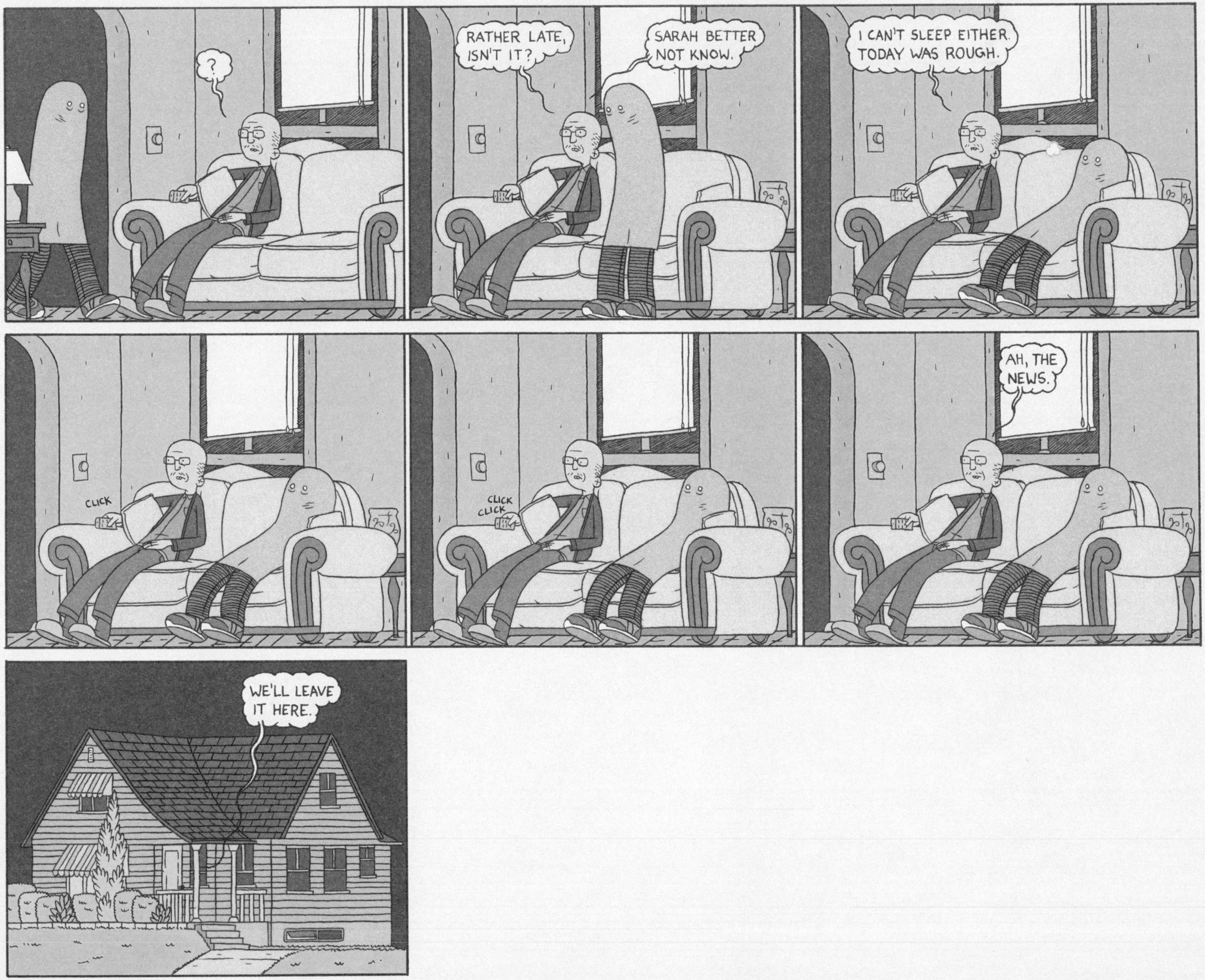
?
RATHER LATE, ISN'T IT?
SARAH BETTER NOT KNOW.
I CAN'T SLEEP EITHER. TODAY WAS ROUGH.
CLICK
CLICK CLICK
AH, THE NEWS.
WE'LL LEAVE IT HERE.

LA BREA WOMAN

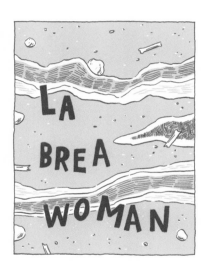

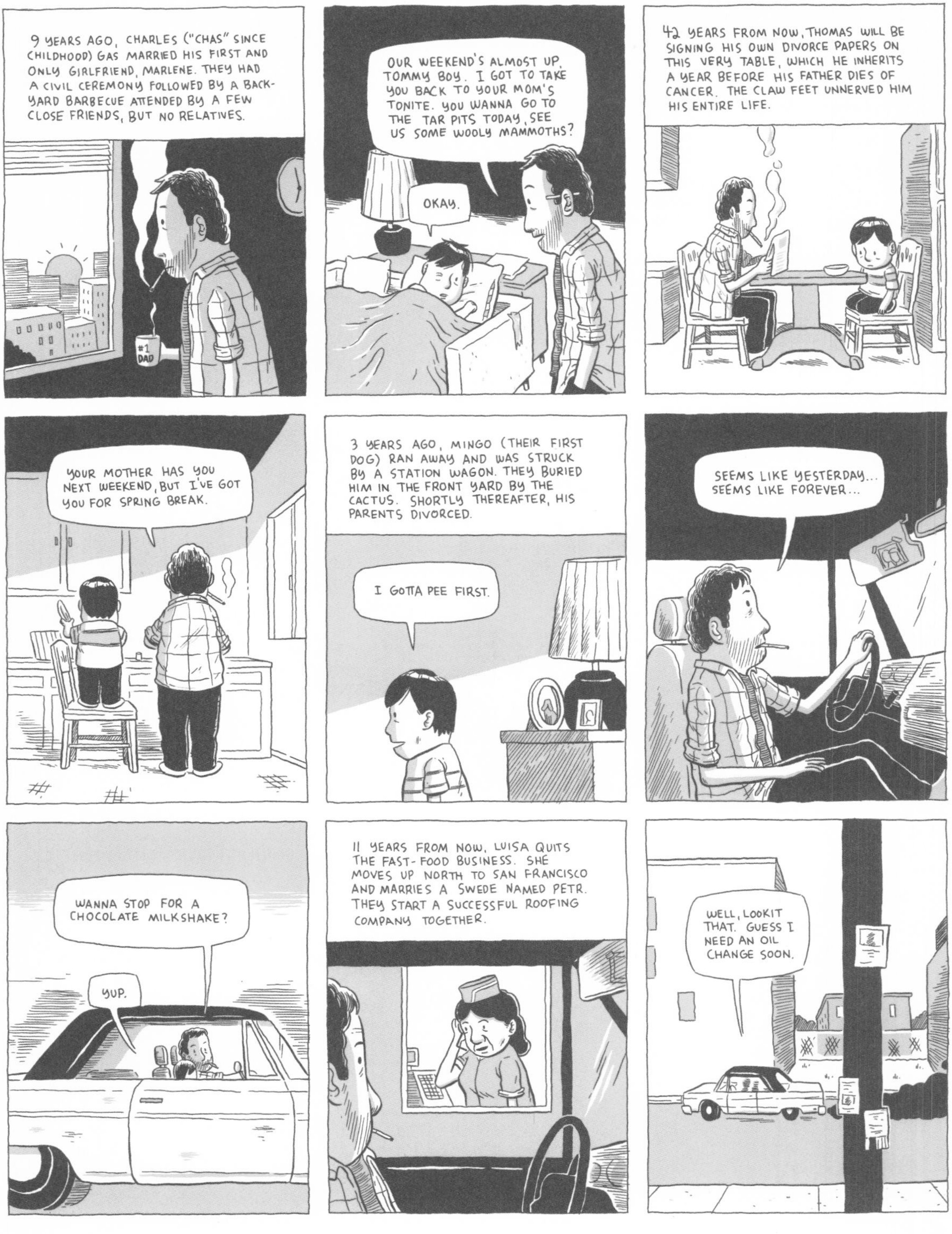
9 YEARS AGO, CHARLES ("CHAS" SINCE CHILDHOOD) GAS MARRIED HIS FIRST AND ONLY GIRLFRIEND, MARLENE. THEY HAD A CIVIL CEREMONY FOLLOWED BY A BACK-YARD BARBECUE ATTENDED BY A FEW CLOSE FRIENDS, BUT NO RELATIVES.
#1 DAD
OUR WEEKEND'S ALMOST UP, TOMMY BOY. I GOT TO TAKE YOU BACK TO YOUR MOM'S TONITE. YOU WANNA GO TO THE TAR PITS TODAY, SEE US SOME WOOLY MAMMOTHS?
OKAY.
42 YEARS FROM NOW, THOMAS WILL BE SIGNING HIS OWN DIVORCE PAPERS ON THIS VERY TABLE, WHICH HE INHERITS A YEAR BEFORE HIS FATHER DIES OF CANCER. THE CLAW FEET UNNERVED HIM HIS ENTIRE LIFE.
YOUR MOTHER HAS YOU NEXT WEEKEND, BUT I'VE GOT YOU FOR SPRING BREAK.
3 YEARS AGO, MINGO (THEIR FIRST DOG) RAN AWAY AND WAS STRUCK BY A STATION WAGON. THEY BURIED HIM IN THE FRONT YARD BY THE CACTUS. SHORTLY THEREAFTER, HIS PARENTS DIVORCED.
I GOTTA PEE FIRST.
SEEMS LIKE YESTERDAY... SEEMS LIKE FOREVER...
WANNA STOP FOR A CHOCOLATE MILKSHAKE?
YUP.
11 YEARS FROM NOW, LUISA QUITS THE FAST-FOOD BUSINESS. SHE MOVES UP NORTH TO SAN FRANCISCO AND MARRIES A SWEDE NAMED PETR. THEY START A SUCCESSFUL ROOFING COMPANY TOGETHER.
WELL, LOOKIT THAT. GUESS I NEED AN OIL CHANGE SOON.

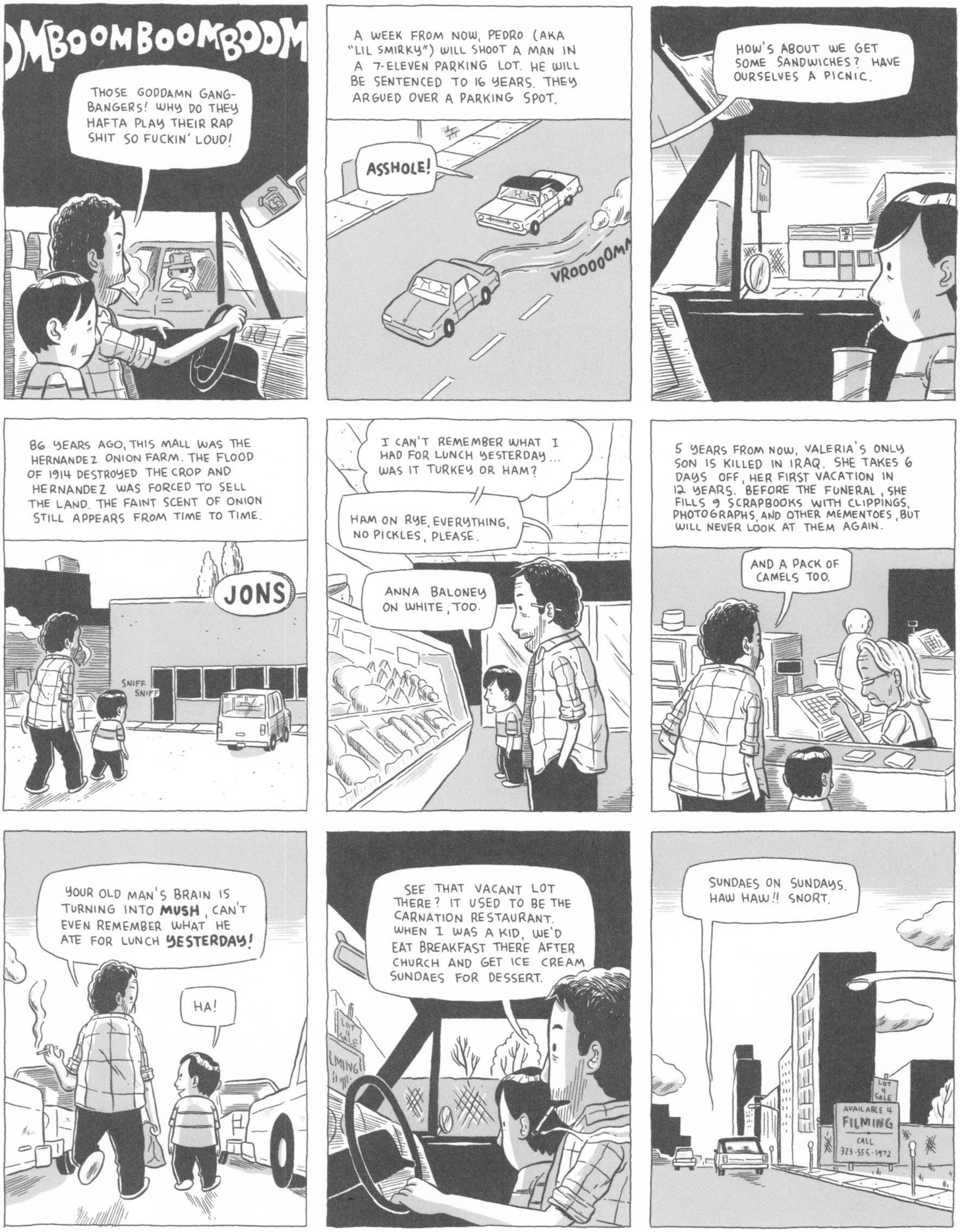

OMBOOMBOOMBOOM
THOSE GODDAMN GANG-BANGERS! WHY DO THEY HAFTA PLAY THEIR RAP SHIT SO FUCKIN' LOUD!
A WEEK FROM NOW, PEDRO (AKA "LIL SMIRKY") WILL SHOOT A MAN IN A 7-ELEVEN PARKING LOT. HE WILL BE SENTENCED TO 16 YEARS. THEY ARGUED OVER A PARKING SPOT.
ASSHOLE!
VROOOOOMM
HOW'S ABOUT WE GET SOME SANDWICHES? HAVE OURSELVES A PICNIC.
86 YEARS AGO, THIS MALL WAS THE HERNANDEZ ONION FARM. THE FLOOD OF 1914 DESTROYED THE CROP AND HERNANDEZ WAS FORCED TO SELL THE LAND. THE FAINT SCENT OF ONION STILL APPEARS FROM TIME TO TIME.
JONS
SNIFF SNIFF
I CAN'T REMEMBER WHAT I HAD FOR LUNCH YESTERDAY... WAS IT TURKEY OR HAM?
HAM ON RYE, EVERYTHING, NO PICKLES, PLEASE.
ANNA BALONEY ON WHITE, TOO.
5 YEARS FROM NOW, VALERIA'S ONLY SON IS KILLED IN IRAQ. SHE TAKES 6 DAYS OFF, HER FIRST VACATION IN 12 YEARS. BEFORE THE FUNERAL, SHE FILLS 9 SCRAPBOOKS WITH CLIPPINGS, PHOTOGRAPHS, AND OTHER MEMENTOES, BUT WILL NEVER LOOK AT THEM AGAIN.
AND A PACK OF CAMELS TOO.
YOUR OLD MAN'S BRAIN IS TURNING INTO MUSH, CAN'T EVEN REMEMBER WHAT HE ATE FOR LUNCH YESTERDAY!
HA!
SEE THAT VACANT LOT THERE? IT USED TO BE THE CARNATION RESTAURANT. WHEN I WAS A KID, WE'D EAT BREAKFAST THERE AFTER CHURCH AND GET ICE CREAM SUNDAES FOR DESSERT.
SUNDAES ON SUNDAYS. HAW HAW!! SNORT.
LOT 4 SALE
AVAILABLE 4 FILMING CALL 323-555-1972

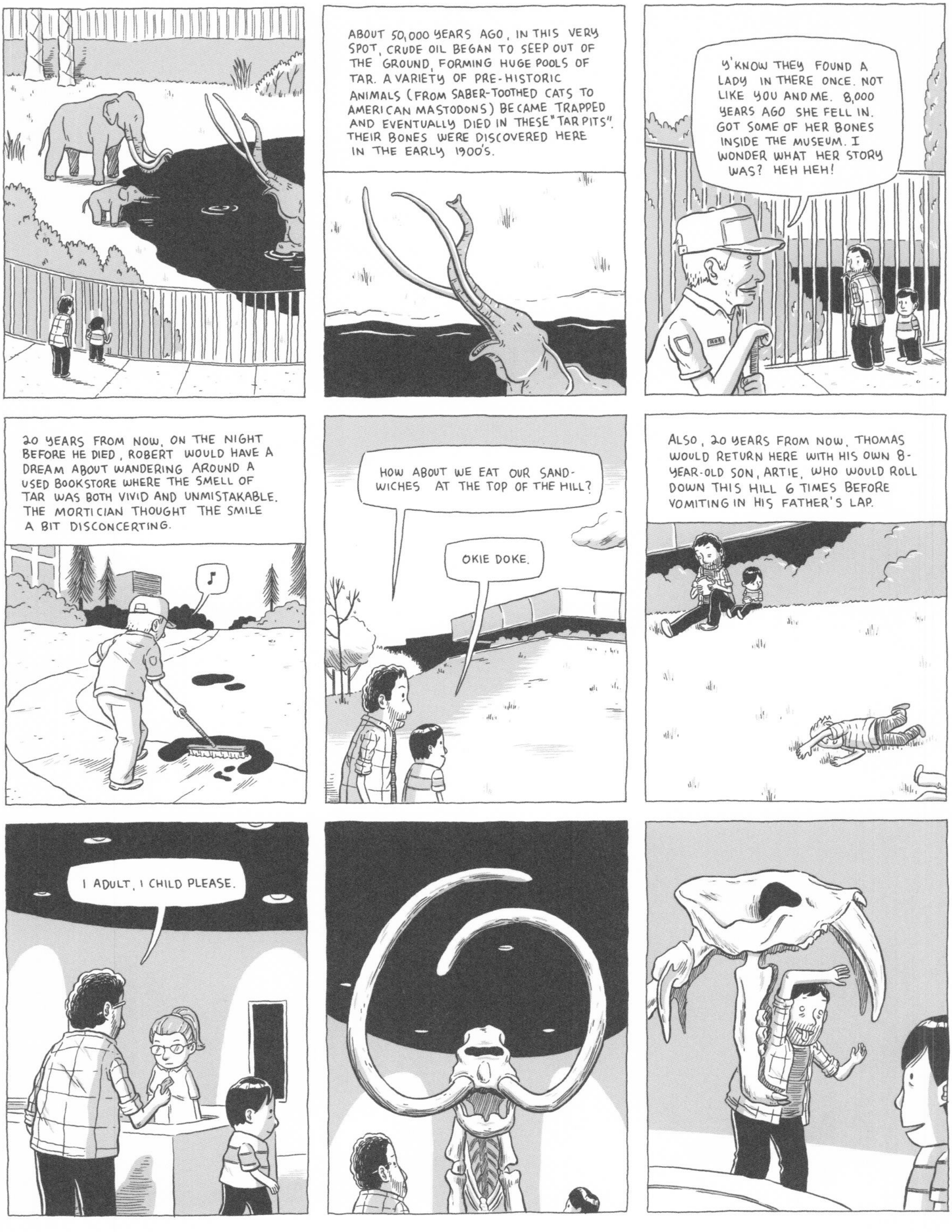
ABOUT 50,000 YEARS AGO, IN THIS VERY SPOT, CRUDE OIL BEGAN TO SEEP OUT OF THE GROUND, FORMING HUGE POOLS OF TAR. A VARIETY OF PRE-HISTORIC ANIMALS (FROM SABER-TOOTHED CATS TO AMERICAN MASTODONS) BECAME TRAPPED AND EVENTUALLY DIED IN THESE "TAR PITS". THEIR BONES WERE DISCOVERED HERE IN THE EARLY 1900'S.
Y'KNOW THEY FOUND A LADY IN THERE ONCE. NOT LIKE YOU AND ME. 8,000 YEARS AGO SHE FELL IN. GOT SOME OF HER BONES INSIDE THE MUSEUM. I WONDER WHAT HER STORY WAS? HEH HEH!
20 YEARS FROM NOW, ON THE NIGHT BEFORE HE DIED, ROBERT WOULD HAVE A DREAM ABOUT WANDERING AROUND A USED BOOKSTORE WHERE THE SMELL OF TAR WAS BOTH VIVID AND UNMISTAKABLE. THE MORTICIAN THOUGHT THE SMILE A BIT DISCONCERTING.
♪
HOW ABOUT WE EAT OUR SAND-WICHES AT THE TOP OF THE HILL?
OKIE DOKE.
ALSO, 20 YEARS FROM NOW, THOMAS WOULD RETURN HERE WITH HIS OWN 8-YEAR-OLD SON, ARTIE, WHO WOULD ROLL DOWN THIS HILL 6 TIMES BEFORE VOMITING IN HIS FATHER'S LAP.
1 ADULT, 1 CHILD PLEASE.

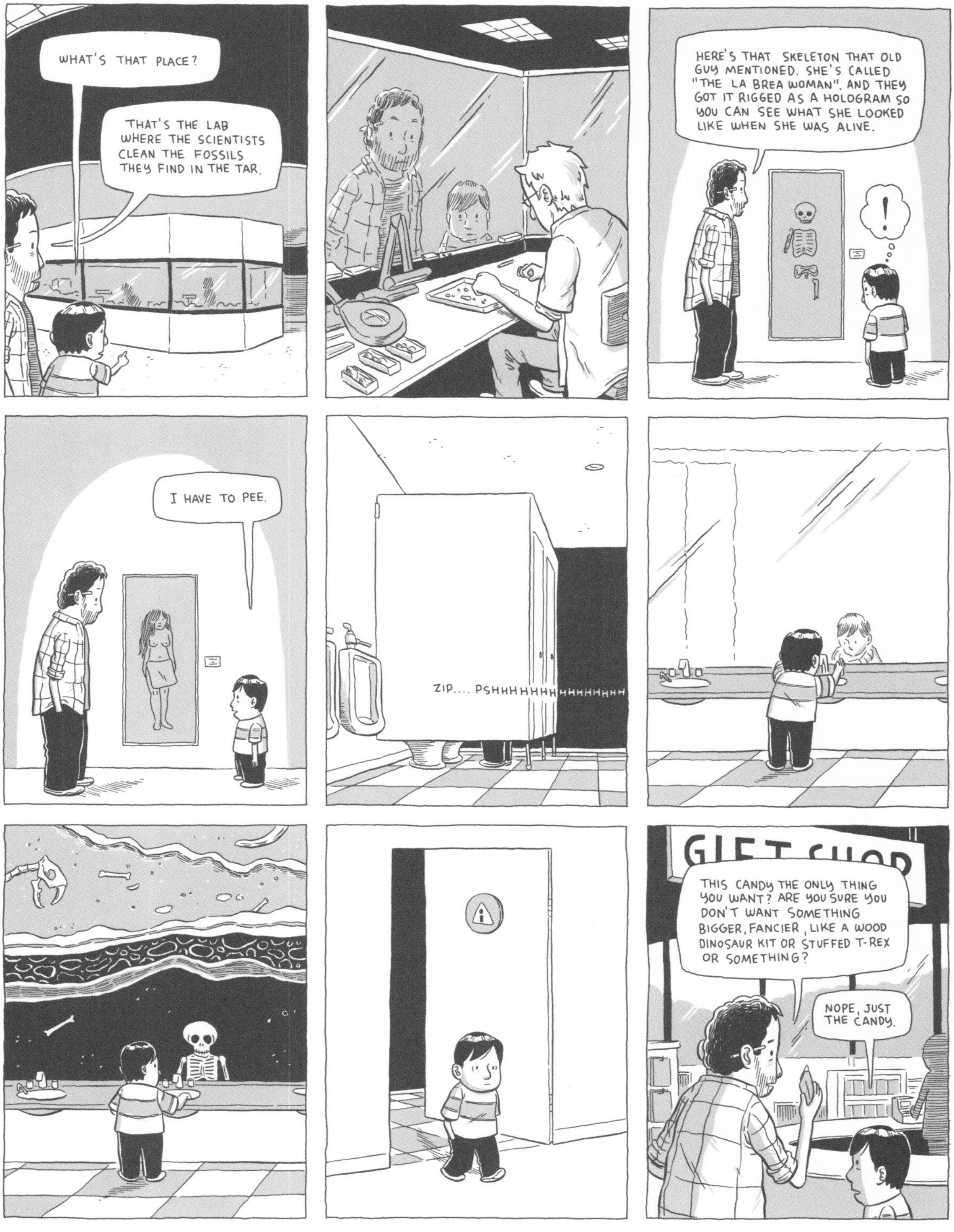
WHAT'S THAT PLACE?
THAT'S THE LAB WHERE THE SCIENTISTS CLEAN THE FOSSILS THEY FIND IN THE TAR.
HERE'S THAT SKELETON THAT OLD GUY MENTIONED. SHE'S CALLED "THE LA BREA WOMAN". AND THEY GOT IT RIGGED AS A HOLOGRAM SO YOU CAN SEE WHAT SHE LOOKED LIKE WHEN SHE WAS ALIVE.
!
I HAVE TO PEE.
ZIP.... PSHHHHHHHHHHHHHHHH
GIFT SHOP
THIS CANDY THE ONLY THING YOU WANT? ARE YOU SURE YOU DON'T WANT SOMETHING BIGGER, FANCIER, LIKE A WOOD DINOSAUR KIT OR STUFFED T-REX OR SOMETHING?
NOPE, JUST THE CANDY.

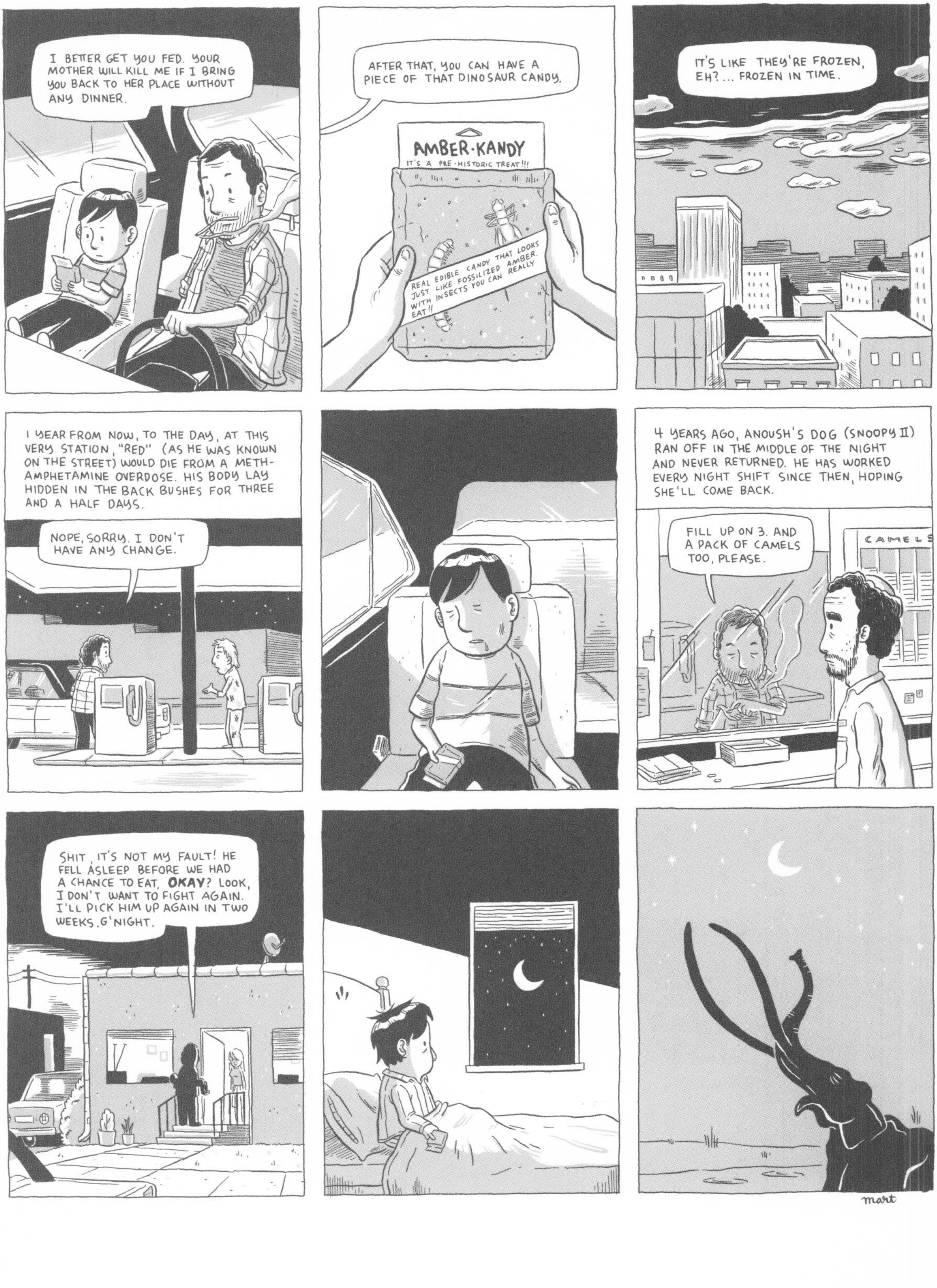

I BETTER GET YOU FED. YOUR MOTHER WILL KILL ME IF I BRING YOU BACK TO HER PLACE WITHOUT ANY DINNER.
AFTER THAT, YOU CAN HAVE A PIECE OF THAT DINOSAUR CANDY.
AMBER·KANDY
IT'S A PRE-HISTORIC TREAT!!!
REAL EDIBLE CANDY THAT LOOKS JUST LIKE FOSSILIZED AMBER. WITH INSECTS YOU CAN REALLY EAT!!
IT'S LIKE THEY'RE FROZEN, EH?... FROZEN IN TIME.
1 YEAR FROM NOW, TO THE DAY, AT THIS VERY STATION, "RED" (AS HE WAS KNOWN ON THE STREET) WOULD DIE FROM A METH-AMPHETAMINE OVERDOSE. HIS BODY LAY HIDDEN IN THE BACK BUSHES FOR THREE AND A HALF DAYS.
NOPE, SORRY. I DON'T HAVE ANY CHANGE.
4 YEARS AGO, ANOUSH'S DOG (SNOOPY II) RAN OFF IN THE MIDDLE OF THE NIGHT AND NEVER RETURNED. HE HAS WORKED EVERY NIGHT SHIFT SINCE THEN, HOPING SHE'LL COME BACK.
FILL UP ON 3. AND A PACK OF CAMELS TOO, PLEASE.
CAMELS
SHIT, IT'S NOT MY FAULT! HE FELL ASLEEP BEFORE WE HAD A CHANCE TO EAT, **OKAY**? LOOK, I DON'T WANT TO FIGHT AGAIN. I'LL PICK HIM UP AGAIN IN TWO WEEKS. G'NIGHT.
mart

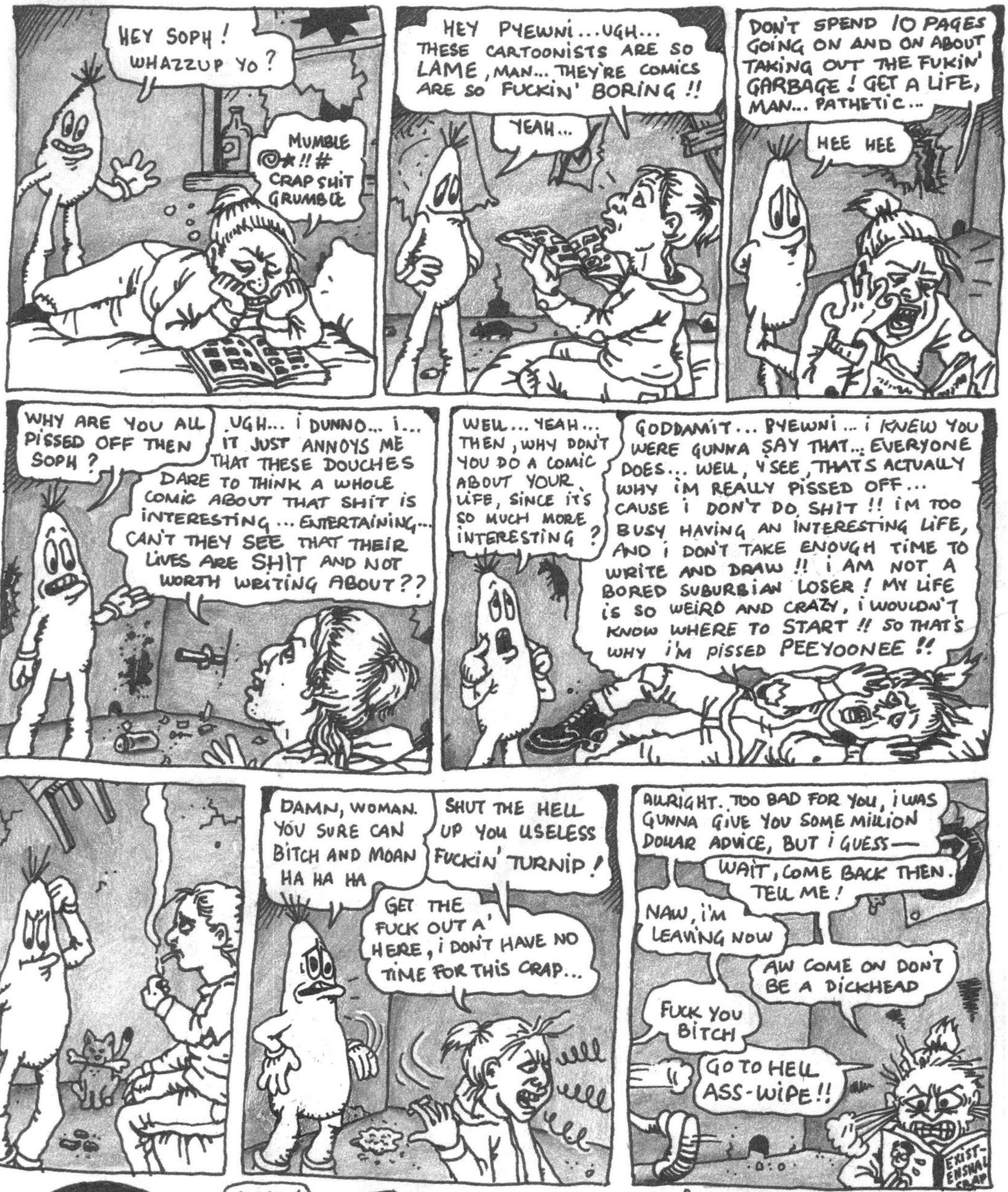
HEY SOPH! WHAZZUP YO?
MUMBLE @*!!# CRAP SHIT GRUMBLE
HEY PYEWNI...UGH... THESE CARTOONISTS ARE SO LAME, MAN... THEY'RE COMICS ARE SO FUCKIN' BORING!!
YEAH...
DON'T SPEND 10 PAGES GOING ON AND ON ABOUT TAKING OUT THE FUKIN' GARBAGE! GET A LIFE, MAN... PATHETIC...
HEE HEE
WHY ARE YOU ALL PISSED OFF THEN SOPH?
UGH... I DUNNO... I... IT JUST ANNOYS ME THAT THESE DOUCHES DARE TO THINK A WHOLE COMIC ABOUT THAT SHIT IS INTERESTING... ENTERTAINING... CAN'T THEY SEE THAT THEIR LIVES ARE SHIT AND NOT WORTH WRITING ABOUT??
WELL... YEAH... THEN, WHY DON'T YOU DO A COMIC ABOUT YOUR LIFE, SINCE IT'S SO MUCH MORE INTERESTING?
GODDAMIT... PYEWNI... I KNEW YOU WERE GUNNA SAY THAT... EVERYONE DOES... WELL, Y'SEE, THAT'S ACTUALLY WHY I'M REALLY PISSED OFF... CAUSE I DON'T DO SHIT!! I'M TOO BUSY HAVING AN INTERESTING LIFE, AND I DON'T TAKE ENOUGH TIME TO WRITE AND DRAW!! I AM NOT A BORED SUBURBIAN LOSER! MY LIFE IS SO WEIRD AND CRAZY, I WOULDN'T KNOW WHERE TO START!! SO THAT'S WHY I'M PISSED PEEYOONEE!!
DAMN, WOMAN. YOU SURE CAN BITCH AND MOAN HA HA HA
SHUT THE HELL UP YOU USELESS FUCKIN' TURNIP!
GET THE FUCK OUT A' HERE, I DON'T HAVE NO TIME FOR THIS CRAP...
ALLRIGHT. TOO BAD FOR YOU, I WAS GUNNA GIVE YOU SOME MILLION DOLLAR ADVICE, BUT I GUESS—
WAIT, COME BACK THEN. TELL ME!
NAW, I'M LEAVING NOW
AW COME ON DON'T BE A DICKHEAD
FUCK YOU BITCH
GO TO HELL ASS-WIPE!!
EXIST-ENSHAL CRAP

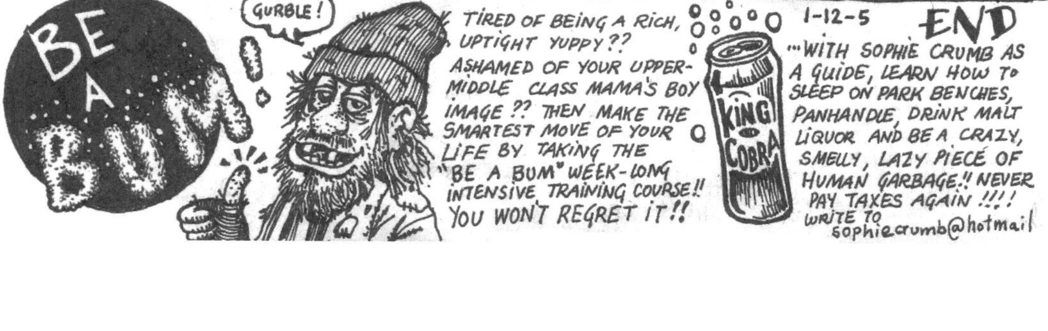
BE A BUM!
GURBLE!
TIRED OF BEING A RICH, UPTIGHT YUPPY?? ASHAMED OF YOUR UPPER-MIDDLE CLASS MAMA'S BOY IMAGE?? THEN MAKE THE SMARTEST MOVE OF YOUR LIFE BY TAKING THE "BE A BUM" WEEK-LONG INTENSIVE TRAINING COURSE!! YOU WON'T REGRET IT!!
KING COBRA
1-12-5
END
...WITH SOPHIE CRUMB AS A GUIDE, LEARN HOW TO SLEEP ON PARK BENCHES, PANHANDLE, DRINK MALT LIQUOR AND BE A CRAZY, SMELLY, LAZY PIECE OF HUMAN GARBAGE!! NEVER PAY TAXES AGAIN!!!!
WRITE TO sophiecrumb@hotmail

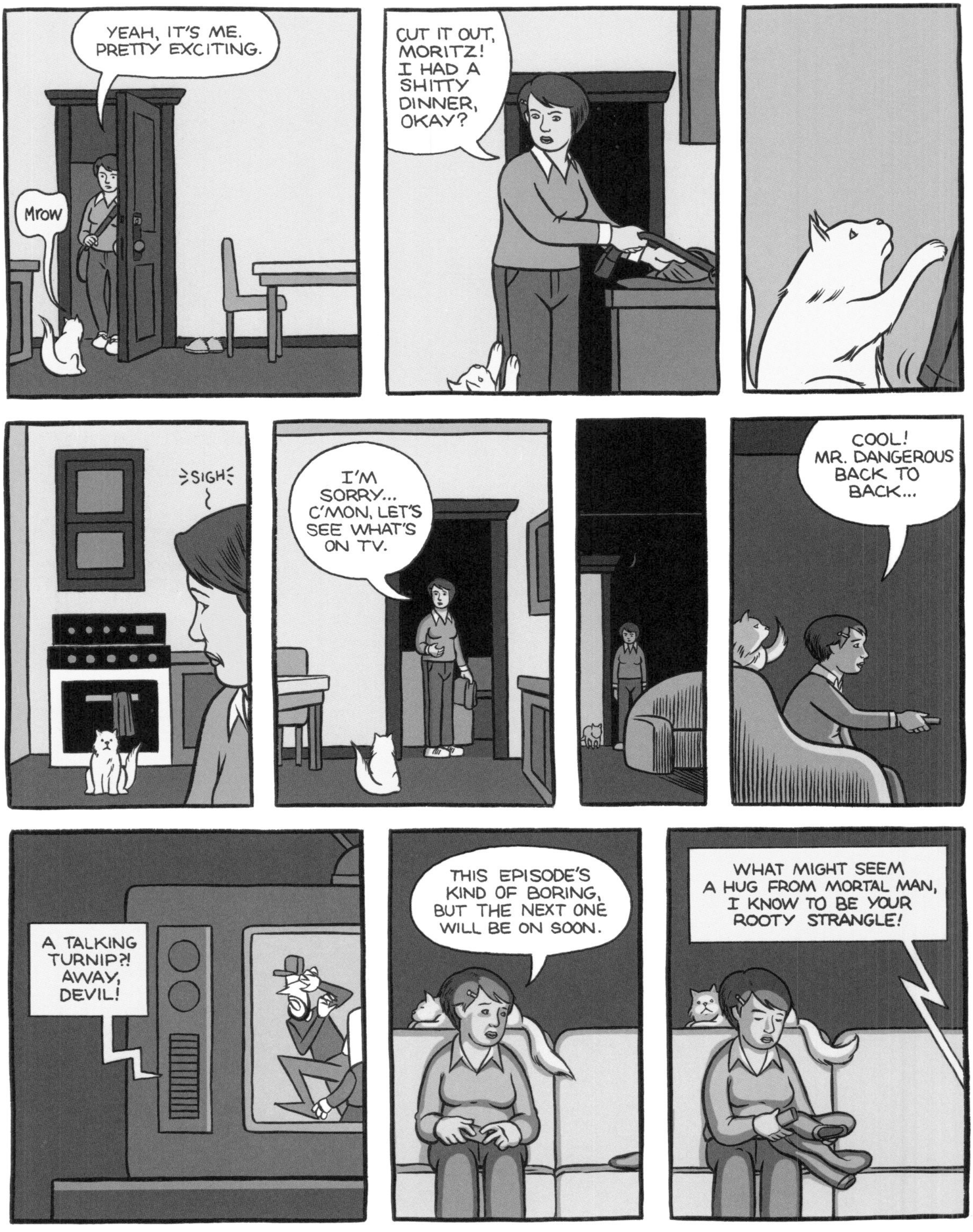
YEAH, IT'S ME. PRETTY EXCITING.
Mrow
CUT IT OUT, MORITZ! I HAD A SHITTY DINNER, OKAY?
SIGH
I'M SORRY... C'MON, LET'S SEE WHAT'S ON TV.
COOL! MR. DANGEROUS BACK TO BACK...
A TALKING TURNIP?! AWAY, DEVIL!
THIS EPISODE'S KIND OF BORING, BUT THE NEXT ONE WILL BE ON SOON.
WHAT MIGHT SEEM A HUG FROM MORTAL MAN, I KNOW TO BE YOUR ROOTY STRANGLE!

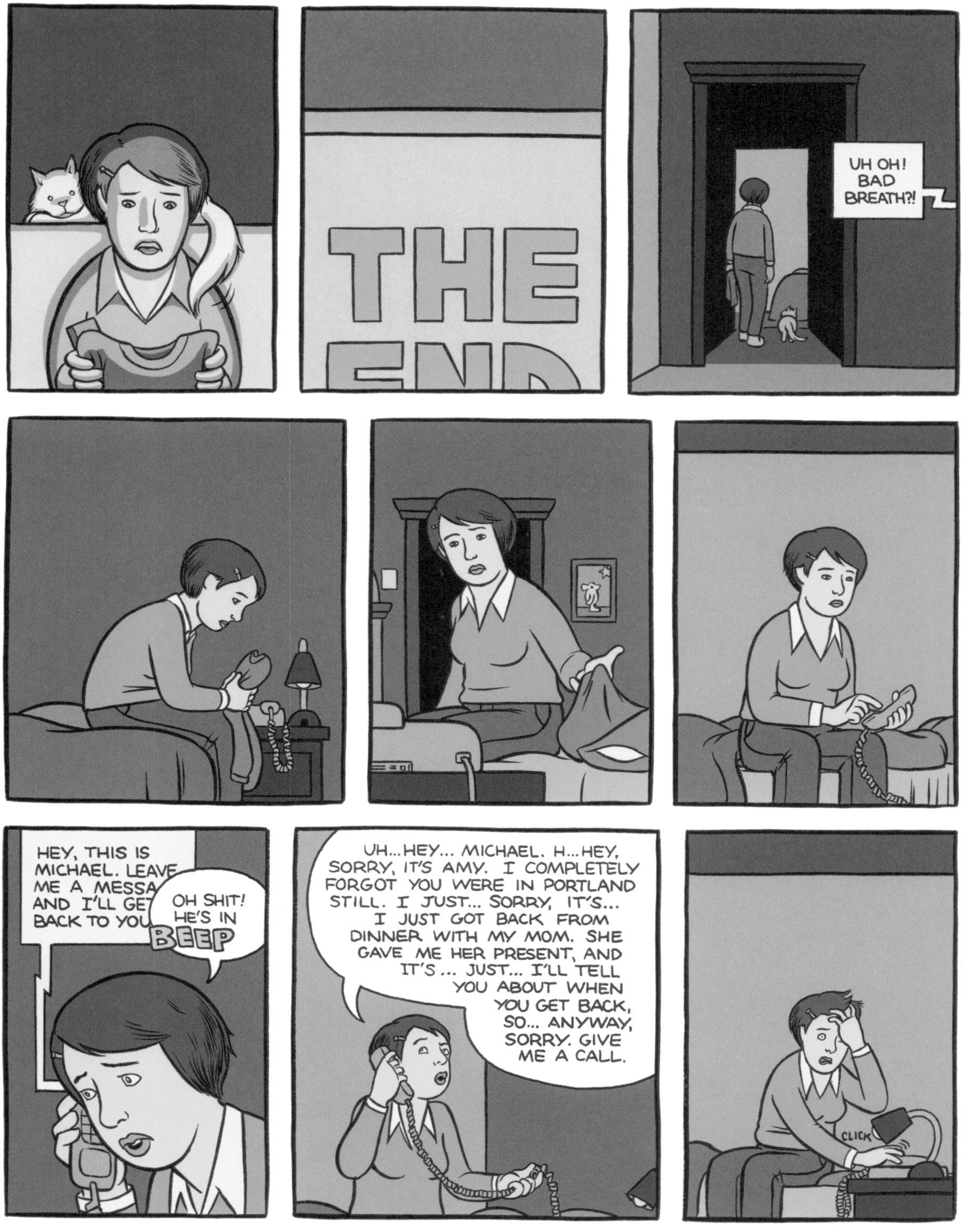

THE END
UH OH! BAD BREATH?!
HEY, THIS IS MICHAEL. LEAVE ME A MESSA AND I'LL GET BACK TO YOU
OH SHIT! HE'S IN
BEEP
UH... HEY... MICHAEL. H... HEY, SORRY, IT'S AMY. I COMPLETELY FORGOT YOU WERE IN PORTLAND STILL. I JUST... SORRY, IT'S... I JUST GOT BACK FROM DINNER WITH MY MOM. SHE GAVE ME HER PRESENT, AND IT'S ... JUST... I'LL TELL YOU ABOUT WHEN YOU GET BACK, SO... ANYWAY, SORRY. GIVE ME A CALL.
CLICK

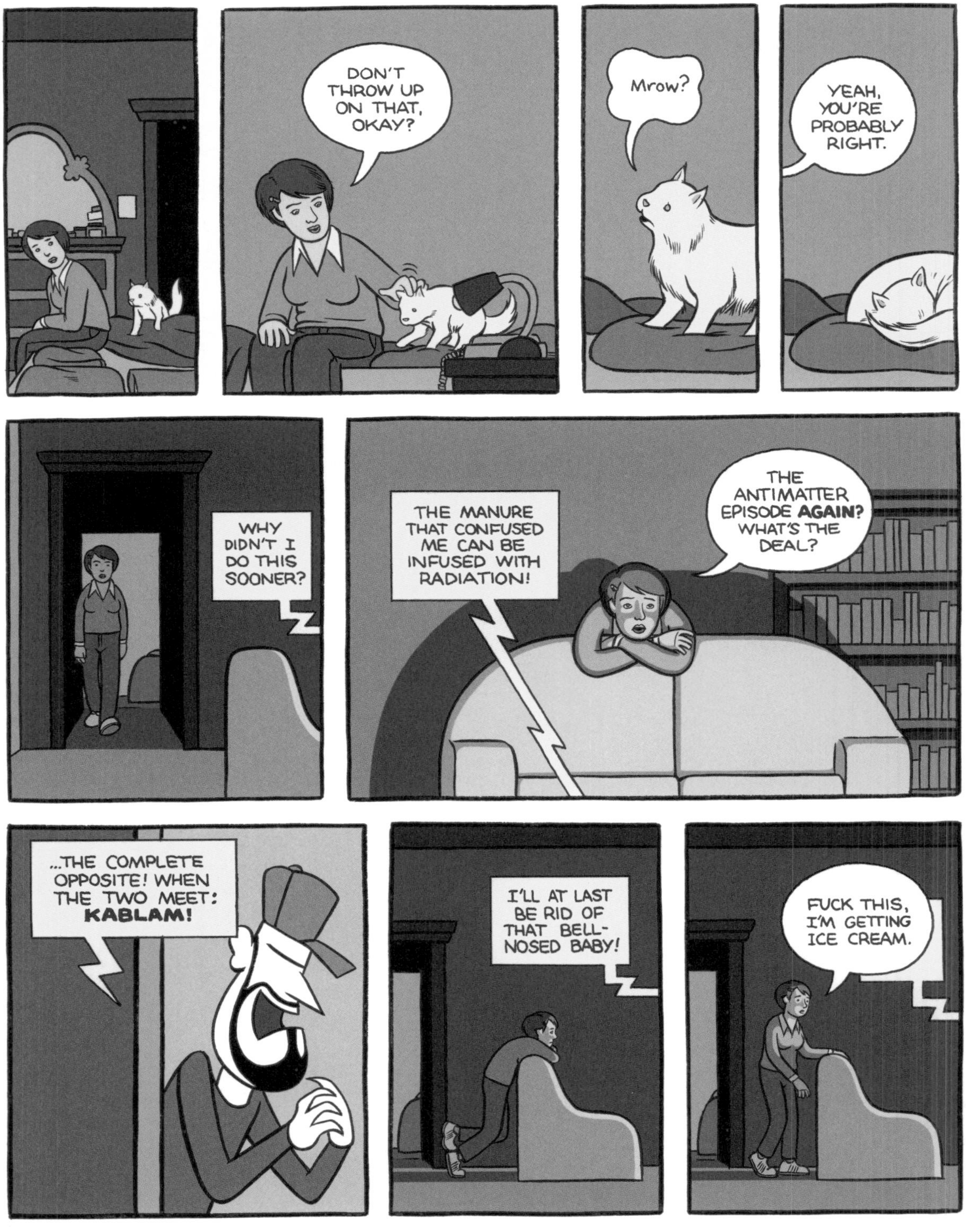

DON'T THROW UP ON THAT, OKAY?
Mrow?
YEAH, YOU'RE PROBABLY RIGHT.
WHY DIDN'T I DO THIS SOONER?
THE MANURE THAT CONFUSED ME CAN BE INFUSED WITH RADIATION!
THE ANTIMATTER EPISODE **AGAIN?** WHAT'S THE DEAL?
...THE COMPLETE OPPOSITE! WHEN THE TWO MEET: **KABLAM!**
I'LL AT LAST BE RID OF THAT BELL-NOSED BABY!
FUCK THIS, I'M GETTING ICE CREAM.

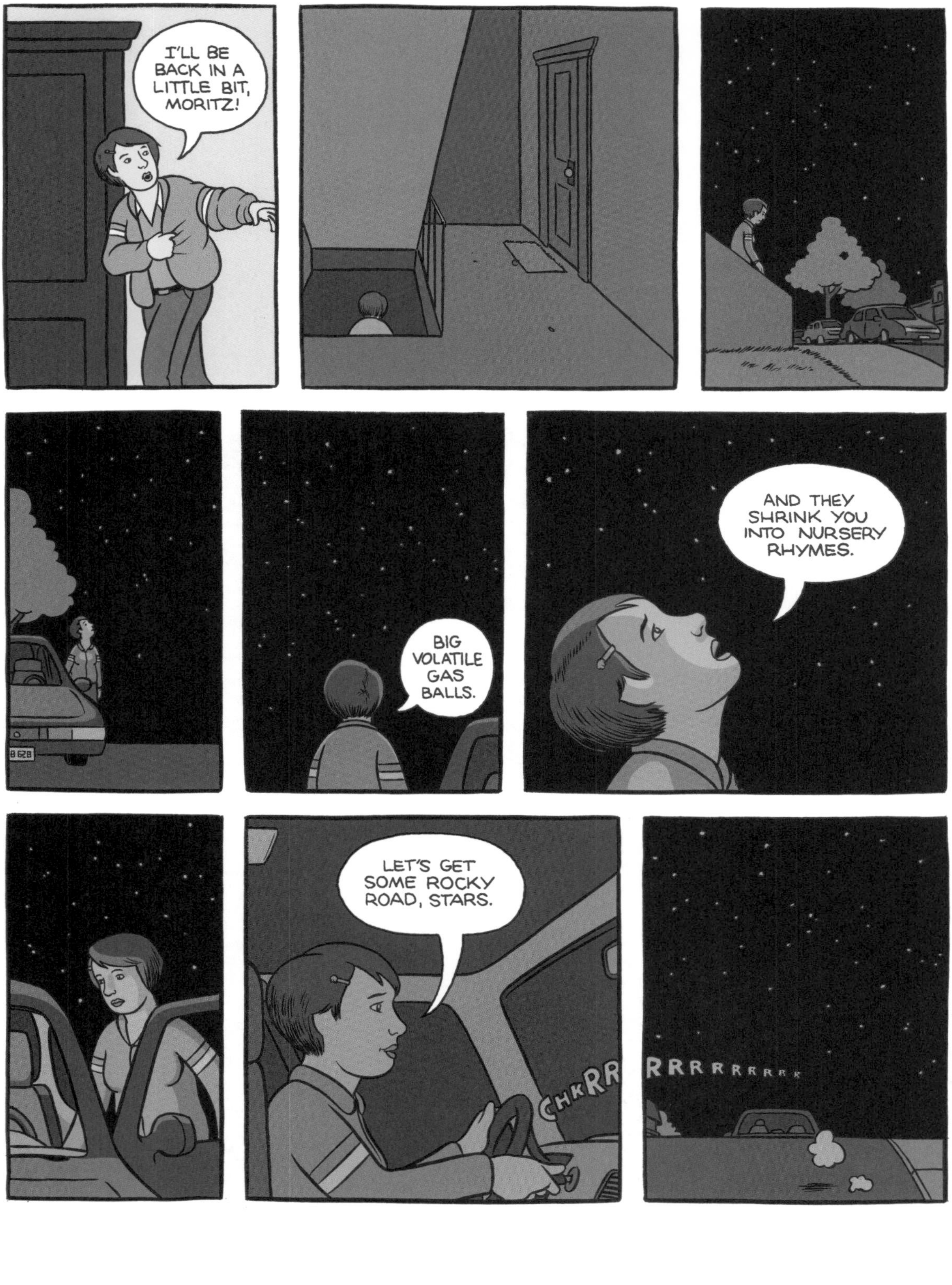
I'LL BE BACK IN A LITTLE BIT, MORITZ!
B 62B
BIG VOLATILE GAS BALLS.
AND THEY SHRINK YOU INTO NURSERY RHYMES.
LET'S GET SOME ROCKY ROAD, STARS.
CHKRRRRRRRRRRRRK

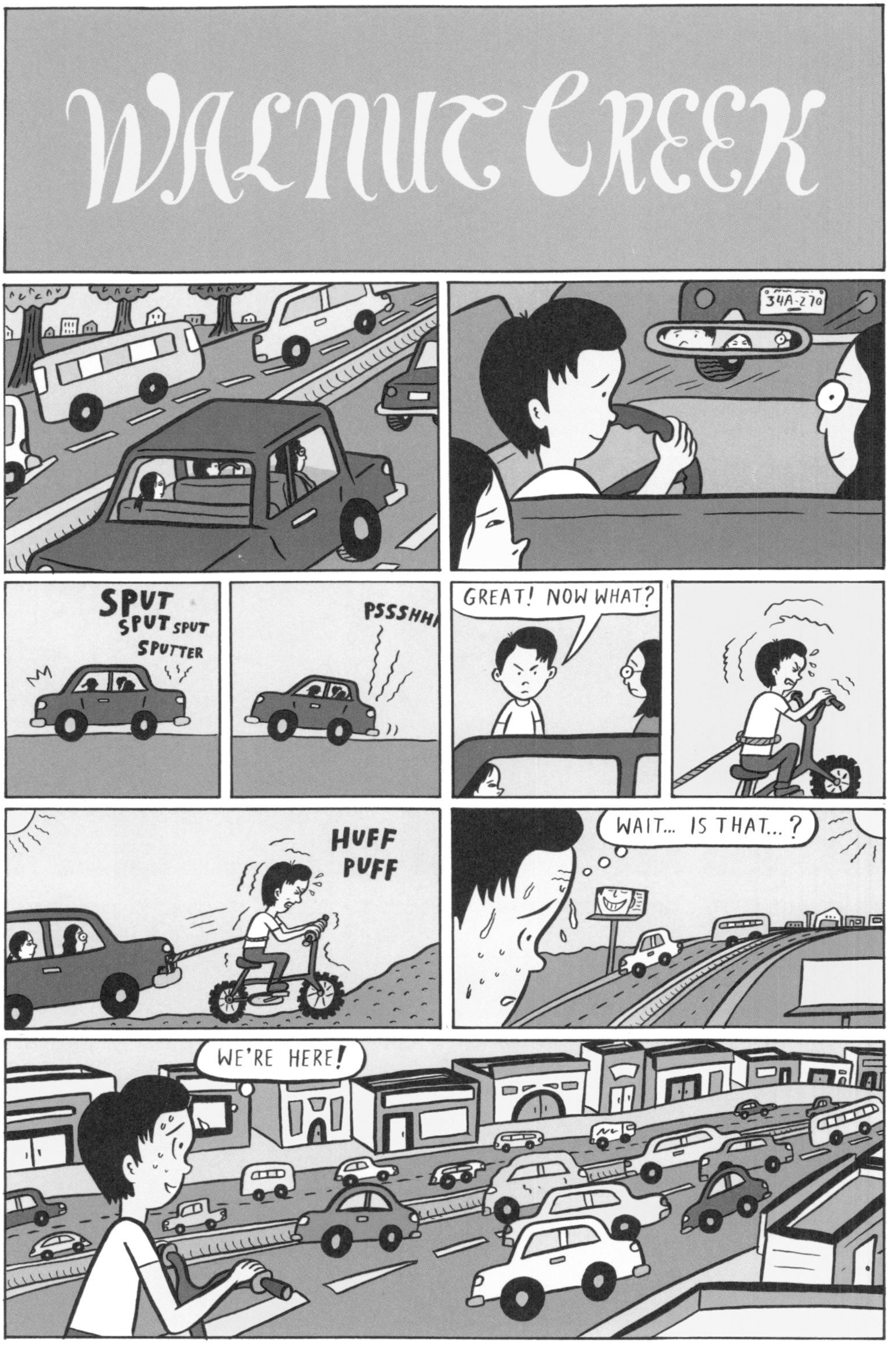
WALNUT CREEK
34A-270
SPUT
SPUT SPUT
SPUTTER
PSSSHH
GREAT! NOW WHAT?
HUFF
PUFF
WAIT... IS THAT...?
WE'RE HERE!

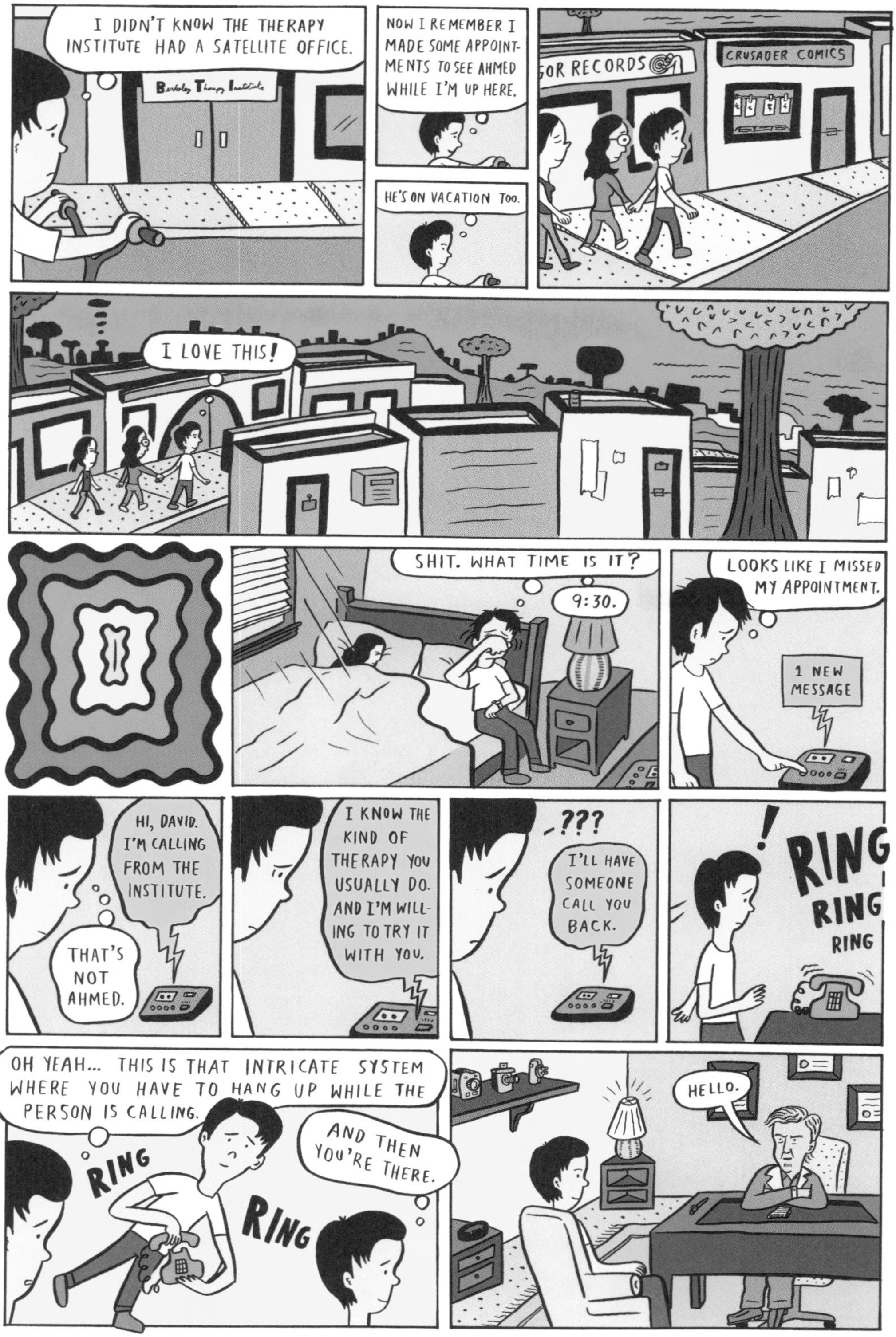
I DIDN'T KNOW THE THERAPY INSTITUTE HAD A SATELLITE OFFICE.
Berkeley Therapy Institute
NOW I REMEMBER I MADE SOME APPOINTMENTS TO SEE AHMED WHILE I'M UP HERE.
HE'S ON VACATION TOO.
GOR RECORDS
CRUSADER COMICS
I LOVE THIS!
SHIT. WHAT TIME IS IT?
9:30.
LOOKS LIKE I MISSED MY APPOINTMENT.
1 NEW MESSAGE
HI, DAVID. I'M CALLING FROM THE INSTITUTE.
THAT'S NOT AHMED.
I KNOW THE KIND OF THERAPY YOU USUALLY DO. AND I'M WILLING TO TRY IT WITH YOU.
???
I'LL HAVE SOMEONE CALL YOU BACK.
!
RING RING RING
OH YEAH... THIS IS THAT INTRICATE SYSTEM WHERE YOU HAVE TO HANG UP WHILE THE PERSON IS CALLING.
RING
RING
AND THEN YOU'RE THERE.
HELLO.

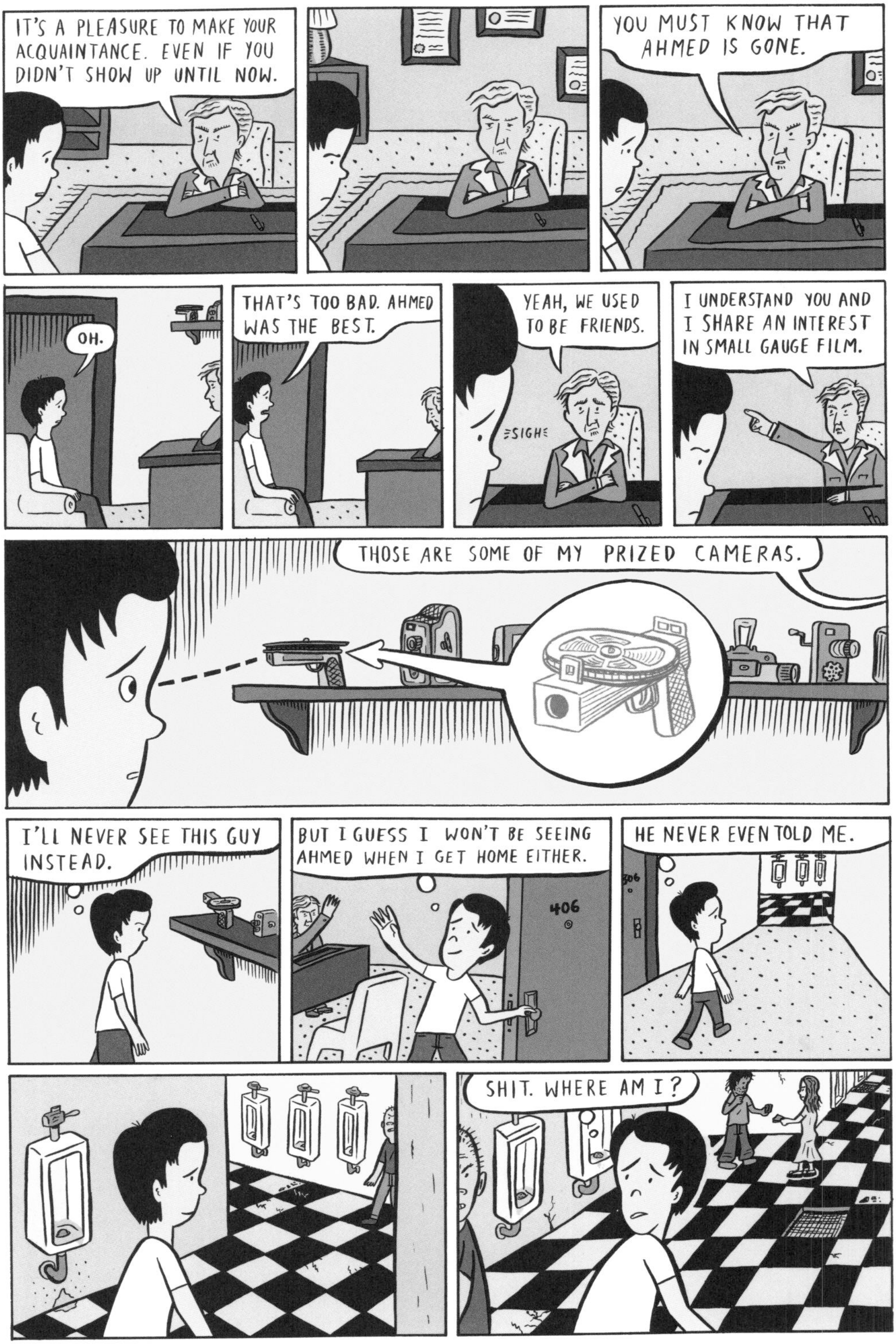
IT'S A PLEASURE TO MAKE YOUR ACQUAINTANCE. EVEN IF YOU DIDN'T SHOW UP UNTIL NOW.
YOU MUST KNOW THAT AHMED IS GONE.
OH.
THAT'S TOO BAD. AHMED WAS THE BEST.
YEAH, WE USED TO BE FRIENDS.
SIGH
I UNDERSTAND YOU AND I SHARE AN INTEREST IN SMALL GAUGE FILM.
THOSE ARE SOME OF MY PRIZED CAMERAS.
I'LL NEVER SEE THIS GUY INSTEAD.
BUT I GUESS I WON'T BE SEEING AHMED WHEN I GET HOME EITHER.
406
HE NEVER EVEN TOLD ME.
306
SHIT. WHERE AM I?

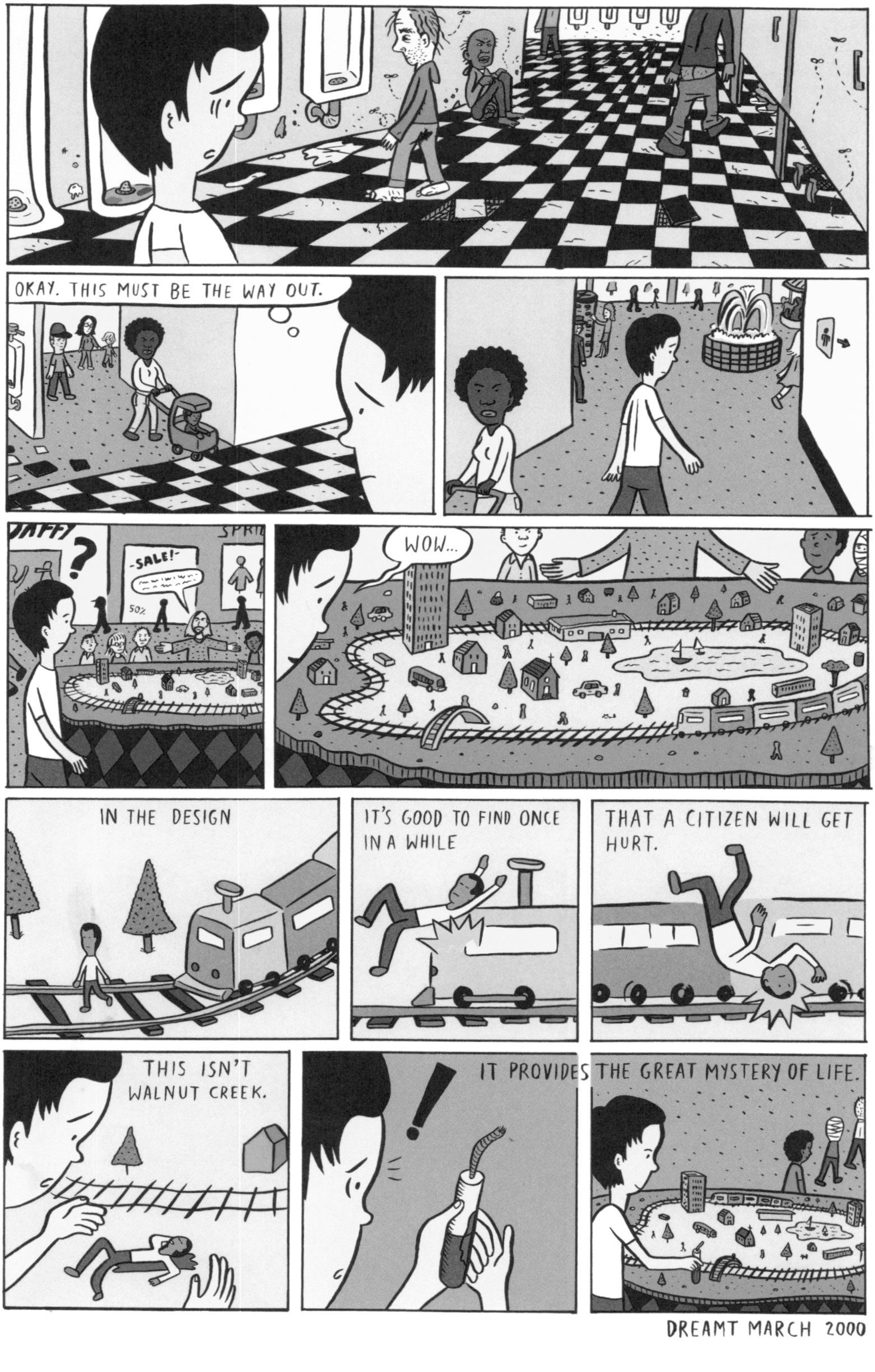

OKAY. THIS MUST BE THE WAY OUT.
-SALE!-
50%
?
WOW...
IN THE DESIGN
IT'S GOOD TO FIND ONCE IN A WHILE
THAT A CITIZEN WILL GET HURT.
THIS ISN'T WALNUT CREEK.
!
IT PROVIDES THE GREAT MYSTERY OF LIFE.

DREAMT MARCH 2000

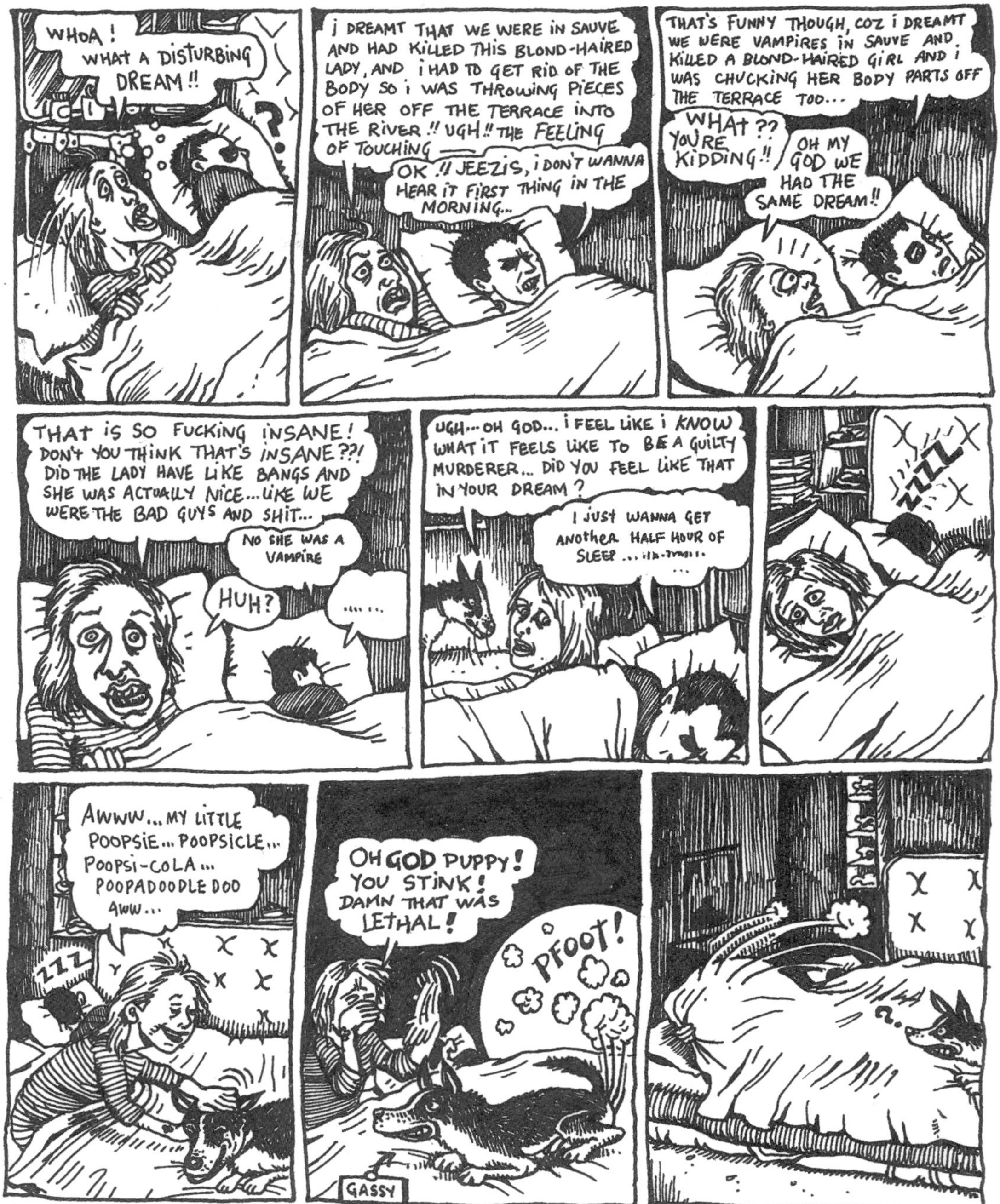
WHOA! WHAT A DISTURBING DREAM!!
I DREAMT THAT WE WERE IN SAUVE AND HAD KILLED THIS BLOND-HAIRED LADY, AND I HAD TO GET RID OF THE BODY SO I WAS THROWING PIECES OF HER OFF THE TERRACE INTO THE RIVER!! UGH!! THE FEELING OF TOUCHING —
OK!! JEEZIS, I DON'T WANNA HEAR IT FIRST THING IN THE MORNING...
THAT'S FUNNY THOUGH, COZ I DREAMT WE WERE VAMPIRES IN SAUVE AND KILLED A BLOND-HAIRED GIRL AND I WAS CHUCKING HER BODY PARTS OFF THE TERRACE TOO...
WHAT?? YOU'RE KIDDING!!
OH MY GOD WE HAD THE SAME DREAM!!
THAT IS SO FUCKING INSANE! DON'T YOU THINK THAT'S INSANE??! DID THE LADY HAVE LIKE BANGS AND SHE WAS ACTUALLY NICE... LIKE WE WERE THE BAD GUYS AND SHIT...
NO SHE WAS A VAMPIRE
HUH?
......
UGH... OH GOD... I FEEL LIKE I KNOW WHAT IT FEELS LIKE TO BE A GUILTY MURDERER... DID YOU FEEL LIKE THAT IN YOUR DREAM?
I JUST WANNA GET ANOTHER HALF HOUR OF SLEEP ...
ZZZZ
AWWW... MY LITTLE POOPSIE... POOPSICLE... POOPSI-COLA... POOPADOODLE DOO AWW...
ZZZ
OH GOD PUPPY! YOU STINK! DAMN THAT WAS LETHAL!
PFOOT!
GASSY

END

... and that's exactly what happened this morning ...

SOPH' CRUMB
JAN. 2006

HOW ARE YOU?

ABOVE, FROM SKETCHBOOK

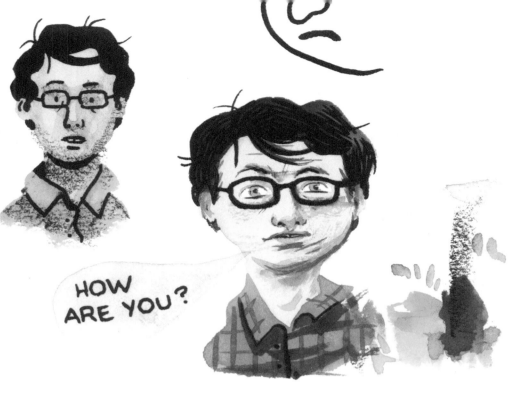

AN INTERVIEW WITH JONATHAN BENNETT

It was practically inevitable *that Jonathan Bennett would become a cartoonist: Growing up in Syosset, a suburb on Long Island, he was a comics geek at an early age, reading newspaper strips first (*Peanuts, Calvin and Hobbes, Ziggy*), then graduating, if that is the word, to shitty Marvel comics at the age of eight or nine. I use the word 'shitty' advisedly since Jonathan admitted to loving Marvel's* Secret Wars II *series, one of the most incontestably awful comics series ever conceived. But apparently nothing could stop the young Master Bennett, not even a love of* Secret Wars II. *He became obsessed, as we all did: He wrote and drew his own X-Men stories, would draw his homework assignments in comic book form when he could get away with it, went to comics conventions with his dad, and even took weekend cartooning classes at the age of 10 or 11.*

His interest waned somewhat when he became a teenager when music (Nirvana, the Pixies, They Might Be Giants, Frank Black, and even "older" bands, he says, like Talking Heads and the Velvet Underground) and starting a band replaced comics as a creative interest. He kept drawing, just not comics. After high school, he attended The Hartford Art School, where his interest was revitalized when he was given a copy of Seth's It's a Good Life If You Don't Weaken, *which was something of a revelation ("I was definitely shocked when I read* It's A Good Life. *I read it in one evening on a train ride…"). He began to realize the artistic possibilities of comics when he started reading more widely — Chester Brown, Charles Burns, Joe Matt, Dave Collier, Chris Ware — but still wasn't sure enough of himself to draw comics full-bore: He drew some sample strips he wanted to submit to the college newspaper but got cold feet and never did. "That was where my comics career began and ended as far as I was concerned in college. I figured I should just be a fan. I'm not meant to do this."*

After he graduated, he and his wife-to-be Amy moved to Brooklyn, where he got a job in a tiny T-shirt factory

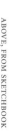

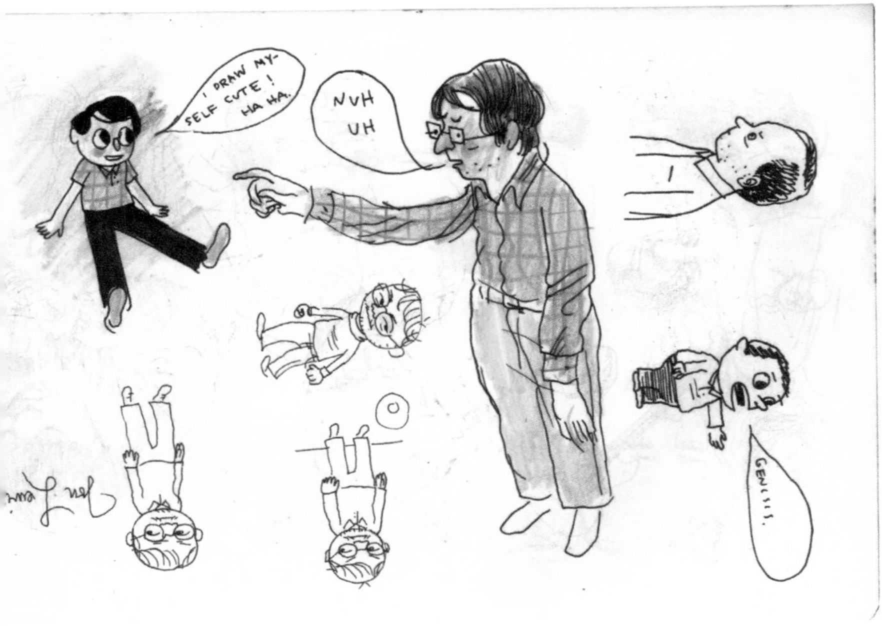

I DRAW MY-
SELF CUTE!
HA HA.
NUH
UH
GENIUS.

ABOVE, FROM SKETCHBOOK

literally spending eight hours a day silkscreening T-shirts — "exactly one year of horribleness" is how he describes it, but which at least inspired him to try to draw a comic about it. From there he got a job at D.K. Publishing as a designer, and had to devote pretty much all his time to leaning how to design books "while putting up a facade like I knew what I was doing" — doing it and faking it at the same time is like two full time jobs, as most of us know, and leaves little time to actually draw comics, so his comics production was put on hold.

Luckily he got laid off three weeks after 9-11 and, using The Jules Feiffer Career Advancement Method, used the time he was subsequently paid unemployment compensation to buckle down and teach himself cartooning. "It was during that brief month and a half of unemployment when I went out and bought a drafting table and finally researched online and found out what pen nibs to buy and practiced with them and started working really hard at trying to draw like a cartoonist." Arguably, this worked.

In 2002 he self-published the first issue of Esoteric Tales *and the second and last issue in 2003. These two small comics were all I'd seen before I invited him to be part of* MOME, *and, in retrospect, look like mere warm-ups to the longer, more formally elaborate work that he's done in* MOME. *His approach to storytelling has congealed: Jonathan's work reminds me of Robert Bresson's in its sparseness, economy, and interiority.*

This interview was conducted in late February, 2006 and edited by Jonathan and myself.

—Gary Groth

JONATHAN BENNETT: I started working on my first comic stories. I made a couple short ones that have since been thrown away and were never published. Then I went to MoCCA [in the summer of 2002] and was introduced to so many more minicomics and other books and stuff like that; I didn't have a table, I just wandered around at that one. But I brought my first *Esoteric Tales* to that.

GARY GROTH: *Because you were something of a designer and because you studied printmaking, you could publish your own comic.*

JB: Yeah, yeah, I think so. I think I just started buying a lot of minicomics around New York at bookstores and comic shops and stuff so I figured out that there was a big community of people making these Xeroxed books and things that were printed on their home printers. I had been working on my own comics from October through June, so I'd been working for like eight months at the time, and threw out a lot of comic strips that didn't come out well, but had practiced enough and gotten confidence enough that I was able to put together a book's worth of material — that first issue. I made that a deadline for myself when I had learned about the show when it was first announced, people were talking about it on the message boards, so I said, "OK, well, I'll make my first comic and I'll hand it out to people at MoCCA."

I can't get anything done without a deadline, so that worked, miraculously. I just started using all my free time, I got out of music, stopped being in band and stuff.

My last band broke up badly, and I just put all my creative energies into comics instead.

GG: *There are only two issues of* Esoteric.

JB: Yeah, pretty much; there's also those two really small minicomics that are sort of *Esoteric Tales* also, they're just smaller.

GG: *They're just really really esoteric tales.*

JB: Those are also self-contained short stories, whereas *Esoteric Tales* is more of a couple of stories in each book. It took a lot longer to produce. I would do those little miniature books in like two weeks, and *Esoteric Tales*, those would take me forever to do because I was just slowly working on random comics and didn't know what I was doing. Eventually, when a comics convention would come up, then I would say, "Oh, I better start finding stuff I can print."

So I didn't really have a plan of what would be in it until I found out there was a comics show coming up and that I have to fill up 16 pages.

GG: *It seems like those first two issues were a learning experience; I can kind of see where you're learning how to develop an inking technique, for example.*

JB: Yeah, definitely, I was trying out all those different things like brushes for the first time. I'd used nibs before, several kinds, and never well, and finally started using different things and trying lettering professionally and buying an Ames guide and all that stuff. Trying to learn how to make things as well crafted as possible and I really was trying really hard even though I look at them now and cringe at a lot of this stuff, but I really tried hard to make them look as professional as I possibly could.

GG: *There seems to be a real break between* Esoteric Tales *and all the work you've done in* MOME *— the first story you did in* MOME *is not dissimilar stylistically to the fourth story you've done in* MOME. *there's a stylistic coherency to all the stuff you did in* MOME *which is quite different from what you did in* Esoteric Tales. *Was that shift a conscious decision or a gradual evolution that looks abrupt?*

JB: I guess you could call it a conscious decision, it was more of a …

GG: *A very deliberate refinement?*

JB: It was just fear; I was afraid, I had never been published before by anyone, so when you guys contacted me about it, I just freaked out and I didn't feel like anything I had printed to date was good enough for a real publisher to have published. I was already very critical of all that stuff, even though it was only a couple of years old. I just made myself work extra hard at trying to make everything better. I was just really freaked out by the whole opportunity that you guys had given me. [*Groth laughs.*] I felt a tremendous amount of pressure.

GG: *I guess that had a good effect on you.*

JB: Yeah, I've read that interview, some publicity thing that I guess Eric [Reynolds] has shared with a few interviews, where he said part of the reason that you guys wanted to put together *MOME* was so that you could get work that otherwise wouldn't have been created out

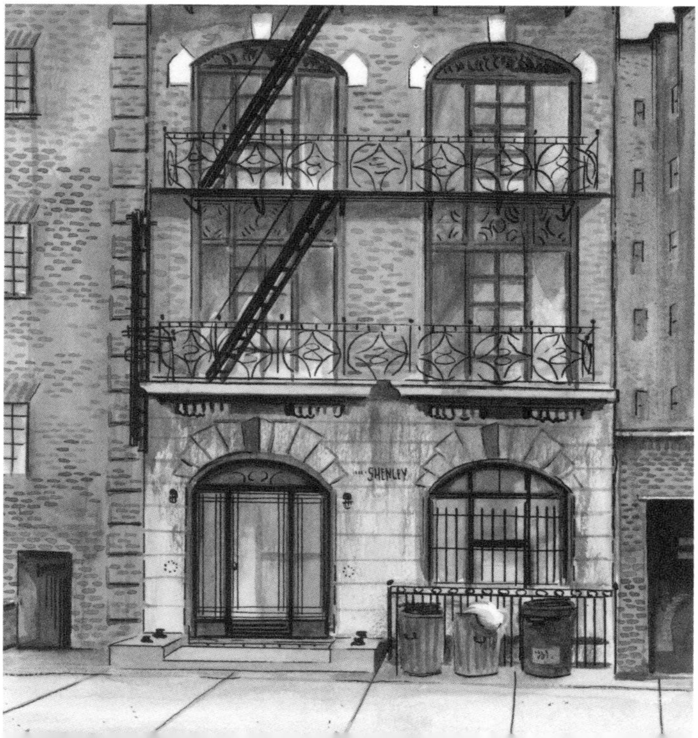
SHENLEY

LEFT, PAINTING USED FOR STORY IN *MOME WINTER 2006*

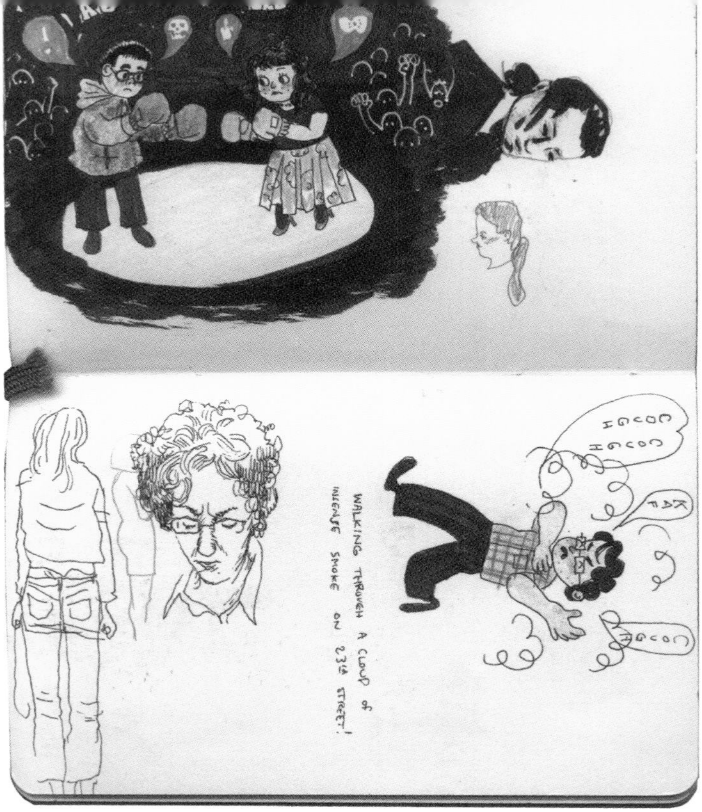
WALKING THROUGH A CLOUD OF INCENSE SMOKE ON 23rd STREET!

ABOVE, FROM SKETCHBOOK

of some newer, under-published cartoonists. I think with me, that's exactly what happened. I never would have written these stories, they weren't kicking around in my head waiting to be written when I had the time or anything like that. These were things that I've had to come up with on the spot because I knew I had a deadline all of a sudden.

It's been really great for me, because it made me work harder and it made me take it seriously on a new level. I was really trying hard, but it upped the ante to have you guys looking over my shoulder and knowing that you'd be reading it, and knowing you guys were committed to publishing whatever it was that we handed in, pretty much.

GG: *Let me ask you how you construct a story. All your stories are around eight to 10 pages or so. You don't write the entire story out first, I assume.*

JB: No, no. I've never worked on anything longer than maybe three pages, or four pages, until I started working on *MOME*. I would do those stories that you saw in *Esoteric Tales*, that were maybe 10 pages long, but really they were on only two sheets of paper and I would chop up the squares and make them — I had these big Chris Ware rip-off style pages with 24 panels on a page, where I was really trying to make it look like one big solid old Sunday newspaper page or something, and then I would reconfigure them to fill up *Esoteric Tales* when a comics show was coming up. Just to fill up 16 pages.

This is the first time that I knew that I'd have to make full pages and make a 10-page story for real, so yeah, I used to write those stories. It's easy to say "OK, this is what's going to happen, it's going to be this brief little anecdote," and I would just make myself a chart. I got this very loose idea of what I would get started with as an opening sequence, and one thing that I would, like thumbnail it out and do a lot of the writing on the page as I get started and not really know where it's going to end up. It's been a weird experiment. Not very well planned at all. Sort of a surprise.

GG: *There's an organic quality to your stories that I wouldn't necessarily think indicates that you have a blueprint before you started drawing. In fact, your stories almost seem like a narrative version of a train of thought — that connections the mind makes routinely becomes a narrative, one things leads to another that leads to another that leads to another.*

JB: Yeah. That's exactly what it is, just trying to think how something has to happen on this page, and trying to further a simple storyline that's going underneath one story that may or may not have a goal or an ending. Trying to keep things interesting visually and not only to allow what's happening to inspire the next panel, and lead to the next section of the story, but also to visually try and use certain points and jump off of them visually. It definitely is an organic sort of thing that grows on the page as each panel leads to the next.

GG: *Right, right. It almost replicates the way you reflect on things when you're driving or when you're on the subway or when you're not focusing on something in particular and your mind starts wandering.*

JB: That's pretty much what it is; I have to sit at the drawing table and let my mind wander in order to come up with another idea. I don't know, it's really weird to try to have that come across. It's weird to me that that comes across reading my comic, because it's not really a train of thought, because all that stuff happens moment to moment, and with the stories, they're taking me weeks and weeks to finish everything. It will take me two weeks to finish one page sometimes, because I only get to work for maybe an hour and a half or three hours at a time each night or something like that. I'm pretty slow at working. But I guess I *write* the page fairly quickly and don't necessarily commit to everything on the page, but have an idea of where it's going to go.

GG: *Do you design the page and lay it out and have the figures placed and then write it, or do you write it —*

JB: Yeah, I usually write the actual thoughts and things being said, those are usually written as they're being lettered, because I can't really think that far ahead, because each panel — I don't know, sometimes I'll only have a panel and I don't know exactly what's going to be in the next panel, I'll just know that on this page, a certain thing will happen by the end of the page, and try and write my way up to that event, and then move on to the next thing and then get past it. I don't really have a method yet, I haven't really figured out why I do things the way that I'm doing them or exactly what I'm doing.

Sometimes I try and just allow the character to write the story for me. They're not really autobiographical stories, I'm not retelling what actually happened in my day, they're sort of things that happen to everyone and have happened to me, so I do have my real-life experience to work off of. But, it would be really boring if I told it as it happened. So instead I'm using circumstances as a springboard. Like, then what could happen, or sometimes I just find it writing itself and not trying to pick what would happen, but instead would feel something else coming. I don't think it happens unconsciously, a lot of the ideas, and then I'll have to sit down and actually write out things.

GG: *It sounds very intuitive.*

JB: I think so. I don't know if that's a good idea or not, and it's hard to count on that, to sit down at the drawing board and hope that something just feels right, or — [*Groth laughs*]. I wish I had it written out, and I wish I could just sit down and then tell the story that I knew I wanted to tell, but it hasn't happened that way yet.

GG: *Well, as long as it works. I don't think there's a 'right' way or a 'wrong' way.*

JB: I guess so, yeah, but I don't even know if it's working [*Groth laughs*], I'm having a hard time evaluating my own work and trying to move ahead and try different things. It's been a difficult, weird process, and it's all because of the page lengths, because I'm just not used to knowing that something is going

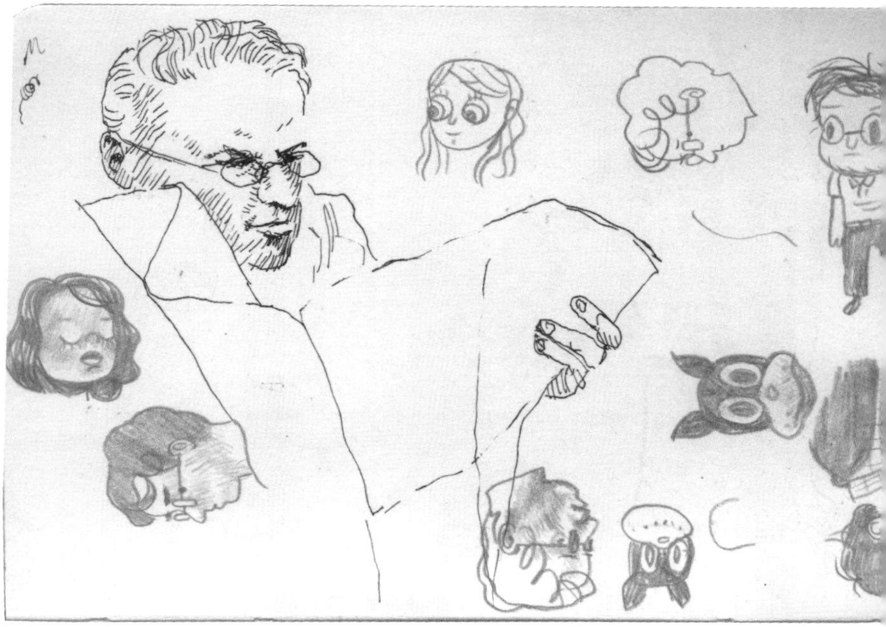

BELOW, FROM SKETCHBOOK

-SHHIIP-

ABOVE, FROM *ESOTERIC TALES* #1

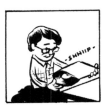

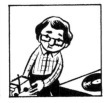

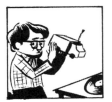

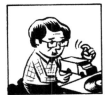

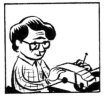

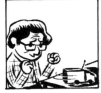

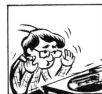

to be 10 pages. I'm getting more used to it, but it's still really weird that it has to keep going and going and going. [*Groth laughs.*] I can't just stop when I feel like something has happened successfully. OK, now I'm on page three. So that's how those stream of consciousness stories emerged, I think.

GG: *When you construct a story, you don't necessarily have beginning, middle, and end, it continues page by page until it ends?*

JB: Sometimes. Sometimes all I will have is the ending. Like with the story in this issue, I had that whole idea of creeping into the mattresses and emerging from them at the end. So I knew that would happen. But all that happens in the last two pages. So, getting up to that point was the tough part. I just knew I didn't want to open up with that happening. So yeah, sometimes the one section of the story that got me started on an idea doesn't necessarily have to be the beginning, middle or end, and all those parts are never there when I've gotten started on a story. It's either knowing that I'm going to work my way up to something and trying to fill in the blanks, or starting off with an idea, using it up, or trying to preserve some part of that idea so that it can also tie into the ending somehow.

GG: *All the characters in the first four stories could be the same character; with the fourth one being the same character maybe 20 years later.*

JB: I feel like that was a huge mistake. I don't know why I made that someone who wasn't myself, or not the same character I've been using, whoever that person is; I don't know if it even feels like it is me or not. It was a weird — I wanted a change visually. I wanted to try something different. So I thought I would try and put it all on someone else's physical body. I don't know if that worked or not, but we'll see.

GG: *In the first three stories, does the main character look like you? Because I don't even know what you look like.*

JB: Yeah, yeah, I think so. It's a caricature. I've been told by people, "You look just like you draw yourself in your comics." And I've also been told by people, "You look nothing like you draw yourself in your comics." [*Groth laughs.*] So I don't know who's right. But yeah, it's definitely based on myself, it's just a little cartoony version of me.

GG: *Now the characters are all microscopically obsessed. They're all pretty insular, and in all the four stories, there're only two other characters.*

JB: Yeah. It's the guy who's picking up junk or whatever?

GG: *Yes, and the other is a girl who has a cameo for one page and then disappears. The stories are primarily one character, either wandering around or reflecting.*

JB: That's true, that's my problem. [*Laughter.*]

GG: *Or your strength.*

JB: Yeah, I don't know.

GG: *So why don't you write stories where characters interact with other human beings?*

JB: I don't know if it's because I just can't do it or I'm afraid to attempt it or what. I think I also spend a lot of time just wandering around alone. That's where I do all my deep thinking. [*Laughs.*]

Who knows; I don't know. I don't want to transcribe conversations in my comics. I hate the idea of that. Eventually I will try my best to do that, to bring in different characters who are interacting, but I have a fear of that, I don't always like that when it's happening in comics. If you don't really have a solid storyline, then it's hard to improve that sort of stuff…for me.

I feel like I'm still learning how to do comics, still trying to learn how to do the basics of it, of writing. I feel like I would need an actual story written down, not necessarily a script, but at least a thumbnail and an idea with a beginning, middle, and end to incorporate other characters like that. I don't know why that is, but the only other characters that I can handle at this point seem to be these people who are on this periphery, edge of things.

GG: *In a way, it seems to me what you're doing is very difficult to do, especially in comics, which is that you are creating a narrative out of the interior of these characters' lives. Basically, it's them thinking to themselves or making connections through observation.*

JB: I think that it allows me to do things visually though, or at least it's made me try and consider the visual side of comics and storytelling instead of just having 12 frames of a talking head or having someone sitting somewhere. It's made me try and keep it a little more interesting, have something else happening visually. So I don't get bored, and so that I feel like there's something worthwhile going on. Whether it's something like a pigeon sideline story that's happening in #2, or flashbacks. I don't know, just having things happening in the environment around me.

GG: *Well, they're interacting with the world, but just not with people in the world.*

JB: Yeah, yeah. Yeah, I can't explain what it is, I think I'm just embarrassed to say that I'm not an experienced enough writer to have taken the plunge. I'm self-obsessed, egotistical, I don't know what the word is. [*Groth laughs.*] I don't know what my problem is, but I definitely want to get away from it, and I tried really hard to begin to break away from it with issue four by making it not myself. But that didn't work, because it became me anyway.

GG: *Your characters almost always start reflecting back to childhood.*

JB: Yeah. I tried to avoid that. It even happened in #4 again. I do not use the same device that I've used in the past, those little like, rip off Sugiura-style manga children. I think it's in the first two stories. I couldn't help but make those connections with the world and how I was interact it with those stories. Those were the things where I see it happening and that's how the writing process happens. That's the connection drawn, and I doodle down the next square, and that's just what it becomes. I just try to let it write itself. I definitely try to avoid doing that though, for a little while. I didn't want to do

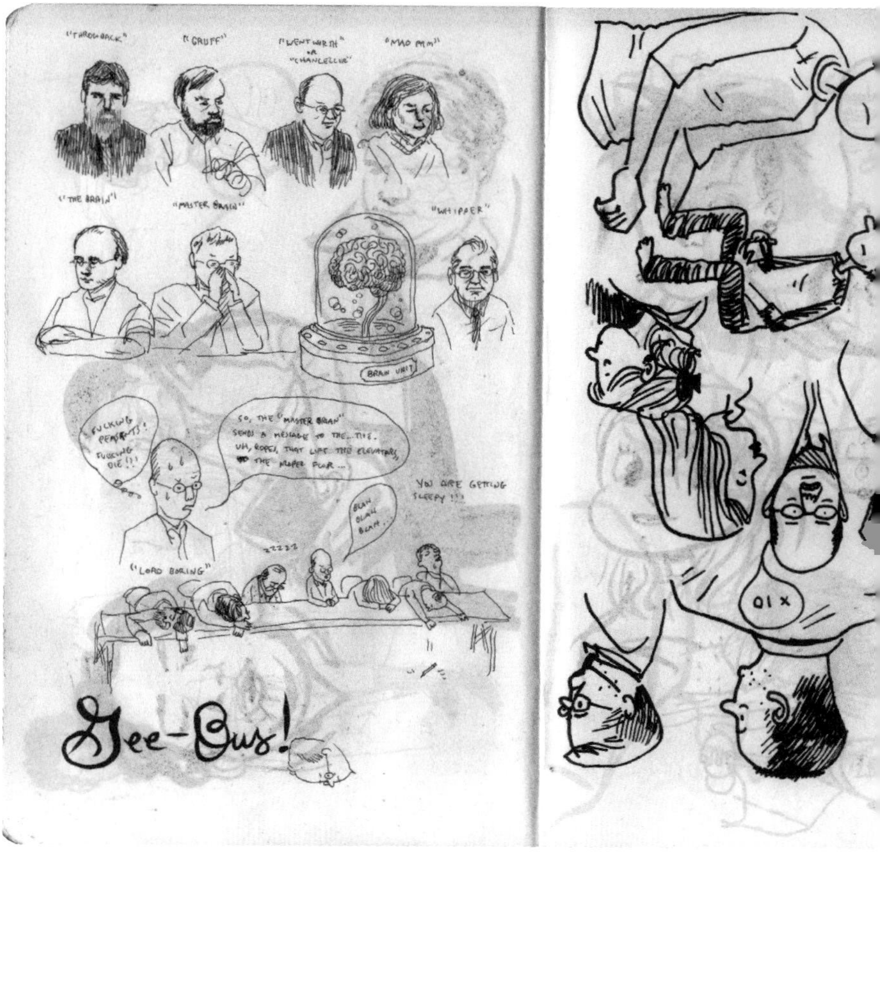
"THROWBACK"
"GRUFF"
"THE BRAIN"
"MASTER BRAIN"
BRAIN UNIT
"LORD BORING"
YOU ARE GETTING SLEEPY !!!
Gee-Bus!

BELOW, FROM SKETCHBOOK

that in #3 or in #4, because I felt like I was doing the same exact thing twice.

GG: *Do you yourself do that? Reflect upon your childhood and relate it to your current life?*

JB: I don't know.

GG: *Is that connection important to you?*

JB: It must be. Definitely, because all those things happen regularly, it's very much my normal train of thought, all those things always pop up, things are always reminding me. I don't know if that's any different for anyone. It seems very natural, I don't feel I'm obsessed with my childhood, or trying to get back to it. I have fond memories of childhood, lots of funny stories that always seem to pop up. So I don't know why that is. I don't feel like there's a particularly interesting reason for it.

GG: *Your characters also have pretty vivid fantasy lives in the sense that they'll imagine themselves, well, talking to an anthropomorphized version of some inanimate object. In* Esoteric Tales, *it was the nib of a pen. I think in the first story, there was something like that. The back of the guy's head was talking to you.*

JB: That's definitely something that I'm guilty of. I have lots of fake conversations with all kinds of inanimate objects or with people who I've never met while I'm wandering around, I just find myself just talking, not out loud, to myself, I definitely have a lot of interior monologues and dialogues with myself. So. It's a weird way of thinking. Strange, I don't know, but I definitely have always brought inanimate objects to life in my brain, I can't help but consider their feelings or whatever it is, because I have really strong reactions to things like that. I get really angry at inanimate objects a lot of the time. [*Laughter.*] So I can't help but put words in their mouth.

GG: *You said that in the story that's in this issue, that you had the last couple of page in your head first. What did that represent, his crawling into the bed and … Back to the womb, or — ?*

JB: That's the obvious connection. I think it's one of those things that was much more random until I decided to start writing the first page and made the obvious connections right there with the title of the story. Yeah, it's more of something I've always done since I was little, just really being fascinated by and always drawn to creeping into really small places. I don't know why that is. I've now been consciously obsessed with it, but I always used to like doing that. Slowly pushing myself through the — my bed in my childhood bedroom was against the wall, and I would always squeeze myself between the crack between the mattress and the wall and slide down until I was under the bed. Slowly pushing the bed off the wall. I remember doing that a lot. Not something I ever did with friends, we didn't play and build caves or anything, and dig underground like Joe Matt apparently did. I don't know, it's one of those things I never have even done in real life. That whole mattress, the dual-mattress womb. I'll have to try that someday if I ever am in a hotel with two mattresses. [*Groth laughs.*] It's probably pretty awesome.

The whole thing could be a product of being a certain age during the Baby Jessica event.

HERE I SIT, WONDERING IF MY FACE LOOKS AS ODD AS IT FEELS RIGHT NOW.
I HAD A MOUTHFUL OF CAVATIES FILLED THIS MORNING.
A NINE-THIRTY DENTIST APPOINTMENT ON THIS, MY LAST "SUMMER FRIDAY" HOME FROM WORK.
WHILE I WALKED TO THE DENTIST, I THOUGHT ABOUT HOW I WOULD BE REALLY RELAXED AND TRY AND SAY WITTY THINGS AND JUST BE REALLY HONEST ABOUT HOW I FEEL ABOUT DENTAL WORK.
GO EASY DOC! I'M A TOTAL WUSS. I CAN'T STAND THE PAIN!
JONATHAN, I'M GOING TO TURN THE PAIN UP TO TEN!!!
HA! HA!
BUT IN REALITY, I SAY LITTLE MORE THAN "YES" AND "NO" AND JUST SIT IN THAT CHAIR LIKE A LOG WAITING FOR THE LUMBER MILL'S SAW. NOT A PEEP. I MOSTLY DREAD THE NOVOCAIN INJECTION.
TAP TAP
BELOW, FROM *ESOTERIC TALES* #2

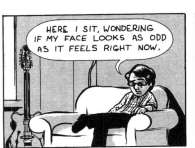

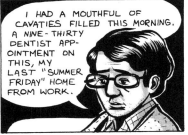

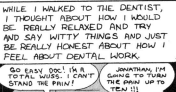

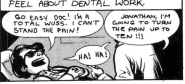

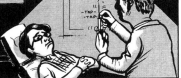

Jessica McClure fell down a well in Texas and I remember staying up really late to see the man with the collapsible collarbones shimmy down the hole to save her. Maybe that's part of it. My mom has told me the story of how they told her they might have to break my collar bone to get me out of her because I was so big. I think that all answers your question. I have a fixation on "tunneling" because of my birth experience and Baby Jessica. I wanted to be the hero who could save the girl, though I think that guy committed suicide when I was in high school.

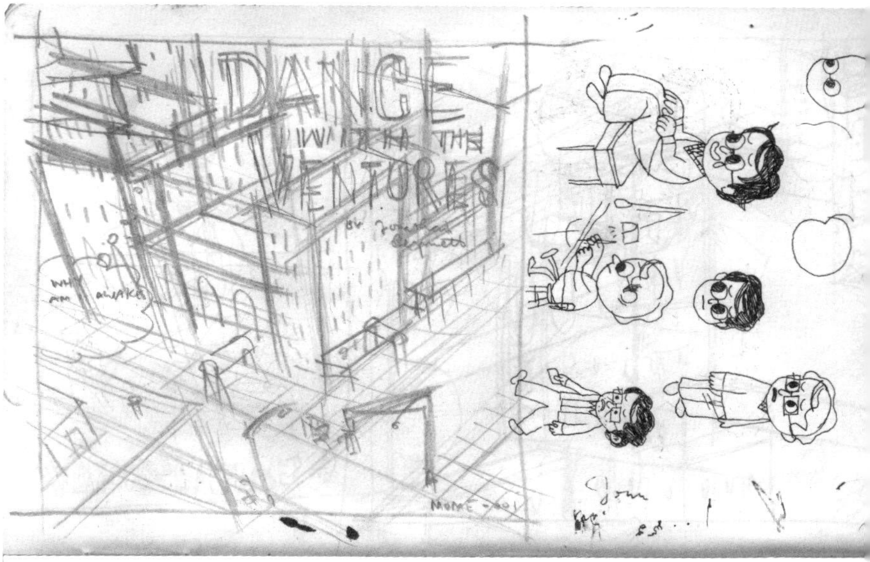
DANCE
VENTURES

ABOVE, FROM SKETCHBOOK

GG: *One of the lamentations I hear from cartoonists is that the sheer labor of drawing comics is so arduous, and it seems like yours would be more arduous than most, because your stories hinge on such inert details: somebody sitting on a park bench or wandering around a neighborhood wondering where he left his cup and so forth. Is it in fact arduous to do that?*

JB: Yeah, it is; it's one of those things where Amy, like I said, goes to the studio, and she spends her 8, 9 or 10 hours at the studio, and then she comes home around the time I get home from the office and then I sit down at my drawing board. Right now, I've been on this writing vacation, since I finished the last *MOME* story, spending my nights working on some freelance illustration jobs and design work, but once I've started on a story, pretty much every night I try to sit down and work for a couple of hours, and she just hates it, you know? She's very supportive and she likes my comics and she likes that I'm doing it and wants me to do it, but she always resents the fact that she's on the couch, trying to relax, just staring at the back of my head. [*Groth laughs.*] She doesn't complain about it too much, but she occasionally gets very sick of it, and I can completely understand because I'm also doing the same thing to myself I feel sometimes. Like, "Why am I doing this?"

I don't know if I even feel like I like what I'm working on at the time, and I just don't know if it's working, I feel like I'm just putting myself through some sort of torture, because it is very time-consuming, and it's not like this energetic, creative experience. You're not in a room with a bunch of people like I was in art school working on prints and everyone's helping each other out with projects and helping make decisions together. It's very isolated and you do it all on your own. Maybe that has something to do with it. I've also been much less social as I've gotten into comics. When you're in a band, then you bring your song out to your friends and you play it for them and then everyone joins in, it's this big social thing, even if only with three people.

GG: *It's a very isolated activity. You must have an enormous amount of discipline.*

JB: I've been working on that. I'm really not that disciplined. I'm lucky if I can get a couple of hours of work out a night.

GG: *What I was referring to was a discipline in the sense that your pacing is so very, I don't know if methodical is the right word, but it's so slow. You don't rush things, is the positive way of putting it. And that, it seems to me, would require discipline, there would seem to be something in the back of your head saying, "Come on, get this thing moving," but you certainly resist that impulse, which I think is one of the*

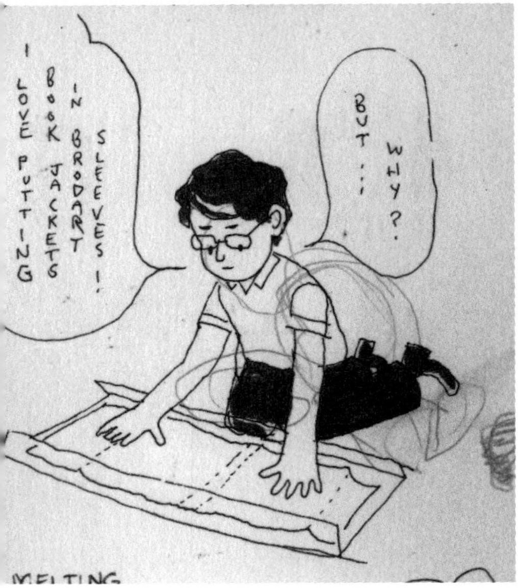
I LOVE PUTTING
BOOK JACKETS
IN BRODART
SLEEVES!
BUT... WHY?

ABOVE, FROM SKETCHBOOK

virtues of your art. It's so observant of the minutiae and the details of daily life.

JB: I think that's more of what I'm excited about, I'm giving myself a story and a dumb situation that's really inconsequential to deal with so that I can just basically bring out details and observe them and have them happen in my comics on their own. Those are the sort of things that seem to write themselves, that I don't really think about too much. They happen casually, and I actually get excited about working and making those things happen, just small details that I didn't foresee, and that weren't part of my one sentence at the top of my blank page of Bristol board, this has to happen on this page, here's the next event.

GG: *Right. Are you always taking mental notes, as you go through your daily routine?*

JB: Not as much as I probably should, because I find myself desperately trying to dredge up a memory that I thought would have been a good idea. And I don't always write them down, but I do always keep a sketchbook around, I usually have one in my bag or my pocket and try to write down ideas. But a lot of the times, they really do write themselves and it's more exciting that way, to not have an idea of, "Oh, wait, I should make sure that this small detail comes out in one of my stories in the future."

Instead, I know that I've seen these things, so I must be taking some sort of unconscious mental notes of them in order to remember them. It's more like when I'm writing the story than I'm almost trying to remember how it happened, even though it didn't necessarily happen *to* me. I'm trying to write down the story as if it were a memory, even if it didn't really happen in any specific order. I may or may not have ever experienced that sort of thing.

GG: *You've got to be extrapolating from memory but changing the context or changing the situation.*

JB: Yeah, because these are all things that I've either witnessed or thought about it, or obsessed over. When they come out, it's usually surprising, and hopefully it will work [*Groth laughs*], I hope that they fit into the story.

GG: *This is how things would unfold if you actually sat on a park bench and watched pigeons for 20 minutes.*

JB: Yeah, exactly, which never really happened. I saw the chicken bone being feasted on by a couple of pigeons a couple of years ago and that was just the seed for a story, but a lot of the stuff in that story, just sort of came out of that story as I was writing it, which worked I guess.

GG: *It seems like a great way to work, really. It gives you free play. I'm always leery of people who create vast blueprints, and then follow them assiduously [Bennett laughs], rather than letting the story itself create more opportunities.*

JB: It's very limiting of course, and I really want to get away from it, at least for a little while, and try to bring two things together at once, so I have another style of working, at least. Because I really don't like being tied down to that and making the same sort of stories.

GG: *I look forward to a story from you with two people in it.*

JB: Yeah. [*Laughs.*] It'll happen, I think. I don't know if it will be any good, but it will happen.

GG: *A cast of two, or a cast of three.*

JB: I think I'll make that jump, hopefully for the next story, I don't know, I haven't even gotten started on it yet.

GG: *We could put that in the press release.*

JB: Yeah. [*Laughs.*] So we'll see, we'll see. I'm working on it. I just feel like I've hardly been doing this at all, even though I've been doing it for a few years now.

M

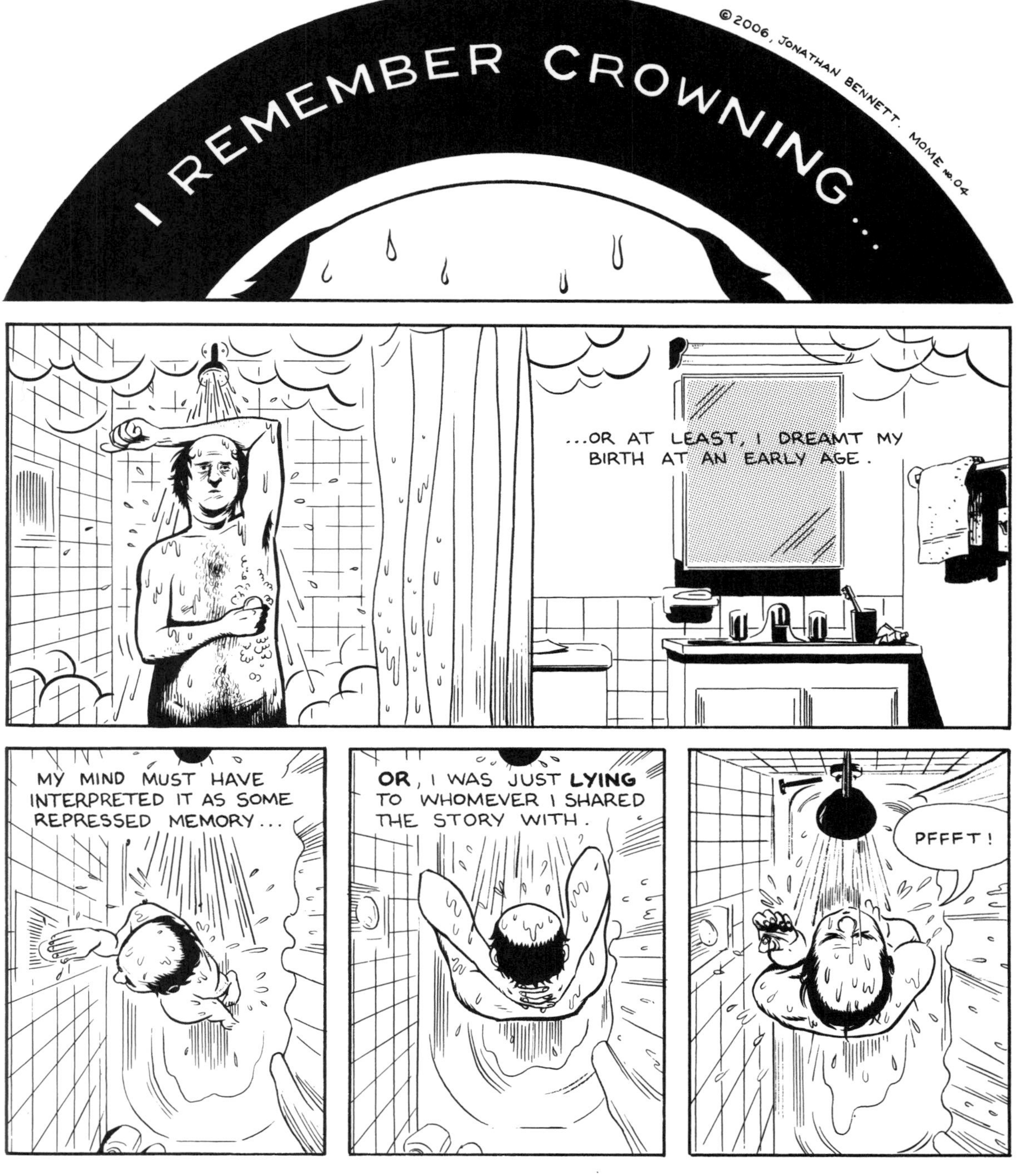

I REMEMBER CROWNING...
©2006, JONATHAN BENNETT. MOME No. 04
...OR AT LEAST, I DREAMT MY BIRTH AT AN EARLY AGE.
MY MIND MUST HAVE INTERPRETED IT AS SOME REPRESSED MEMORY...
OR, I WAS JUST LYING TO WHOMEVER I SHARED THE STORY WITH.
PFFFT!

I REMEMBER BEING SIX...

PERHAPS NOT TOO CLEARLY, BUT THERE ARE MANY **VIVID** MOMENTS FROM... **THIRTY YEARS PAST!**

SO...

—SHHHFFF

AT AGE SIX YOU COULD COUNT ON A SIX YEAR CACHE OF MEMORIES...

eet

EEEEEET

RIGHT?

FUUF

IT'S A **TRAUMATIC** EVENT. THE SORT OF THING YOUR MIND WOULD **CERTAINLY** REPRESS. IS THAT WHY OUR BRAINS DON'T REALLY REMEMBER MUCH UNTIL 12 OR 18 MONTHS? EACH NEW STEP IS SO OVER-WHELMING AND IT **ALL** GETS REPRESSED. SLOWLY YOU BEGIN TO LET YOUR GUARD DOWN, LEARNING TO COPE... BUT, ALL THOSE EAR-LIEST EVENTS ARE STILL IN THERE...

SOMEWHERE.

FFF   FFF

SHF

RUB

FUF   FUF

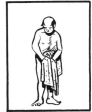

RUB
RUB

OR, THEY'RE GONE. TRULY AND COMPLETELY FORGOTTEN.
SQUEEE
WHATEVER IT IS I'M HOLDING ONTO COULD BE SOME SCENE FROM A MOVIE OR TELEVISION PROGRAM.
seeeee
"THE MIRACLE...
...OF...
LIFE"
POKE
SQUEEET
TAP
eeet!
DID THEY HAVE A NEW-BORN'S P.O.V. SHOT OF AN ACTUAL BIRTH IN THAT FILM? MAYBE I DREAMT THAT TOO.

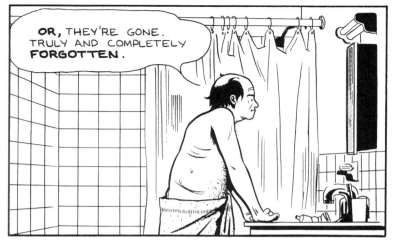

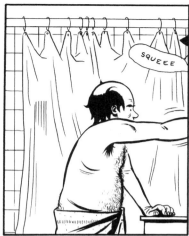

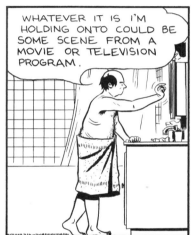

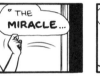

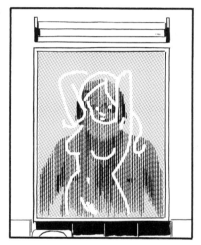

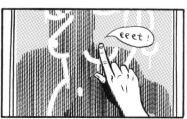

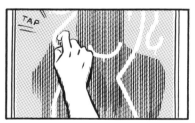

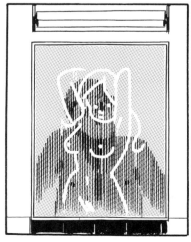

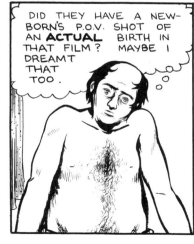

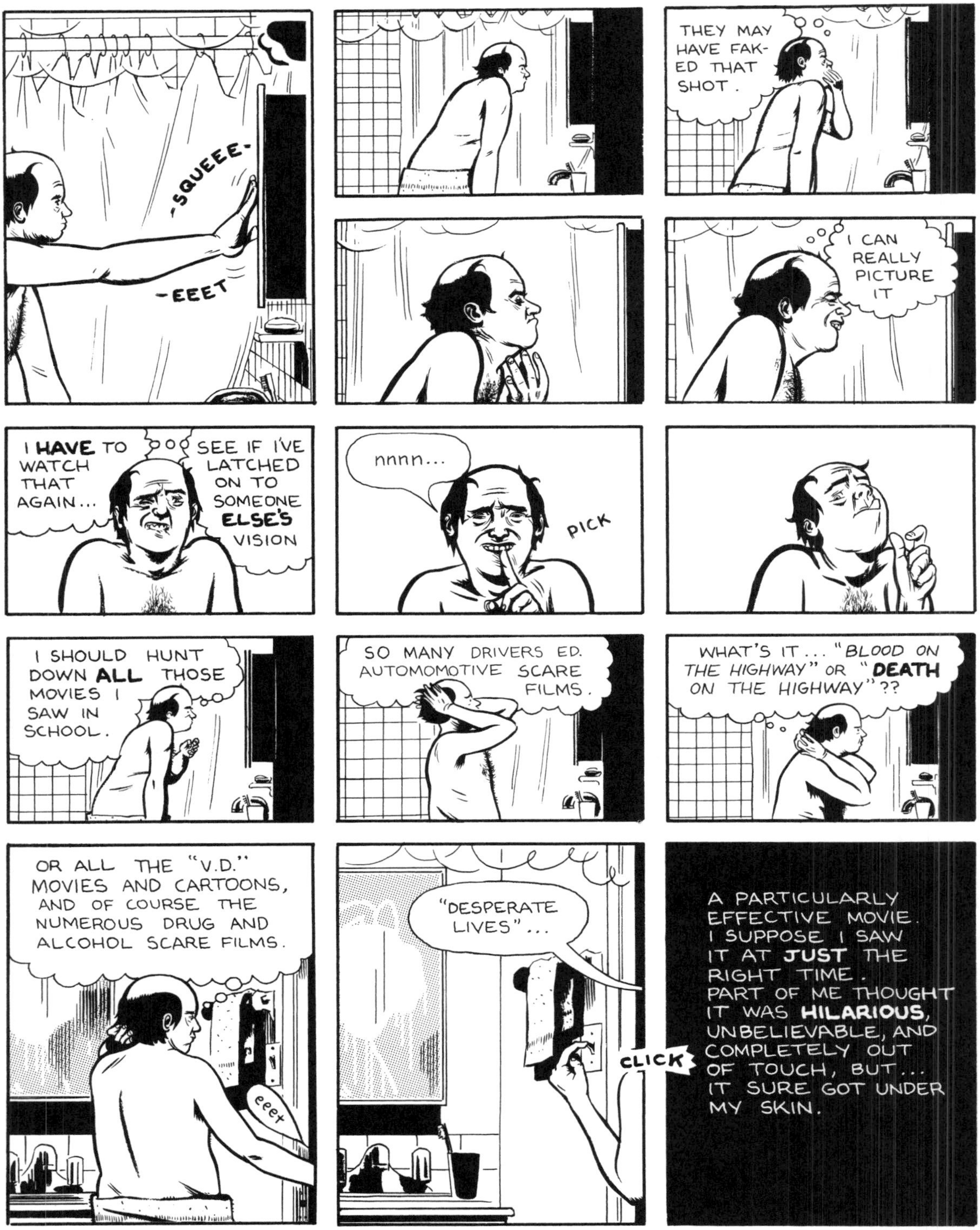
-SQUEEE-
-EEET
THEY MAY HAVE FAK-ED THAT SHOT.
I CAN REALLY PICTURE IT
I HAVE TO WATCH THAT AGAIN...
SEE IF I'VE LATCHED ON TO SOMEONE ELSE'S VISION
nnnn...
PICK
I SHOULD HUNT DOWN ALL THOSE MOVIES I SAW IN SCHOOL.
SO MANY DRIVERS ED. AUTOMOMOTIVE SCARE FILMS.
WHAT'S IT... "BLOOD ON THE HIGHWAY" OR "DEATH ON THE HIGHWAY"??
OR ALL THE "V.D." MOVIES AND CARTOONS, AND OF COURSE THE NUMEROUS DRUG AND ALCOHOL SCARE FILMS.
eeet
"DESPERATE LIVES"...
CLICK
A PARTICULARLY EFFECTIVE MOVIE. I SUPPOSE I SAW IT AT JUST THE RIGHT TIME. PART OF ME THOUGHT IT WAS HILARIOUS, UNBELIEVABLE, AND COMPLETELY OUT OF TOUCH, BUT... IT SURE GOT UNDER MY SKIN.

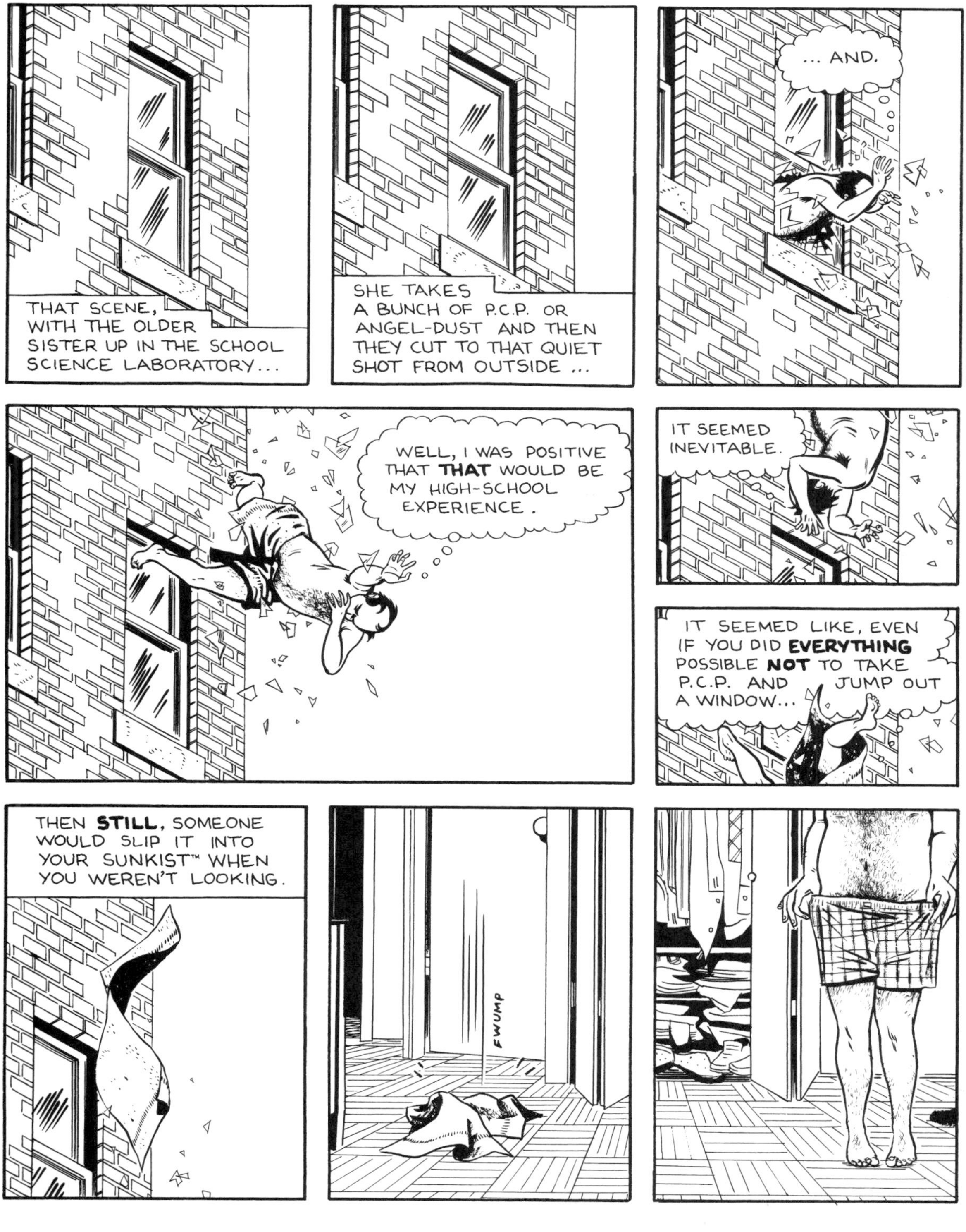
THAT SCENE, WITH THE OLDER SISTER UP IN THE SCHOOL SCIENCE LABORATORY...
SHE TAKES A BUNCH OF P.C.P. OR ANGEL-DUST AND THEN THEY CUT TO THAT QUIET SHOT FROM OUTSIDE ...
... AND.
WELL, I WAS POSITIVE THAT **THAT** WOULD BE MY HIGH-SCHOOL EXPERIENCE.
IT SEEMED INEVITABLE.
IT SEEMED LIKE, EVEN IF YOU DID **EVERYTHING** POSSIBLE **NOT** TO TAKE P.C.P. AND JUMP OUT A WINDOW...
THEN **STILL**, SOMEONE WOULD SLIP IT INTO YOUR SUNKIST™ WHEN YOU WEREN'T LOOKING.
FWUMP

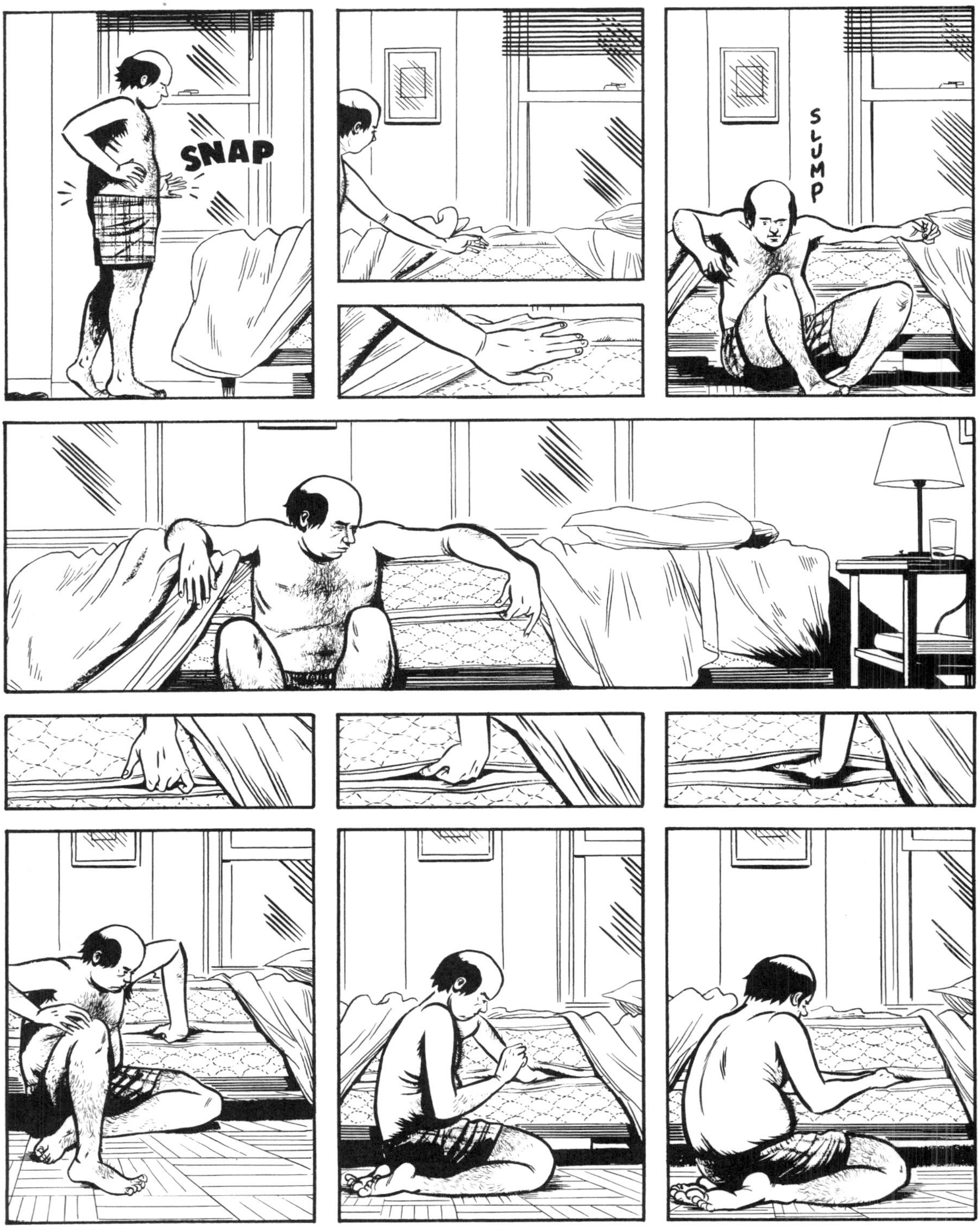
SNAP
SLUMP

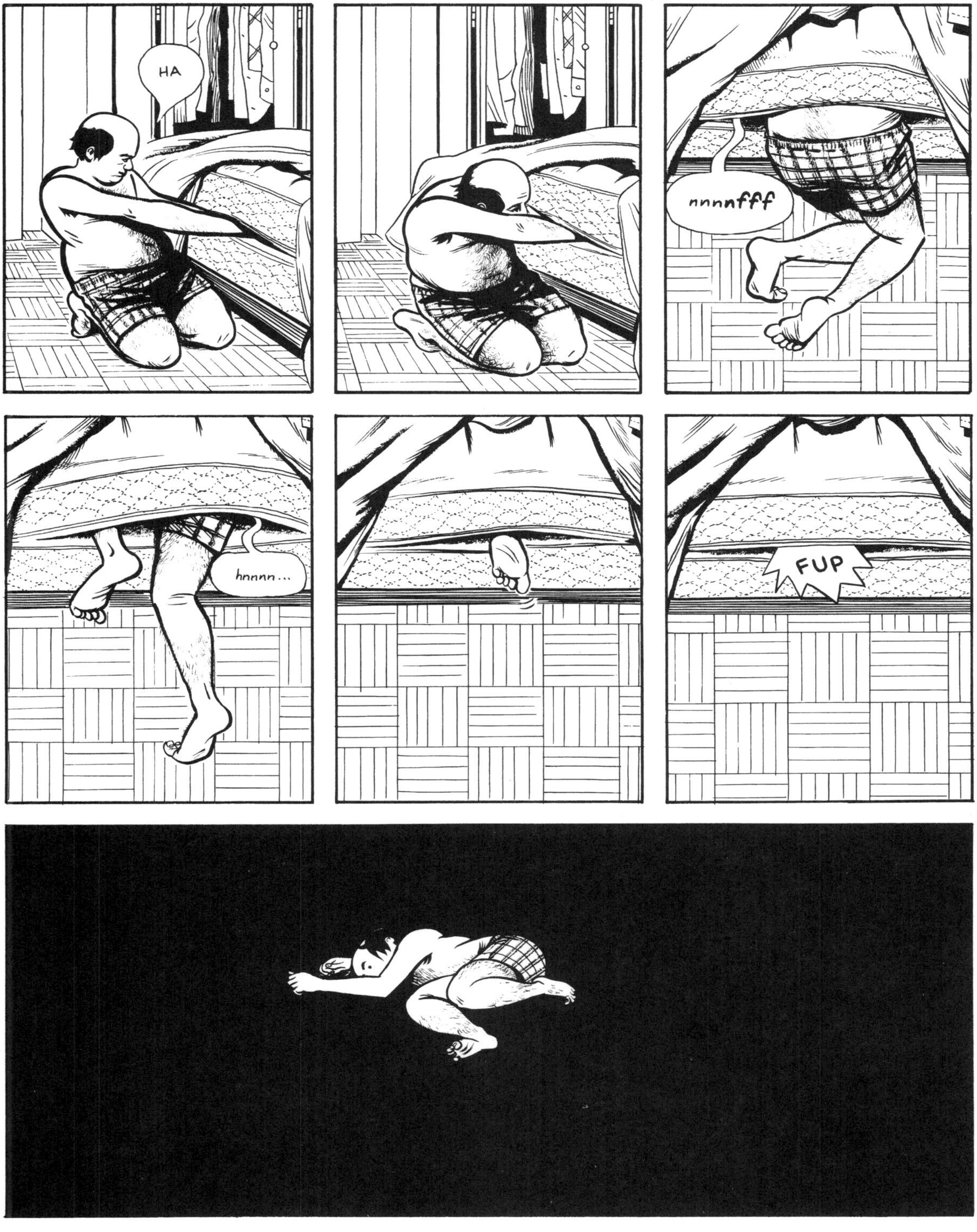
HA
nnnnfff
hnnnn...
FUP

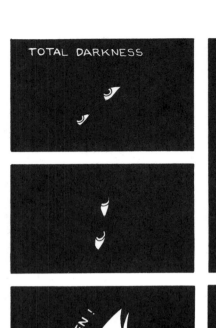

TOTAL DARKNESS

IN DARKNESS LIKE THIS, DISTANT MEMORIES COME TO ME WITH **ASTOUNDING** CLARITY.

I CAN **TASTE** ORANGE SODA DRAWN THROUGH A **TWIZZLER**™.

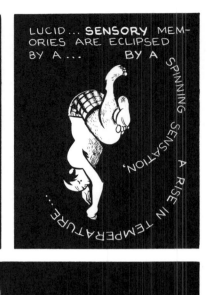

LUCID... **SENSORY** MEMORIES ARE ECLIPSED BY A ... BY A SPINNING SENSATION, A RISE IN TEMPERATURE...

...A LACK OF OXYGEN!

GUH! NNNNNNN

THRUST!

HNNNNN

AH!

huf huf

huf huf... THE FLOOR... IS **FREEZING**.

THE END

SOMETHING WAS BEWILDERINGLY DIFFERENT ABOUT MARTIN. HIS FACE WAS POINTIER, MAYBE?

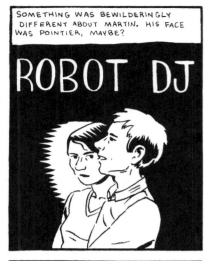

ROBOT DJ

OR MAYBE HIS POOFY HAIR MADE HIS FEATURES LOOK MORE ANGULAR. OR HE WAS THINNER. OR HE HELD HIMSELF MORE ERECT.

HE SEEMED MORE SOLID. SOMETHING MUST HAVE HAPPENED TO HIM. DID HE FALL IN LOVE?

WHAT?

MORE TANGIBLY CHANGED WAS GREGORY. OVER SUMMER VACATION HE'D SUDDENLY TRANSFORMED FROM A BACKGROUND KID TO A SUBSTANTIAL AND SLIGHTLY DISTURBING PRESENCE.

HEY! WHERE'VE YOU BEEN?

OUT BACK.

PARTICULARLY TROUBLING WAS HIS DEVOTION TO THE READS. HOW DID THAT HAPPEN?

YOU KNOW, I WAS INTO THEM WHEN I WAS YOUR AGE TOO.

'INTO' WAS AN UNDERSTATEMENT. AT FIFTEEN I TOOK NOONE SERIOUSLY, NOT MY TEACHERS, NOT MY PARENTS, NOT THE KIDS AT SCHOOL, ONLY SAMMY ABRAMS.

IT WAS THE COMBINATION OF NERDINESS AND POETRY, AND HIS INIMITABLE LILTING, MEWLING VOICE. HE WAS JUST LIKE ME, ONLY MORE AWKWARDLY BOLD.

IT WAS HIS SONG 'ROBOT DJ' THAT MADE ME WANT TO HAVE A RADIO SHOW. IT WAS KRISTIN WHO HAD THE NERVE TO CALL THE STATION MANAGER AT KCMU TO SET UP AN INTERVIEW.

IT'S TRUE, WE'RE YOUNG. BUT WE CAN OFFER A UNIQUE PERSPECTIVE.

YOU KNOW, SEVENTY PERCENT OF YOUR LISTENERS ARE UNDER TWENTY-FOUR...

'ROBOT DJ' WAS OUR THEME SONG. WE BANTERED, STAGED SKITS, TOLD JOKES. WE WERE HIGH SCHOOL CELEBRITIES.

AND NOW, KRISTIN IS GOING TO RECITE FOR US A HUMOROUS POEM. ISN'T THAT RIGHT, KRISTIN?

BUT FIRST, IVY IS GOING TO DEMONSTRATE FOR US HER IMPERSONATION OF THE MATING CALL OF THE OCELOT.

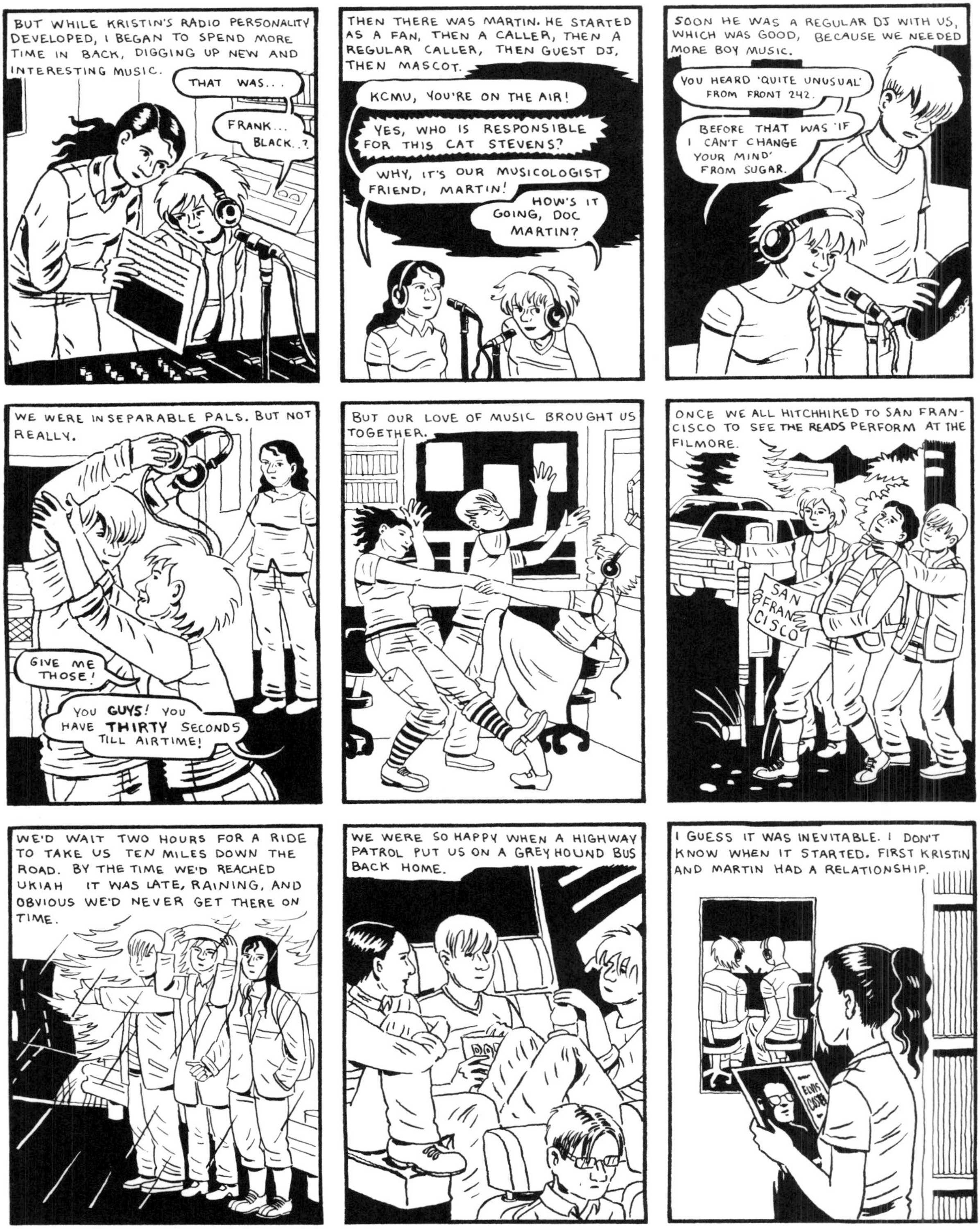
BUT WHILE KRISTIN'S RADIO PERSONALITY DEVELOPED, I BEGAN TO SPEND MORE TIME IN BACK, DIGGING UP NEW AND INTERESTING MUSIC.
THAT WAS...
FRANK... BLACK..?
THEN THERE WAS MARTIN. HE STARTED AS A FAN, THEN A CALLER, THEN A REGULAR CALLER, THEN GUEST DJ, THEN MASCOT.
KCMU, YOU'RE ON THE AIR!
YES, WHO IS RESPONSIBLE FOR THIS CAT STEVENS?
WHY, IT'S OUR MUSICOLOGIST FRIEND, MARTIN!
HOW'S IT GOING, DOC MARTIN?
SOON HE WAS A REGULAR DJ WITH US, WHICH WAS GOOD, BECAUSE WE NEEDED MORE BOY MUSIC.
YOU HEARD 'QUITE UNUSUAL' FROM FRONT 242.
BEFORE THAT WAS 'IF I CAN'T CHANGE YOUR MIND' FROM SUGAR.
WE WERE INSEPARABLE PALS. BUT NOT REALLY.
GIVE ME THOSE!
YOU GUYS! YOU HAVE THIRTY SECONDS TILL AIRTIME!
BUT OUR LOVE OF MUSIC BROUGHT US TOGETHER.
ONCE WE ALL HITCHHIKED TO SAN FRANCISCO TO SEE THE READS PERFORM AT THE FILMORE.
SAN FRANCISCO
WE'D WAIT TWO HOURS FOR A RIDE TO TAKE US TEN MILES DOWN THE ROAD. BY THE TIME WE'D REACHED UKIAH IT WAS LATE, RAINING, AND OBVIOUS WE'D NEVER GET THERE ON TIME.
WE WERE SO HAPPY WHEN A HIGHWAY PATROL PUT US ON A GREYHOUND BUS BACK HOME.
I GUESS IT WAS INEVITABLE. I DON'T KNOW WHEN IT STARTED. FIRST KRISTIN AND MARTIN HAD A RELATIONSHIP.
ELVIS COSTELLO

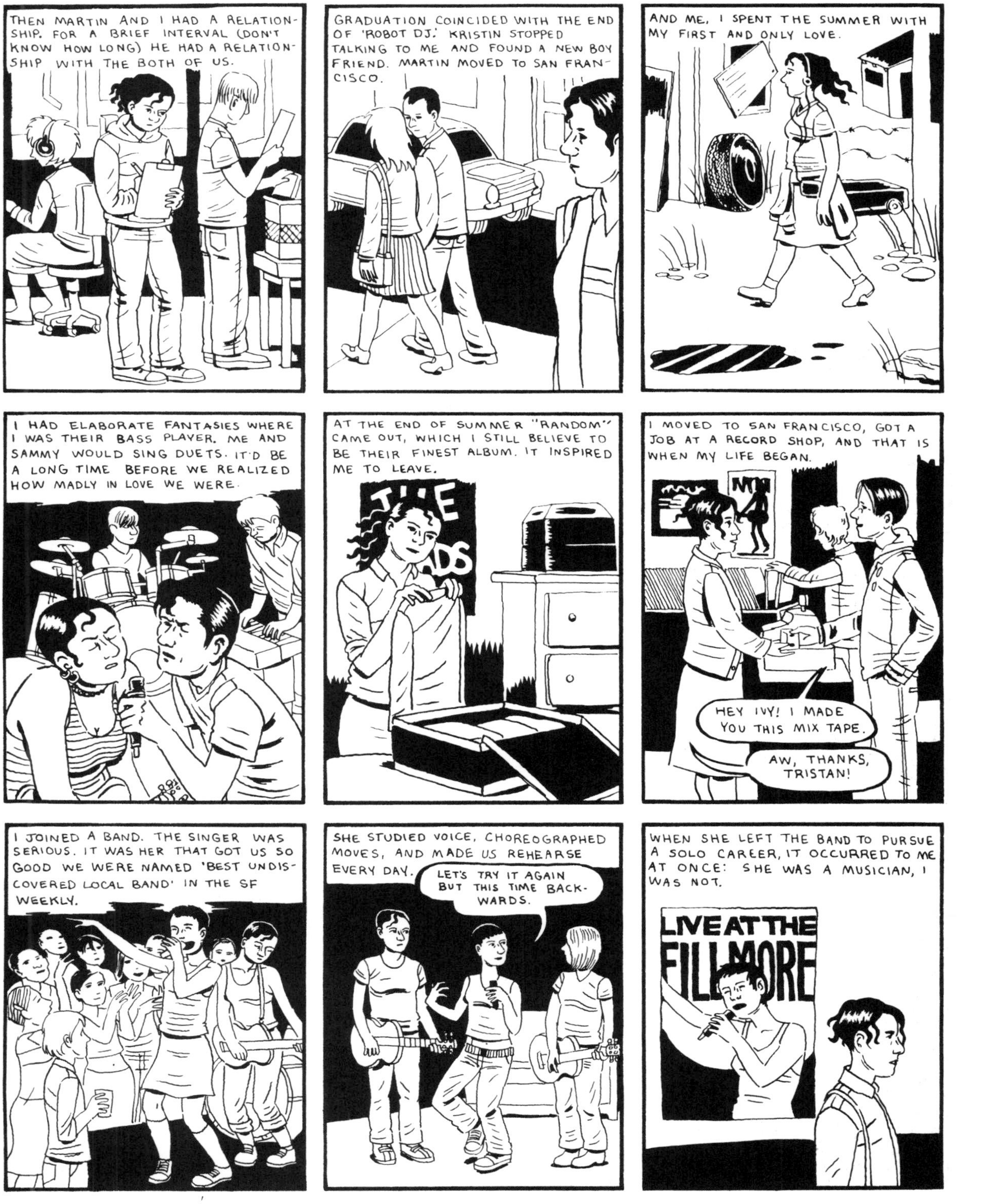
THEN MARTIN AND I HAD A RELATIONSHIP. FOR A BRIEF INTERVAL (DON'T KNOW HOW LONG) HE HAD A RELATIONSHIP WITH THE BOTH OF US.
GRADUATION COINCIDED WITH THE END OF 'ROBOT DJ.' KRISTIN STOPPED TALKING TO ME AND FOUND A NEW BOY FRIEND. MARTIN MOVED TO SAN FRANCISCO.
AND ME, I SPENT THE SUMMER WITH MY FIRST AND ONLY LOVE.
I HAD ELABORATE FANTASIES WHERE I WAS THEIR BASS PLAYER. ME AND SAMMY WOULD SING DUETS. IT'D BE A LONG TIME BEFORE WE REALIZED HOW MADLY IN LOVE WE WERE.
AT THE END OF SUMMER "RANDOM" CAME OUT, WHICH I STILL BELIEVE TO BE THEIR FINEST ALBUM. IT INSPIRED ME TO LEAVE.
I MOVED TO SAN FRANCISCO, GOT A JOB AT A RECORD SHOP, AND THAT IS WHEN MY LIFE BEGAN.
HEY IVY! I MADE YOU THIS MIX TAPE.
AW, THANKS, TRISTAN!
I JOINED A BAND. THE SINGER WAS SERIOUS. IT WAS HER THAT GOT US SO GOOD WE WERE NAMED 'BEST UNDISCOVERED LOCAL BAND' IN THE SF WEEKLY.
SHE STUDIED VOICE, CHOREOGRAPHED MOVES, AND MADE US REHEARSE EVERY DAY.
LET'S TRY IT AGAIN BUT THIS TIME BACKWARDS.
WHEN SHE LEFT THE BAND TO PURSUE A SOLO CAREER, IT OCCURRED TO ME AT ONCE: SHE WAS A MUSICIAN, I WAS NOT.
LIVE AT THE FILLMORE

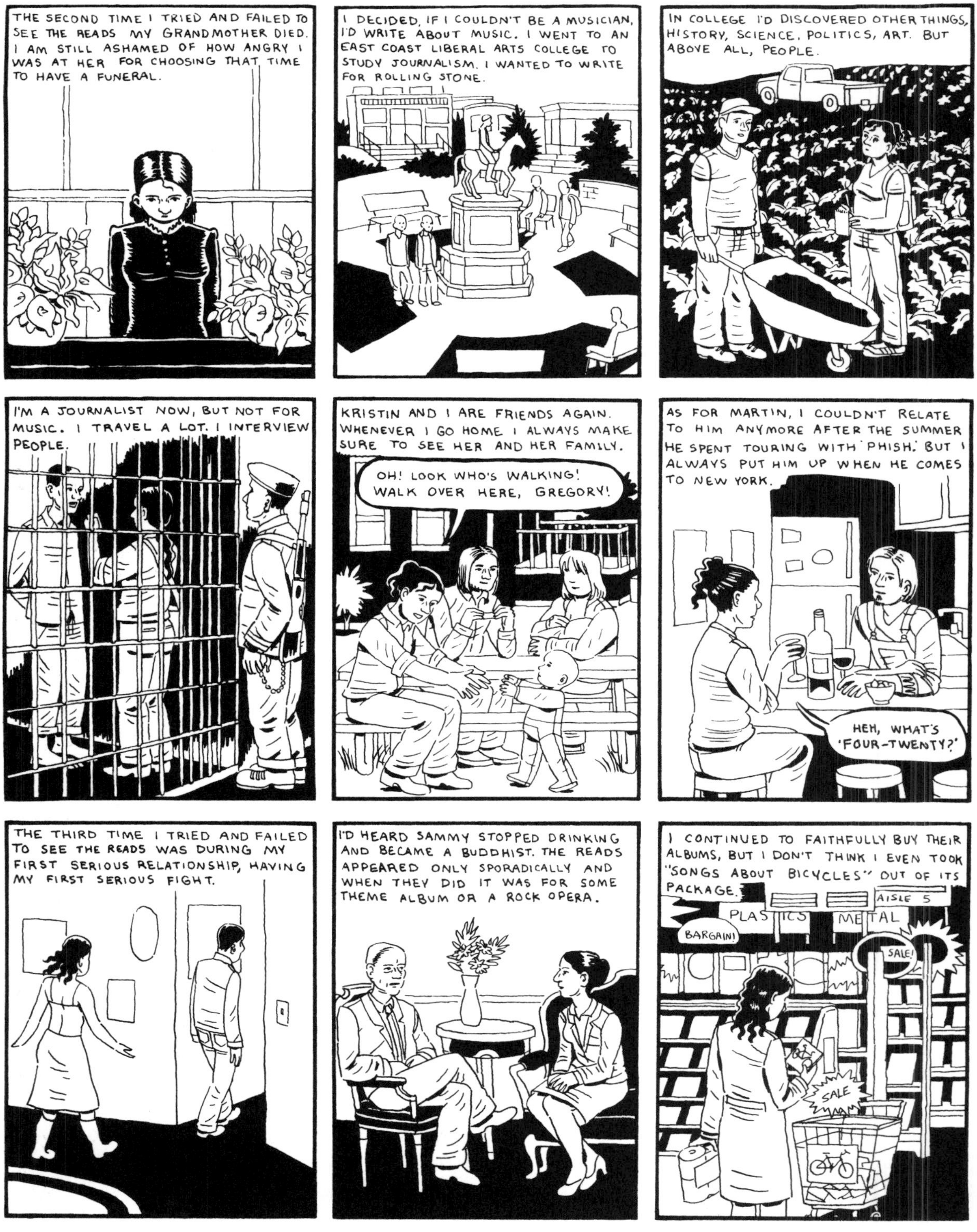
THE SECOND TIME I TRIED AND FAILED TO SEE THE READS MY GRANDMOTHER DIED. I AM STILL ASHAMED OF HOW ANGRY I WAS AT HER FOR CHOOSING THAT TIME TO HAVE A FUNERAL.
I DECIDED, IF I COULDN'T BE A MUSICIAN, I'D WRITE ABOUT MUSIC. I WENT TO AN EAST COAST LIBERAL ARTS COLLEGE TO STUDY JOURNALISM. I WANTED TO WRITE FOR ROLLING STONE.
IN COLLEGE I'D DISCOVERED OTHER THINGS, HISTORY, SCIENCE, POLITICS, ART. BUT ABOVE ALL, PEOPLE.
I'M A JOURNALIST NOW, BUT NOT FOR MUSIC. I TRAVEL A LOT. I INTERVIEW PEOPLE.
KRISTIN AND I ARE FRIENDS AGAIN. WHENEVER I GO HOME I ALWAYS MAKE SURE TO SEE HER AND HER FAMILY.
OH! LOOK WHO'S WALKING! WALK OVER HERE, GREGORY!
AS FOR MARTIN, I COULDN'T RELATE TO HIM ANYMORE AFTER THE SUMMER HE SPENT TOURING WITH "PHISH." BUT I ALWAYS PUT HIM UP WHEN HE COMES TO NEW YORK.
HEH, WHAT'S 'FOUR-TWENTY?'
THE THIRD TIME I TRIED AND FAILED TO SEE THE READS WAS DURING MY FIRST SERIOUS RELATIONSHIP, HAVING MY FIRST SERIOUS FIGHT.
I'D HEARD SAMMY STOPPED DRINKING AND BECAME A BUDDHIST. THE READS APPEARED ONLY SPORADICALLY AND WHEN THEY DID IT WAS FOR SOME THEME ALBUM OR A ROCK OPERA.
I CONTINUED TO FAITHFULLY BUY THEIR ALBUMS, BUT I DON'T THINK I EVEN TOOK "SONGS ABOUT BICYCLES" OUT OF ITS PACKAGE.
AISLE 5
PLASTICS
METAL
BARGAIN!
SALE!
SALE

AND NOW, HERE WE WERE, A BIG REUNION.

WHERE'D GREGORY GO?

THE OPENING BAND WAS AN EARNEST YOUNG PUNK GROUP FROM BALTIMORE.

I WAS WALKING DOWN THE **STREET** AND THIS **FASCIST** FUCKIN COP **STOPPED** ME IN MY **TRACKS** AND HE SAID TO ME

ONCE I WOULD'VE LIKED THEM. ONCE THEY WOULD'VE MADE ME CRINGE. NOW I LIKED THEM AGAIN.

WHAT? YOU GOTTA ADMIT THEY'RE CATCHY.

THE READS HADN'T AGED WELL.

THOSE AREN'T THEM! THE REAL READS ARE **YOUNG** AND HANDSOME!

THERE MUST BE SOME MISTAKE!

MORE SHOCKING WAS SAMMY. HE LOOKED EVEN YOUNGER THAN ME!

EVERYONE GOT OLD EXCEPT SAMMY!

HE WAS NOTHING LIKE I'D REMEMBERED HIM. HAD BUDDHISM KEPT HIM YOUNG? WAS HE DOING YOGA? TAI-CHI?

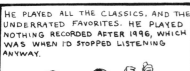

HE PLAYED ALL THE CLASSICS, AND THE UNDERRATED FAVORITES. HE PLAYED NOTHING RECORDED AFTER 1996, WHICH WAS WHEN I'D STOPPED LISTENING ANYWAY.

I DIDN'T WANT ANYTHING NEW. I WANTED A WEIRD SIMULACRUM OF WHAT WE ONCE HAD.

IT FELT LIKE SAMMY WAS SINGING DIRECTLY TO ME, WITH HIS INIMITABLE LILTING, MEWLING VOICE.

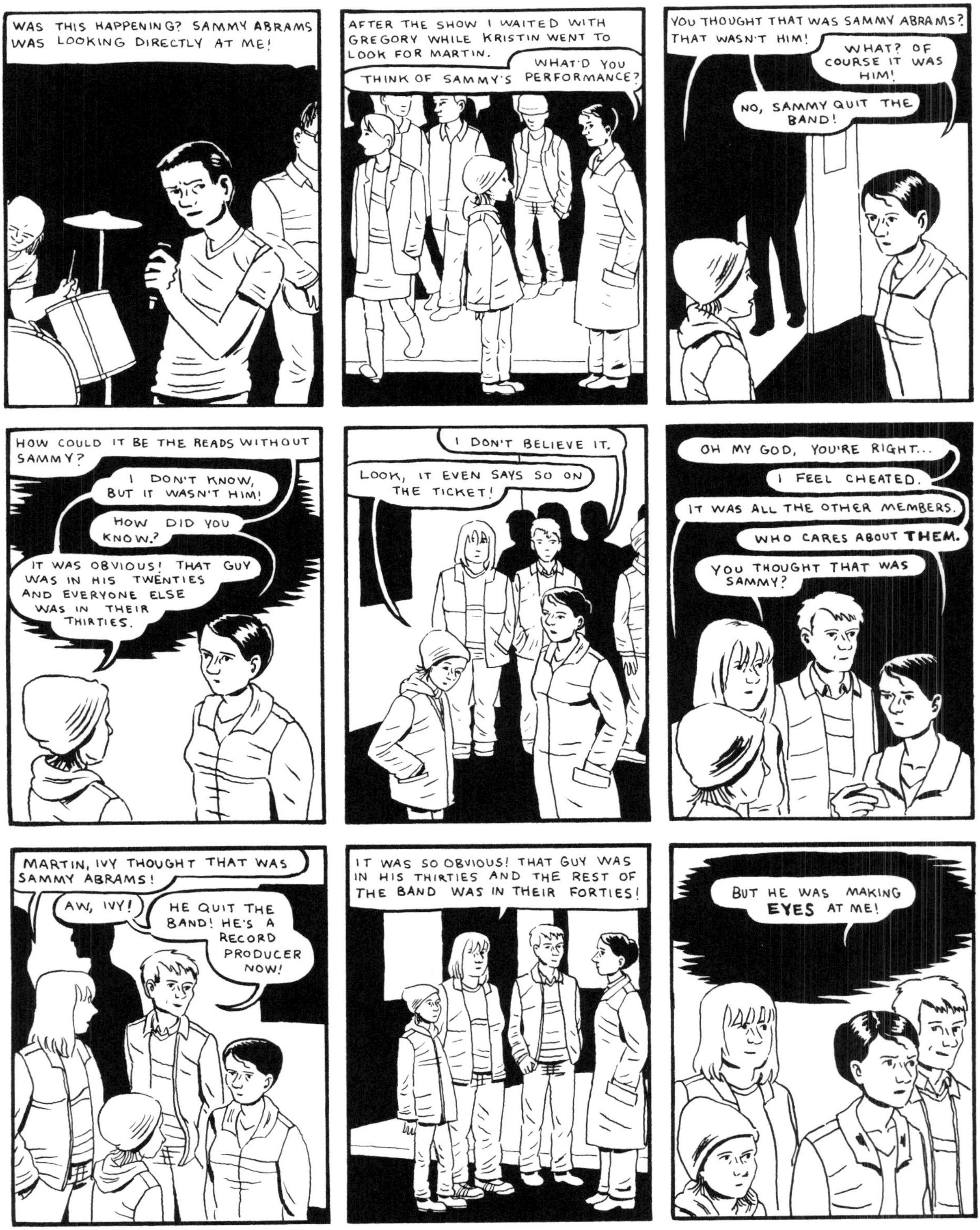
WAS THIS HAPPENING? SAMMY ABRAMS WAS LOOKING DIRECTLY AT ME!
AFTER THE SHOW I WAITED WITH GREGORY WHILE KRISTIN WENT TO LOOK FOR MARTIN.
WHAT'D YOU THINK OF SAMMY'S PERFORMANCE?
YOU THOUGHT THAT WAS SAMMY ABRAMS? THAT WASN'T HIM!
WHAT? OF COURSE IT WAS HIM!
NO, SAMMY QUIT THE BAND!
HOW COULD IT BE THE READS WITHOUT SAMMY?
I DON'T KNOW, BUT IT WASN'T HIM!
HOW DID YOU KNOW?
IT WAS OBVIOUS! THAT GUY WAS IN HIS TWENTIES AND EVERYONE ELSE WAS IN THEIR THIRTIES.
I DON'T BELIEVE IT.
LOOK, IT EVEN SAYS SO ON THE TICKET!
OH MY GOD, YOU'RE RIGHT...
I FEEL CHEATED.
IT WAS ALL THE OTHER MEMBERS.
WHO CARES ABOUT THEM.
YOU THOUGHT THAT WAS SAMMY?
MARTIN, IVY THOUGHT THAT WAS SAMMY ABRAMS!
AW, IVY!
HE QUIT THE BAND! HE'S A RECORD PRODUCER NOW!
IT WAS SO OBVIOUS! THAT GUY WAS IN HIS THIRTIES AND THE REST OF THE BAND WAS IN THEIR FORTIES!
BUT HE WAS MAKING EYES AT ME!

WHAT WERE THEY THINKING
AND ALSO,
WHAT THEY WERE THINKING
I'M VERY CONCERNED WITH BEING GOOD ENOUGH

WHAT HAVE I EVER REALLY ACCOMPLISHED WITH MY LIFE?

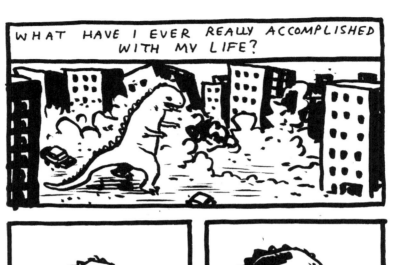

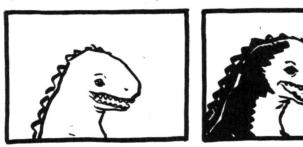

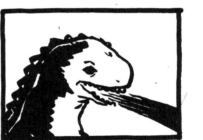

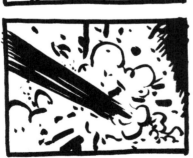

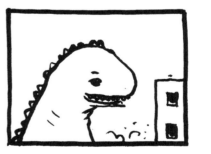

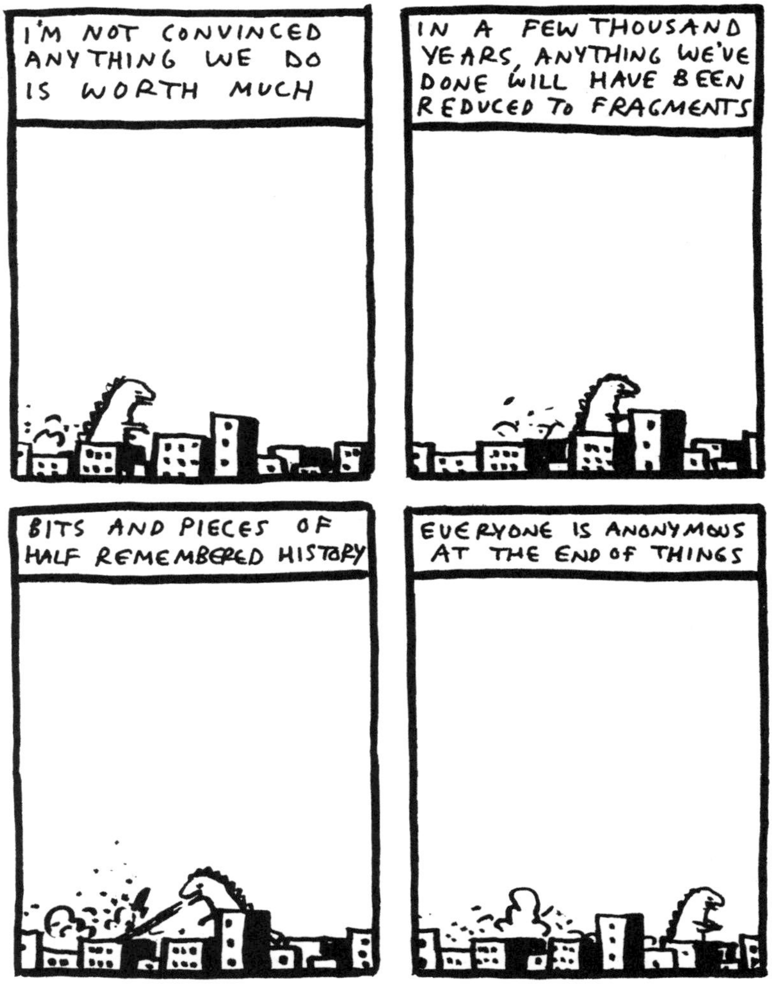
I'M NOT CONVINCED ANYTHING WE DO IS WORTH MUCH
IN A FEW THOUSAND YEARS, ANYTHING WE'VE DONE WILL HAVE BEEN REDUCED TO FRAGMENTS
BITS AND PIECES OF HALF REMEMBERED HISTORY
EVERYONE IS ANONYMOUS AT THE END OF THINGS

WHATEVER WE INTEND
GETS LOST

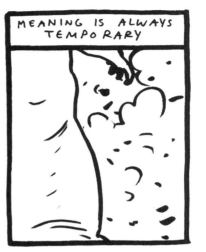

MEANING IS ALWAYS
TEMPORARY

SOCIETY IS JUST AN
ACCUMULATION OF THESE
BROKEN PIECES

SOMETIMES I THINK SO MUCH ABOUT BAD THINGS THAT MIGHT HAPPEN, IT'S AS IF THEY HAVE

I HAVE A VERY FERTILE IMAGINATION

THERE ARE A LOT OF BAD THINGS THAT COULD HAPPEN

I'M SORRY IF I HOLD YOU RESPONSIBLE

FOR THINGS

YOU HAVEN'T DONE

NOTHING ALL THAT BAD CAN REALLY HAPPEN
IT'S ALL PREDETERMINED BY PHYSICS

I'M A "TORTURED SOUL"
I CAN'T HELP IT, BUT I DON'T WANT TO BE HURT
I STILL FIND MYSELF FALLING IN LOVE, I JUST DON'T WANT TO SCREW THINGS UP AGAIN
I JUST DON'T UNDERSTAND WHAT SHE MEANS WHEN SHE SAYS I'M MAKING EXCUSES FOR MY BEHAVIOR AND I'M PATHETIC WHEN I CAN'T HELP HOW I FEEL

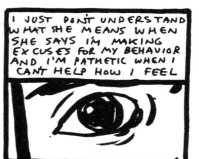

THE CONCEPT OF ETERNITY IN COMBINATION WITH THE IDEA THAT DEATH MEANS CEASING TO EXIST AS A CONSCIOUS BEING IS HORRIFYING

REAAHHHTTT

IT'S HARD NOT TO FEEL LIKE YOU'RE ALONE

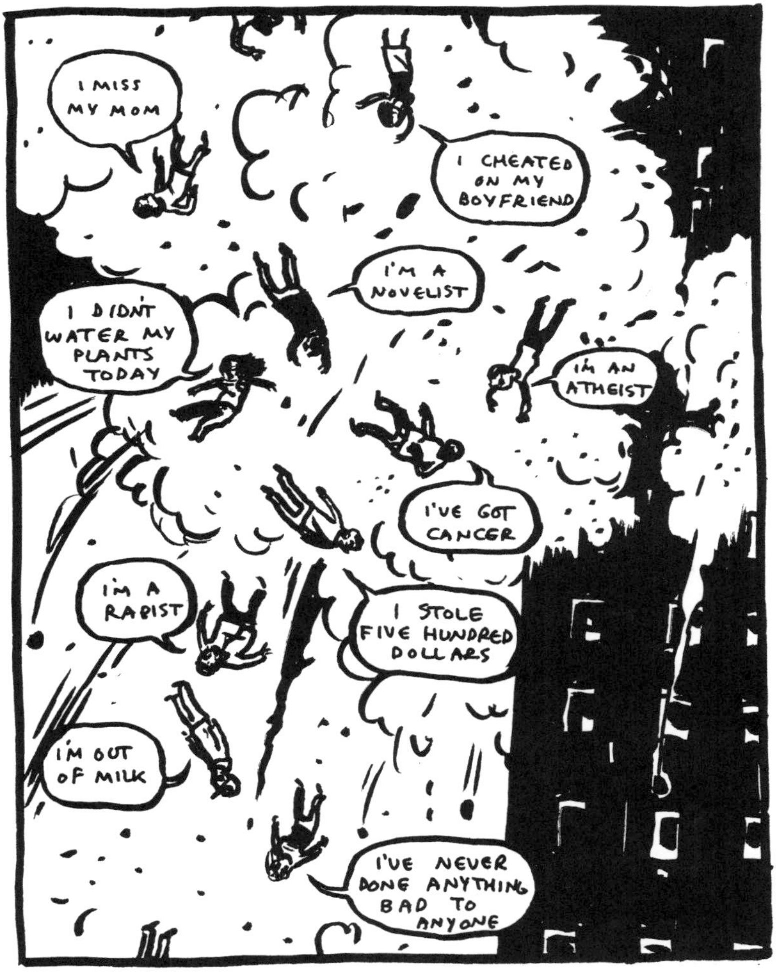
I MISS MY MOM
I CHEATED ON MY BOYFRIEND
I'M A NOVELIST
I DIDN'T WATER MY PLANTS TODAY
I'M AN ATHEIST
I'VE GOT CANCER
I'M A RAPIST
I STOLE FIVE HUNDRED DOLLARS
I'M OUT OF MILK
I'VE NEVER DONE ANYTHING BAD TO ANYONE

THE PASSAGE OF TIME IS AN ILLUSION CREATED BY CONSCIOUSNESS

ON THE SCALE OF THE UNIVERSE, THE MEAGER COLLECTION OF PARTICLES CONSTITUTING A SINGLE LIFE IS RELATIVELY EQUIVALENT TO NOTHING

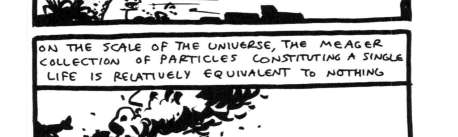

OF COURSE, THE PRACTICAL IMPLICATIONS OF THIS IN EVERY DAY LIFE ARE NEGLIGIBLE

SOMETIMES
LET'S GO!
I'M AMAZED AT WHAT I FIND MYSELF CAPABLE OF

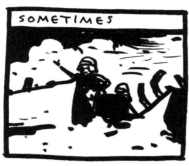

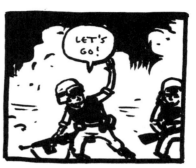

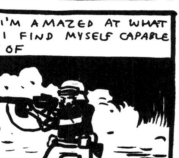

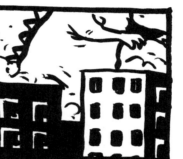

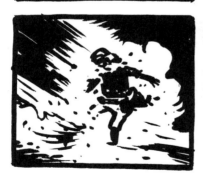

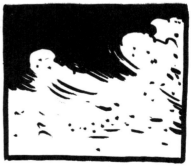

I THINK IT'S TRUE THAT THE KEY TO FINDING HAPPINESS IS BEING ABLE TO GIVE UP ALL DESIRE

OR MAYBE THAT'S JUST ANOTHER WAY OF SAYING THAT YOU DON'T CARE

I CAN'T REALLY IMAGINE A WORLD WITHOUT LIFE SO IT'S ODD THAT I'M SO CONSTANTLY WORRIED ABOUT MY OWN

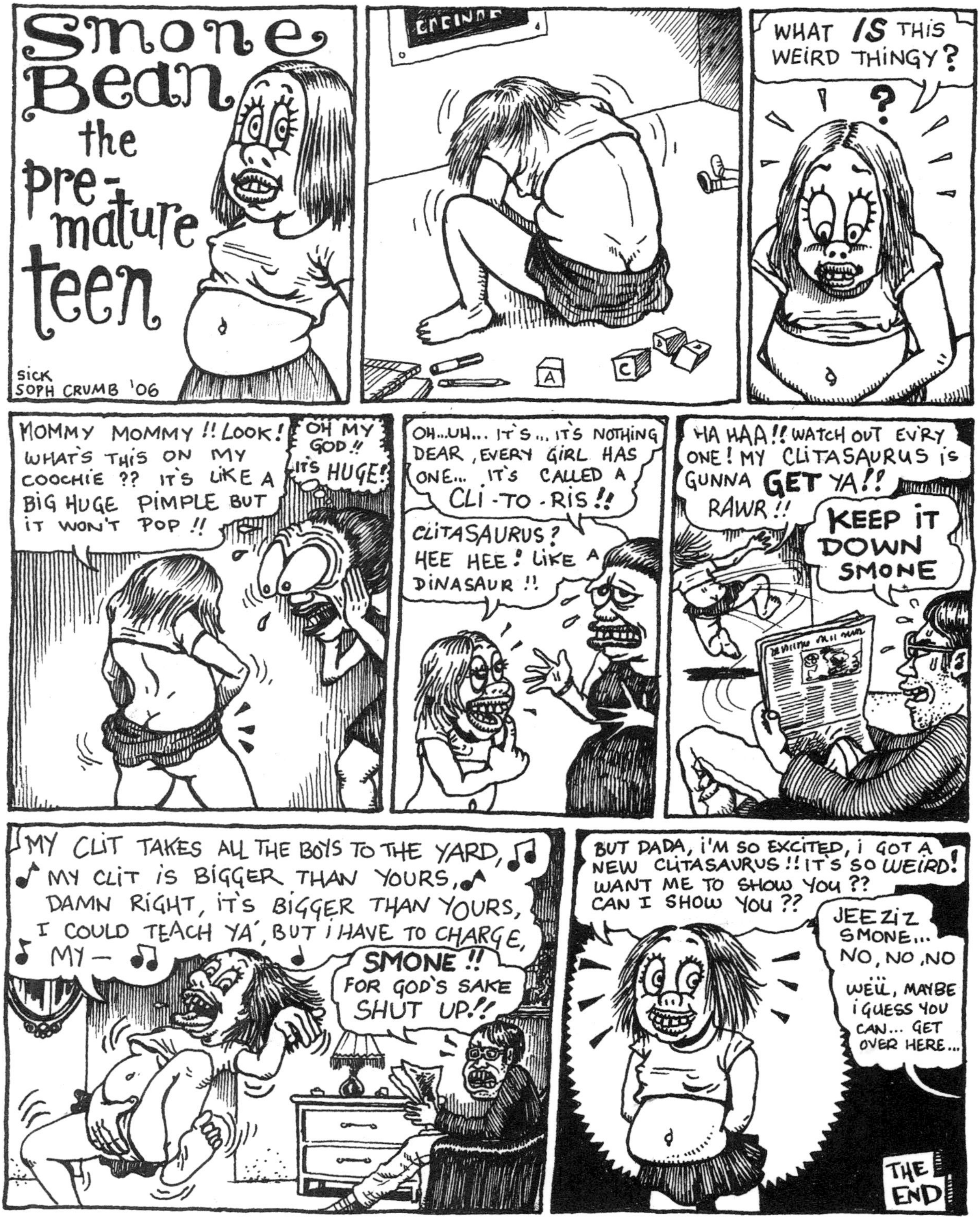
Smone Bean the pre-mature teen
SICK SOPH CRUMB '06
WHAT IS THIS WEIRD THINGY?
MOMMY MOMMY !! LOOK! WHAT'S THIS ON MY COOCHIE ?? IT'S LIKE A BIG HUGE PIMPLE BUT IT WON'T POP !!
OH MY GOD !! IT'S HUGE!
OH...UH... IT'S... IT'S NOTHING DEAR, EVERY GIRL HAS ONE... IT'S CALLED A CLI-TO-RIS !!
CLITASAURUS? HEE HEE! LIKE A DINASAUR !!
HA HAA!! WATCH OUT EV'RY ONE! MY CLITASAURUS IS GUNNA GET YA!! RAWR !!
KEEP IT DOWN SMONE
MY CLIT TAKES ALL THE BOYS TO THE YARD, MY CLIT IS BIGGER THAN YOURS, DAMN RIGHT, IT'S BIGGER THAN YOURS, I COULD TEACH YA', BUT I HAVE TO CHARGE, MY—
SMONE !! FOR GOD'S SAKE SHUT UP!!
BUT DADA, I'M SO EXCITED, I GOT A NEW CLITASAURUS !! IT'S SO WEIRD! WANT ME TO SHOW YOU ?? CAN I SHOW YOU ??
JEEZIZ SMONE... NO, NO, NO
WELL, MAYBE I GUESS YOU CAN... GET OVER HERE...
THE END

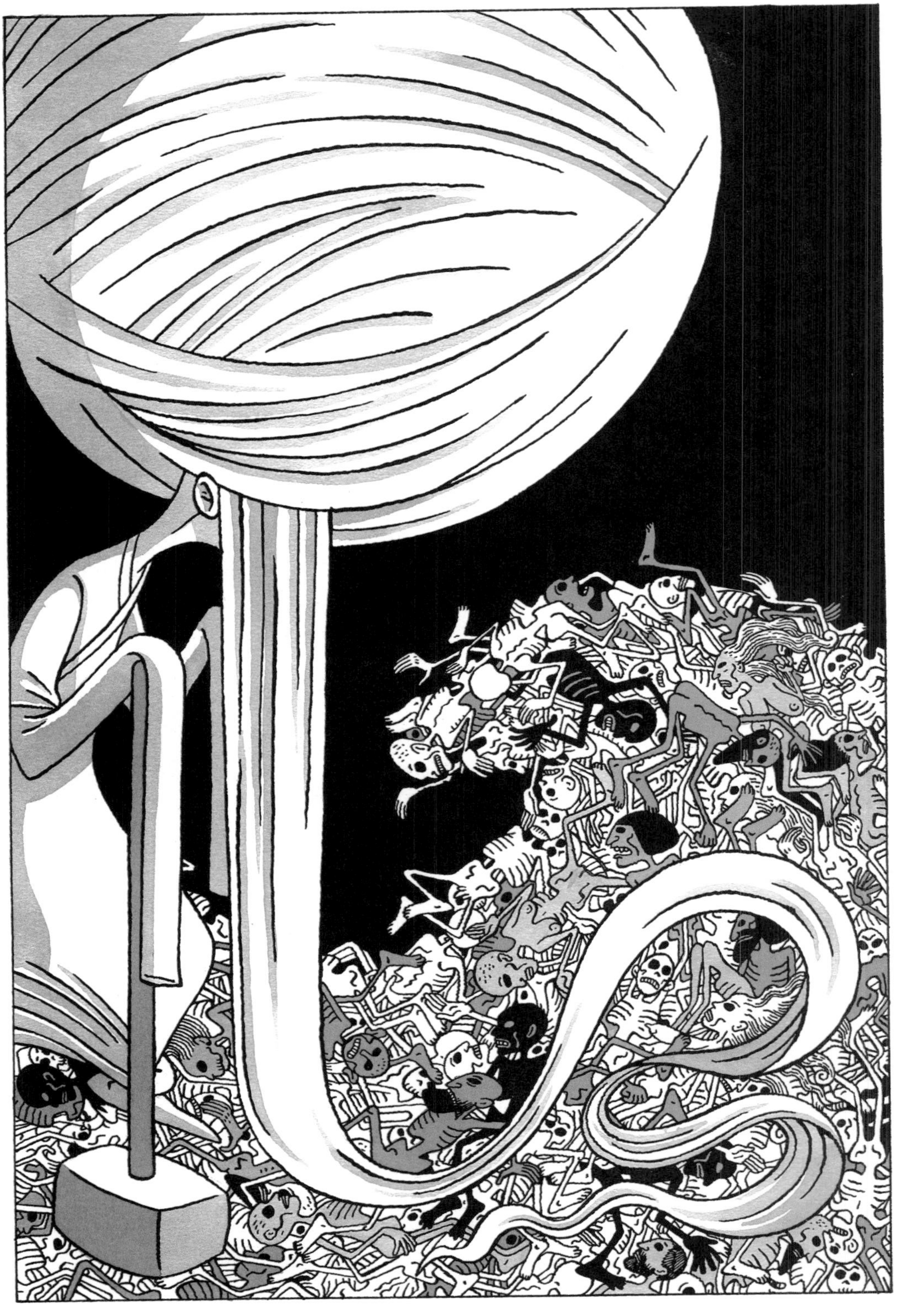

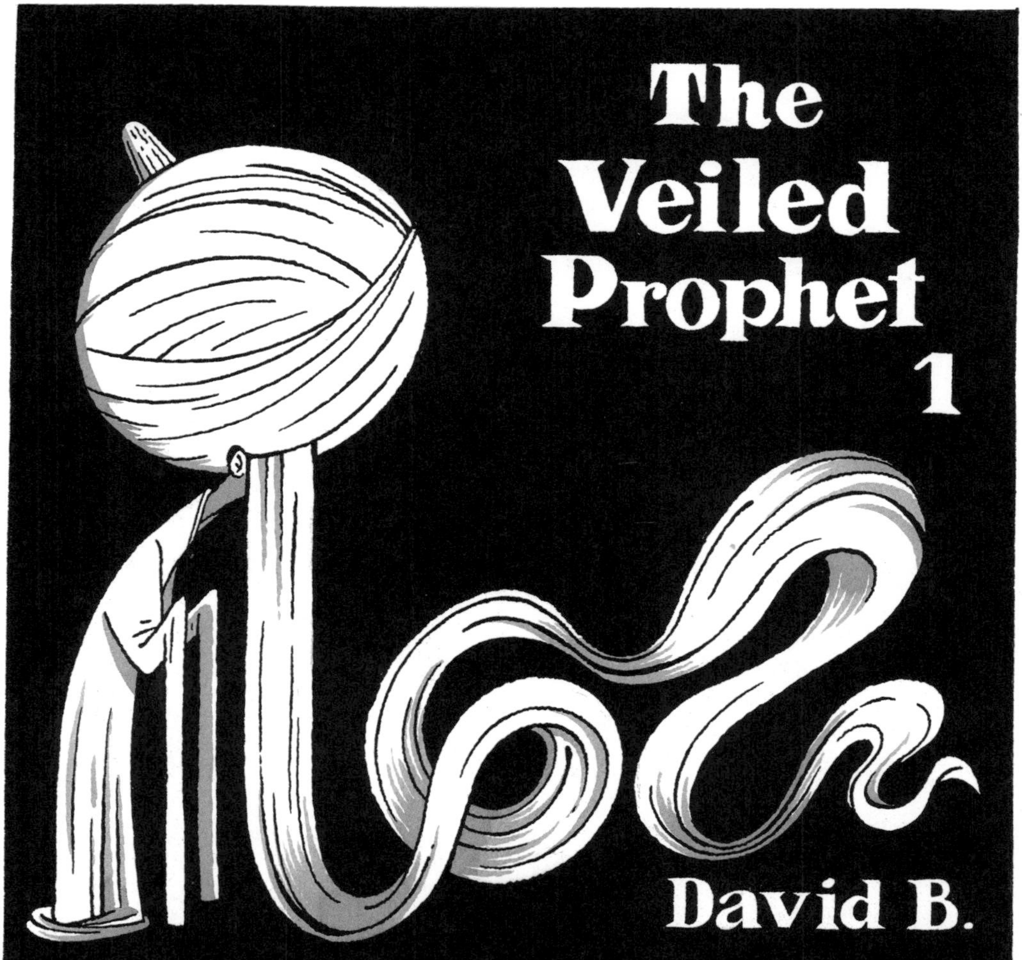
The Veiled Prophet 1
David B.

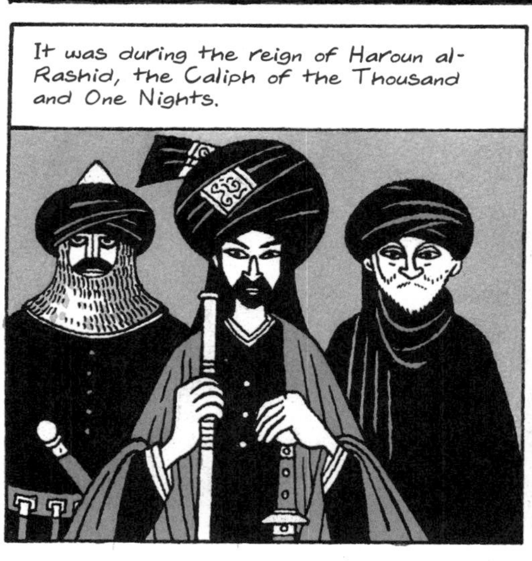
It was during the reign of Haroun al-Rashid, the Caliph of the Thousand and One Nights.

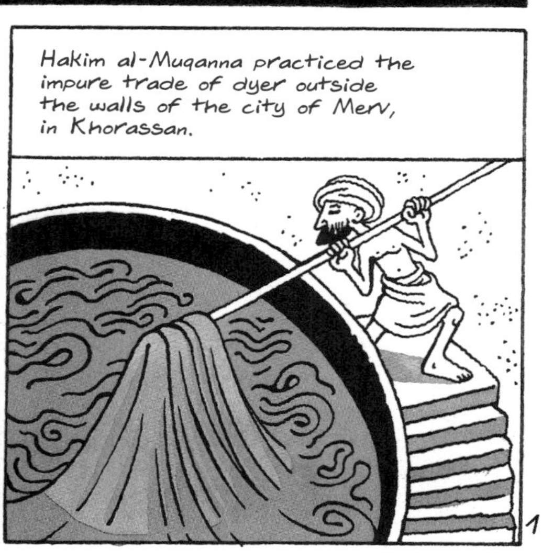
Hakim al-Muqanna practiced the impure trade of dyer outside the walls of the city of Merv, in Khorassan.

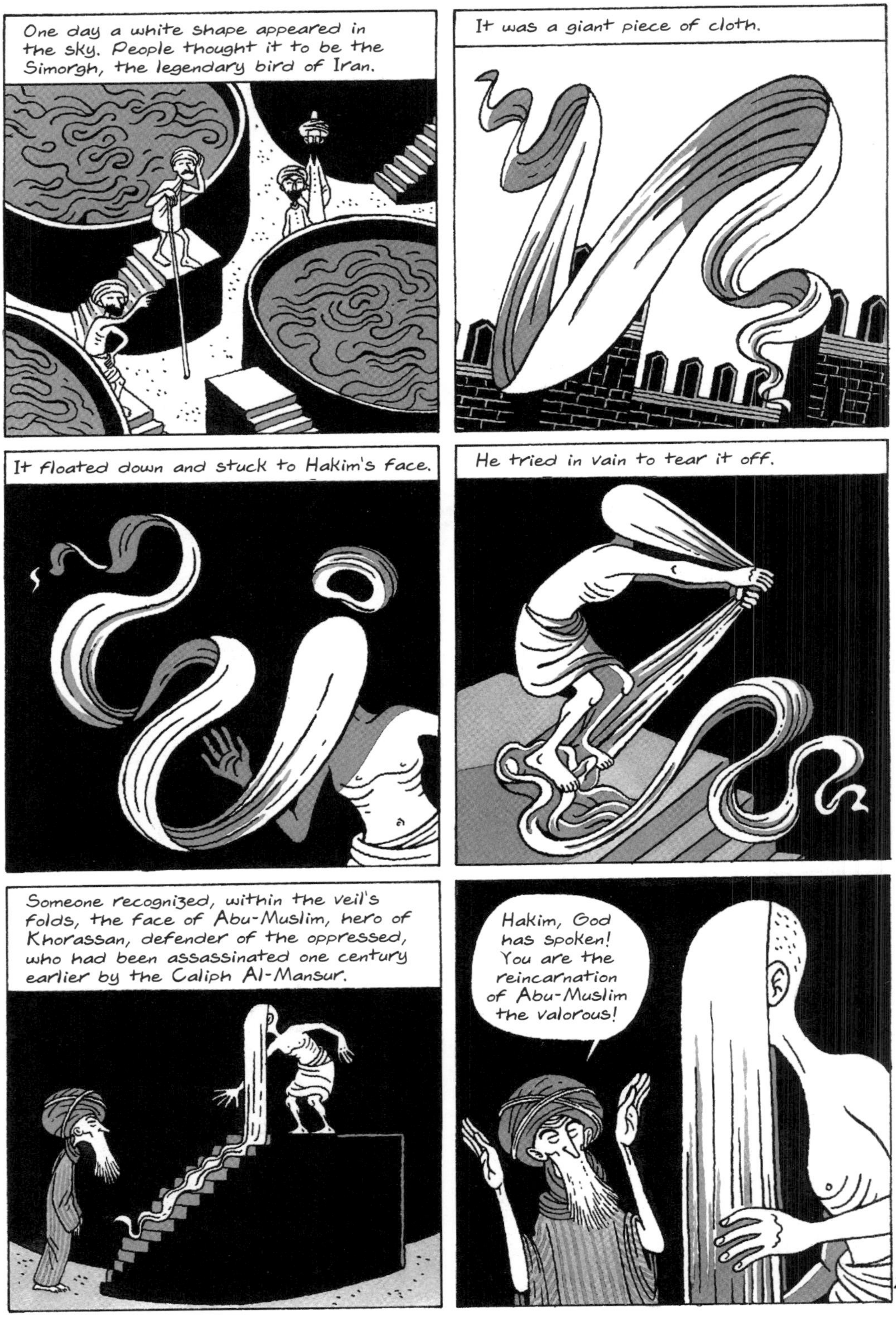
One day a white shape appeared in the sky. People thought it to be the Simorgh, the legendary bird of Iran.
It was a giant piece of cloth.
It floated down and stuck to Hakim's face.
He tried in vain to tear it off.
Someone recognized, within the veil's folds, the face of Abu-Muslim, hero of Khorassan, defender of the oppressed, who had been assassinated one century earlier by the Caliph Al-Mansur.
Hakim, God has spoken! You are the reincarnation of Abu-Muslim the valorous!
2

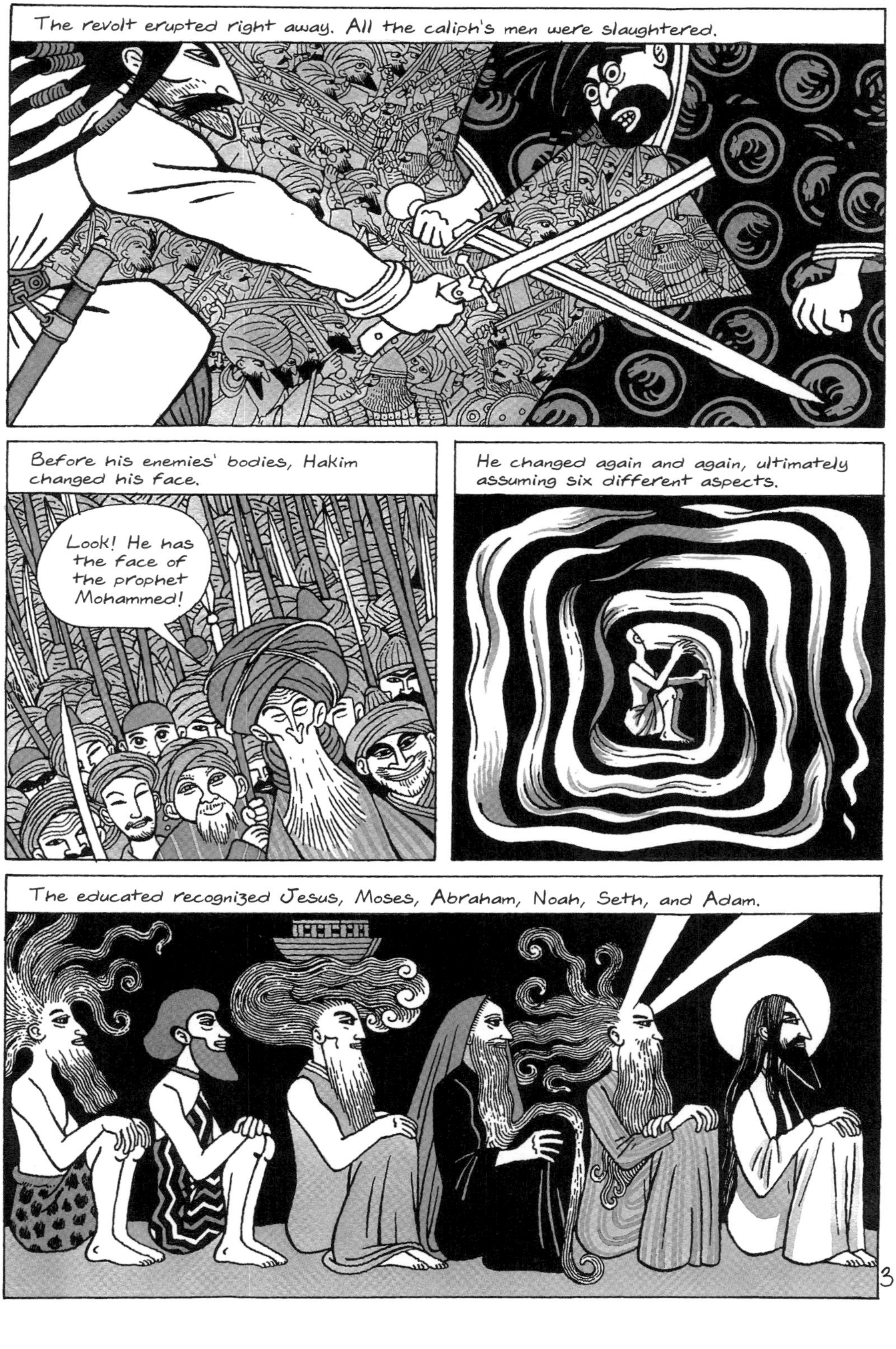
The revolt erupted right away. All the caliph's men were slaughtered.
Before his enemies' bodies, Hakim changed his face.
Look! He has the face of the prophet Mohammed!
He changed again and again, ultimately assuming six different aspects.
The educated recognized Jesus, Moses, Abraham, Noah, Seth, and Adam.

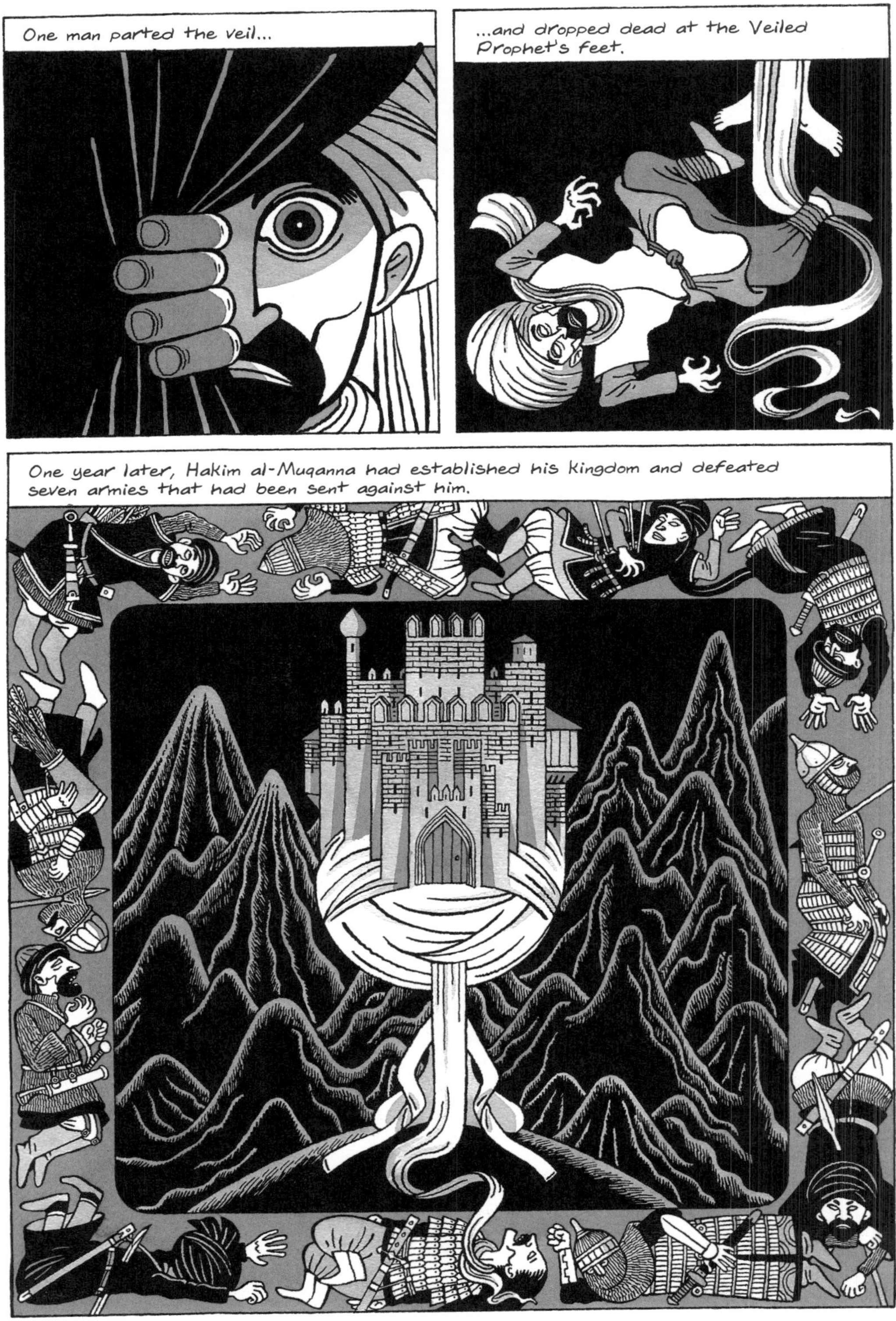

One man parted the veil...
...and dropped dead at the Veiled Prophet's feet.
One year later, Hakim al-Muqanna had established his kingdom and defeated seven armies that had been sent against him.

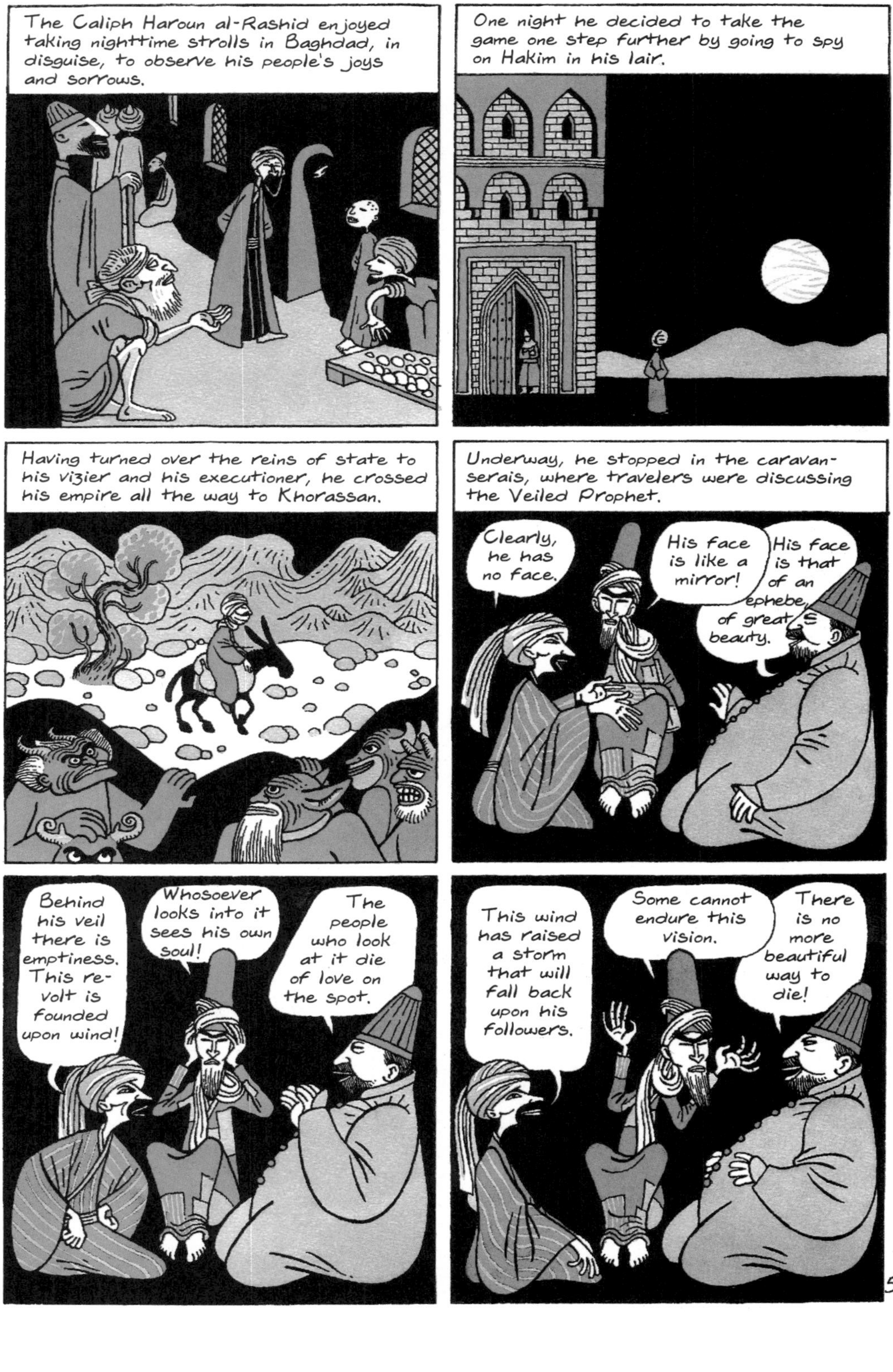
The Caliph Haroun al-Rashid enjoyed taking nighttime strolls in Baghdad, in disguise, to observe his people's joys and sorrows.
One night he decided to take the game one step further by going to spy on Hakim in his lair.
Having turned over the reins of state to his vizier and his executioner, he crossed his empire all the way to Khorassan.
Underway, he stopped in the caravan-serais, where travelers were discussing the Veiled Prophet.
Clearly, he has no face.
His face is like a mirror!
His face is that of an ephebe of great beauty.
Behind his veil there is emptiness. This revolt is founded upon wind!
Whosoever looks into it sees his own soul!
The people who look at it die of love on the spot.
This wind has raised a storm that will fall back upon his followers.
Some cannot endure this vision.
There is no more beautiful way to die!

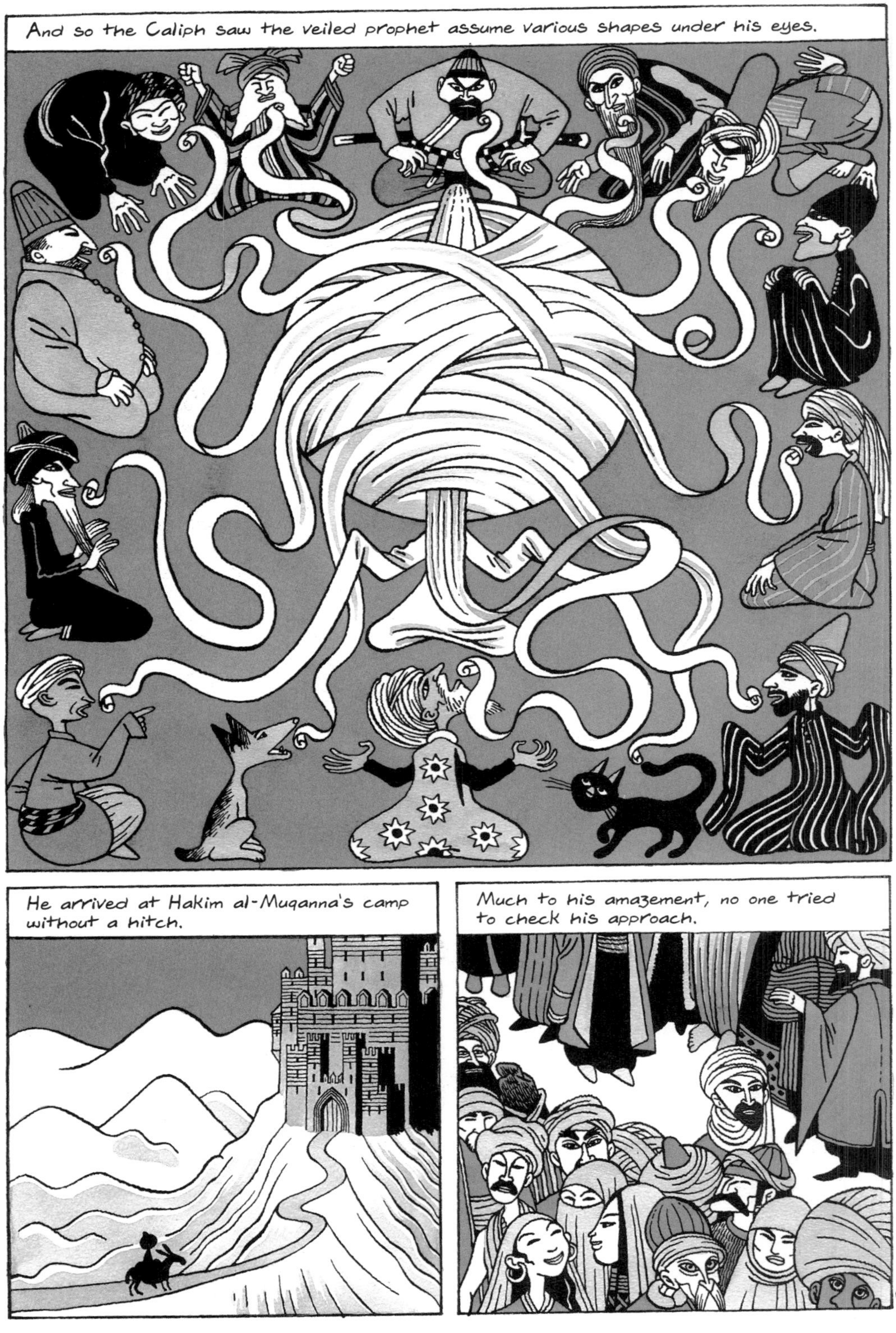
And so the Caliph saw the veiled prophet assume various shapes under his eyes.
He arrived at Hakim al-Muqanna's camp without a hitch.
Much to his amazement, no one tried to check his approach.

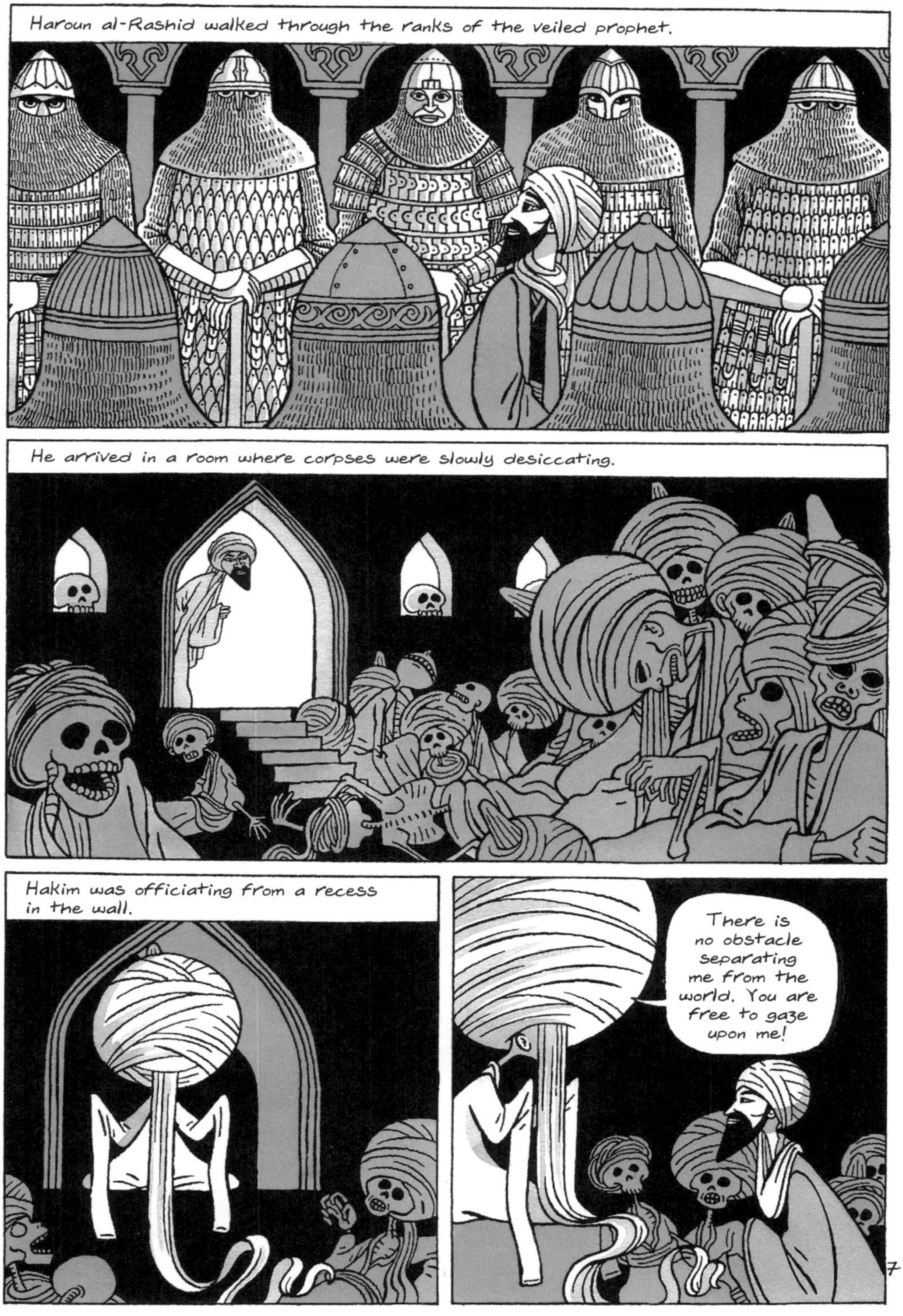
Haroun al-Rashid walked through the ranks of the veiled prophet.
He arrived in a room where corpses were slowly desiccating.
Hakim was officiating from a recess in the wall.
There is no obstacle separating me from the world. You are free to gaze upon me!

Behind you, the corpses of those who dared.

And before you, a thrilling mystery.

I have come but to bring you a present, O Prophet!

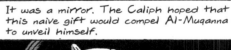

It was a mirror. The Caliph hoped that this naive gift would compel Al-Muqanna to unveil himself.

He slipped the mirror under his veil.

When he handed it back to Haroun al Rashid the mirror's face was dark.

Every day, the veiled prophet would preach to his troops.

This world does not exist! It is an illusion!

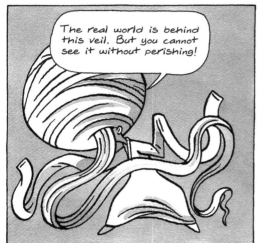

The real world is behind this veil. But you cannot see it without perishing!

Here, there is neither law nor religion. The violation of every law is the first step toward the real world.

At night, he disposed of the women in his harem as if he were plowing a field.

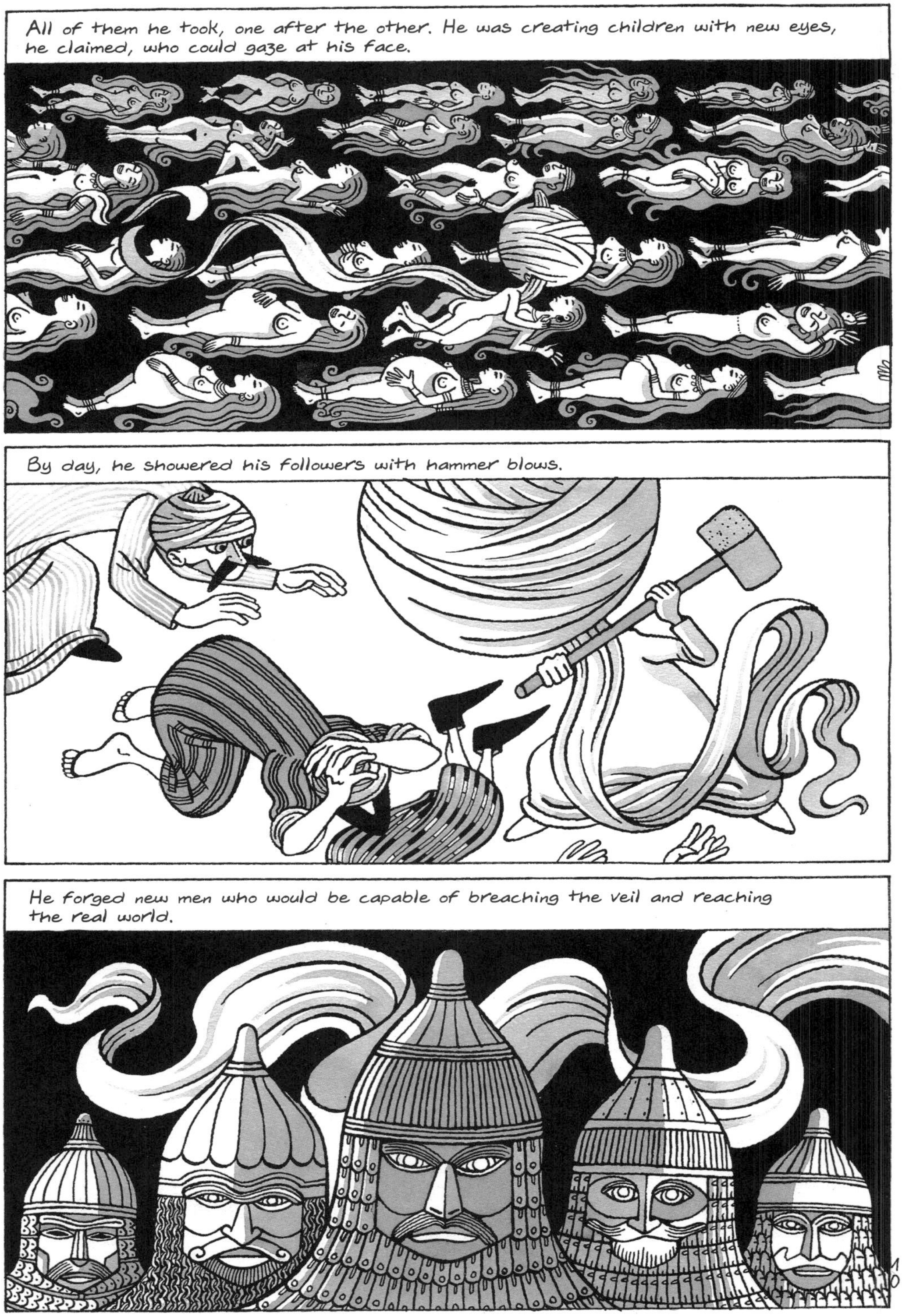
All of them he took, one after the other. He was creating children with new eyes, he claimed, who could gaze at his face.
By day, he showered his followers with hammer blows.
He forged new men who would be capable of breaching the veil and reaching the real world.

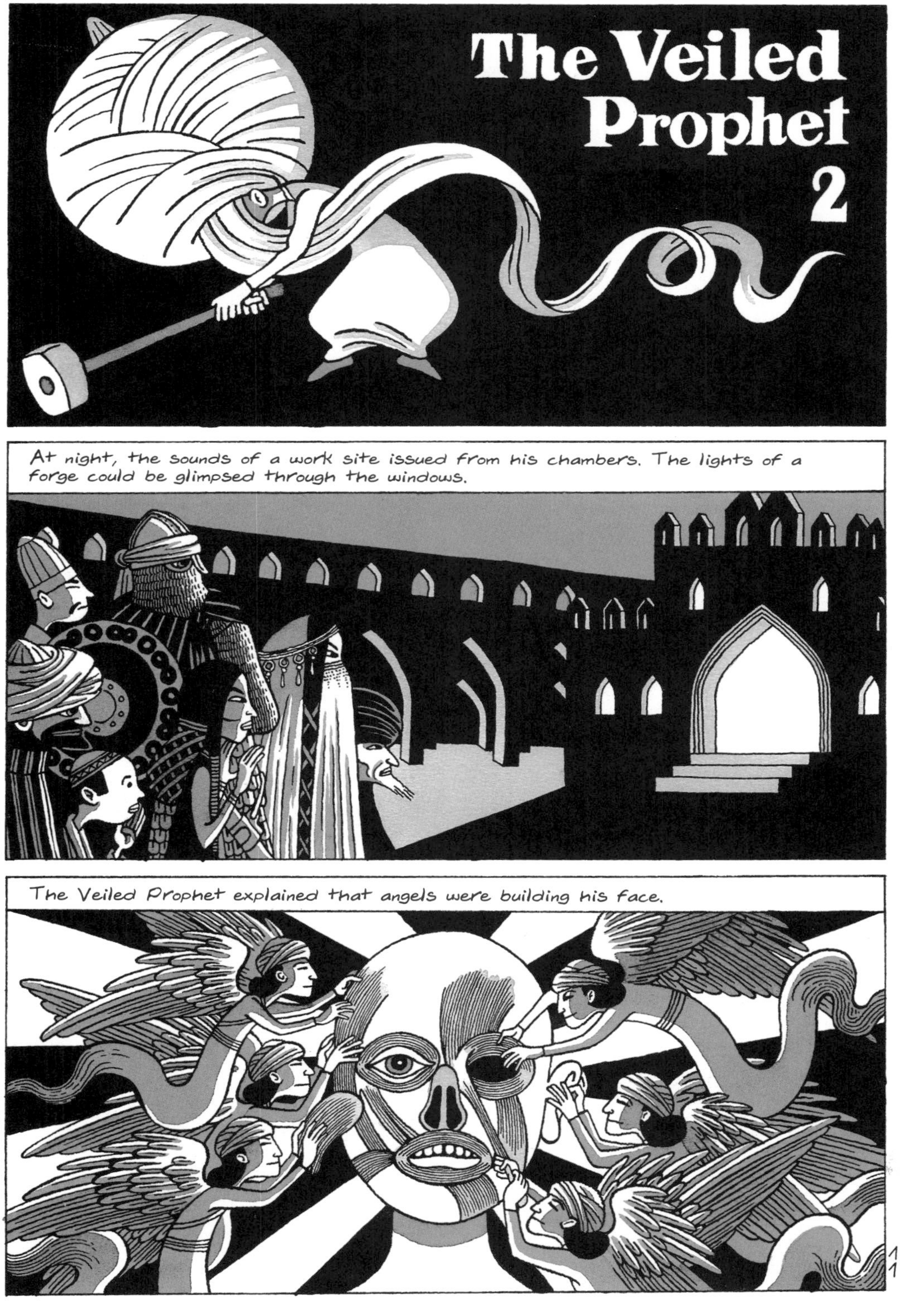
The Veiled Prophet 2
At night, the sounds of a work site issued from his chambers. The lights of a forge could be glimpsed through the windows.
The Veiled Prophet explained that angels were building his face.
11

Now al-Muqanna proclaimed himself to be the entire world incarnate. He demanded to be worshiped as such.

Some faithful had yoked themselves to this task and spent their days and their nights enumerating his infinite names.

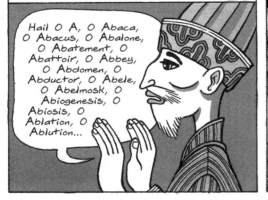

Hail O A, O Abaca, O Abacus, O Abalone, O Abatement, O Abattoir, O Abbey, O Abdomen, O Abductor, O Abele, O Abelmosk, O Abiogenesis, O Abiosis, O Ablation, O Ablution...

This "Road of the Names," as it was called, was strewn with corpses.

One evening, the Prophet announced that God was preparing a new flood and that he, Hakim al-Muqanna, would be its instrument.

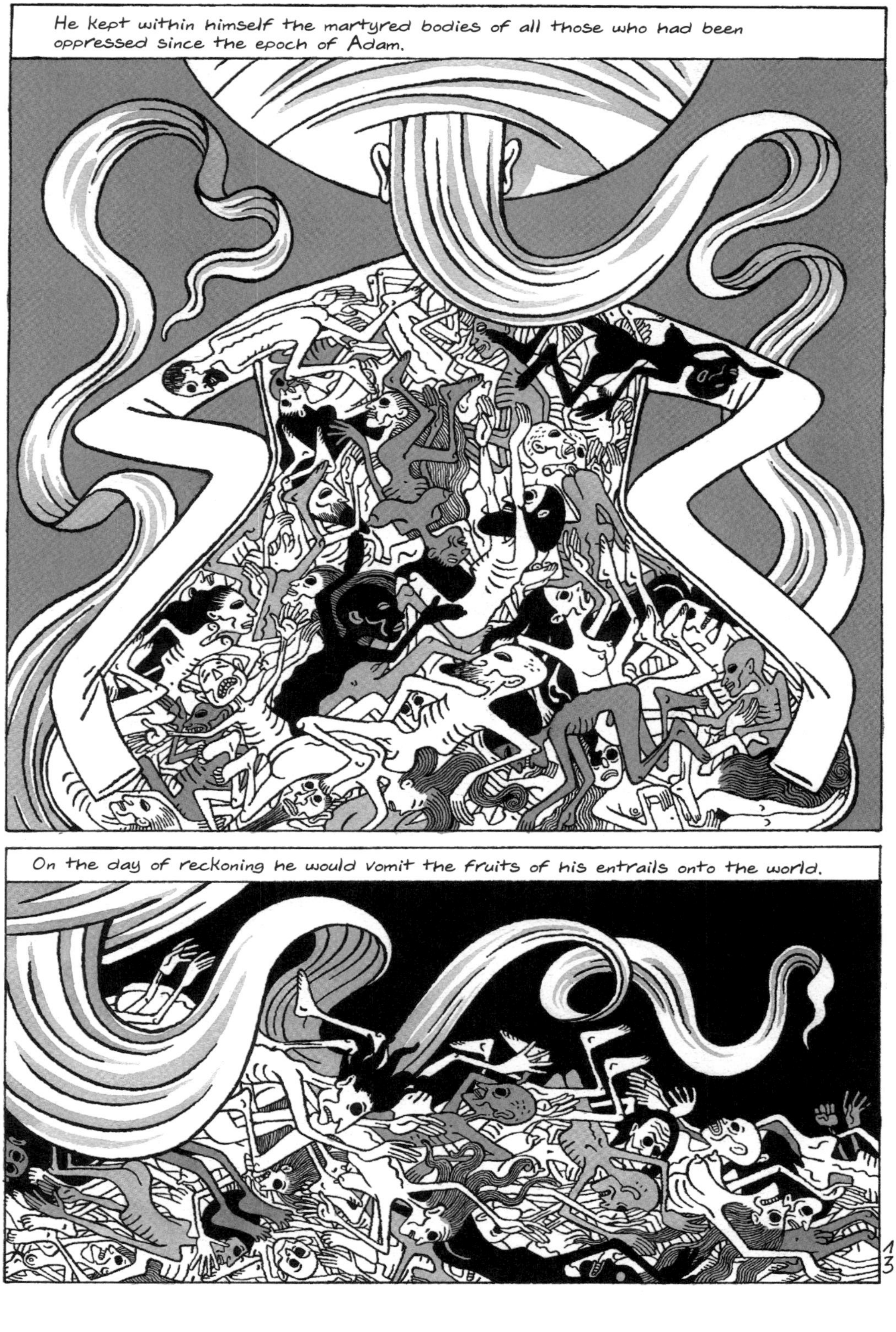
He kept within himself the martyred bodies of all those who had been oppressed since the epoch of Adam.
On the day of reckoning he would vomit the fruits of his entrails onto the world.

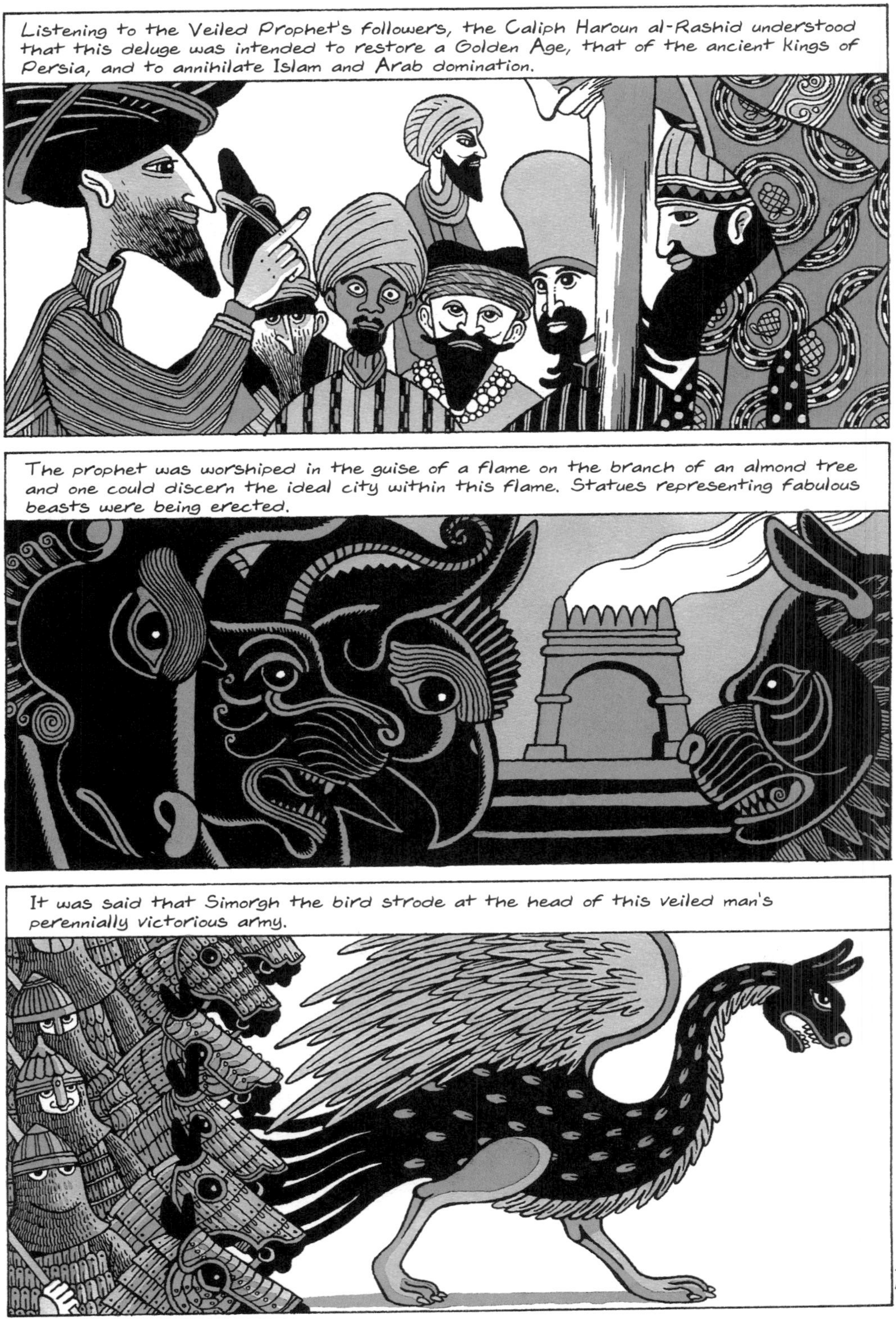
Listening to the Veiled Prophet's followers, the Caliph Haroun al-Rashid understood that this deluge was intended to restore a Golden Age, that of the ancient Kings of Persia, and to annihilate Islam and Arab domination.
The prophet was worshiped in the guise of a flame on the branch of an almond tree and one could discern the ideal city within this flame. Statues representing fabulous beasts were being erected.
It was said that Simorgh the bird strode at the head of this veiled man's perennially victorious army.

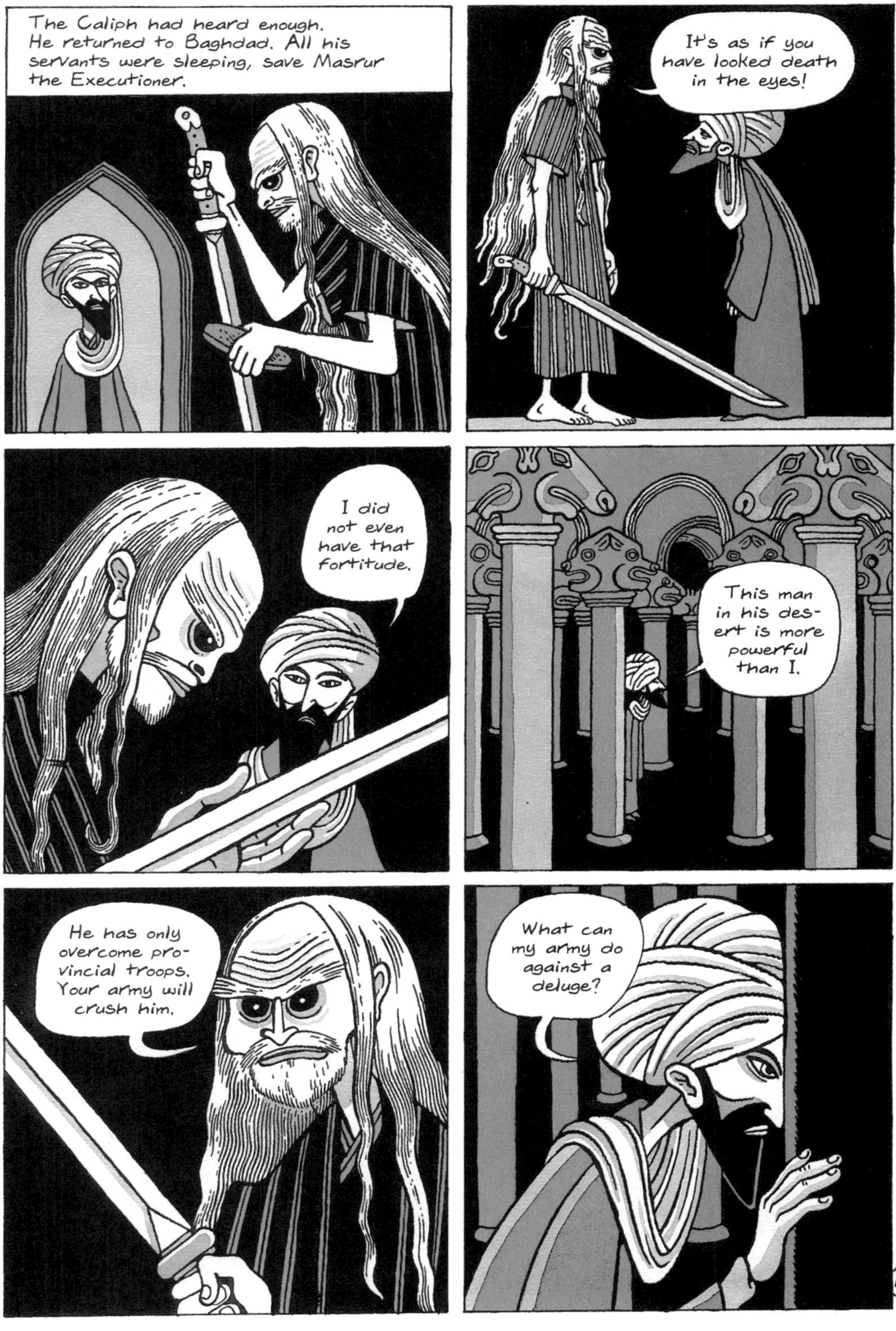

The Caliph had heard enough. He returned to Baghdad. All his servants were sleeping, save Masrur the Executioner.
It's as if you have looked death in the eyes!
I did not even have that fortitude.
This man in his desert is more powerful than I.
He has only overcome provincial troops. Your army will crush him.
What can my army do against a deluge?

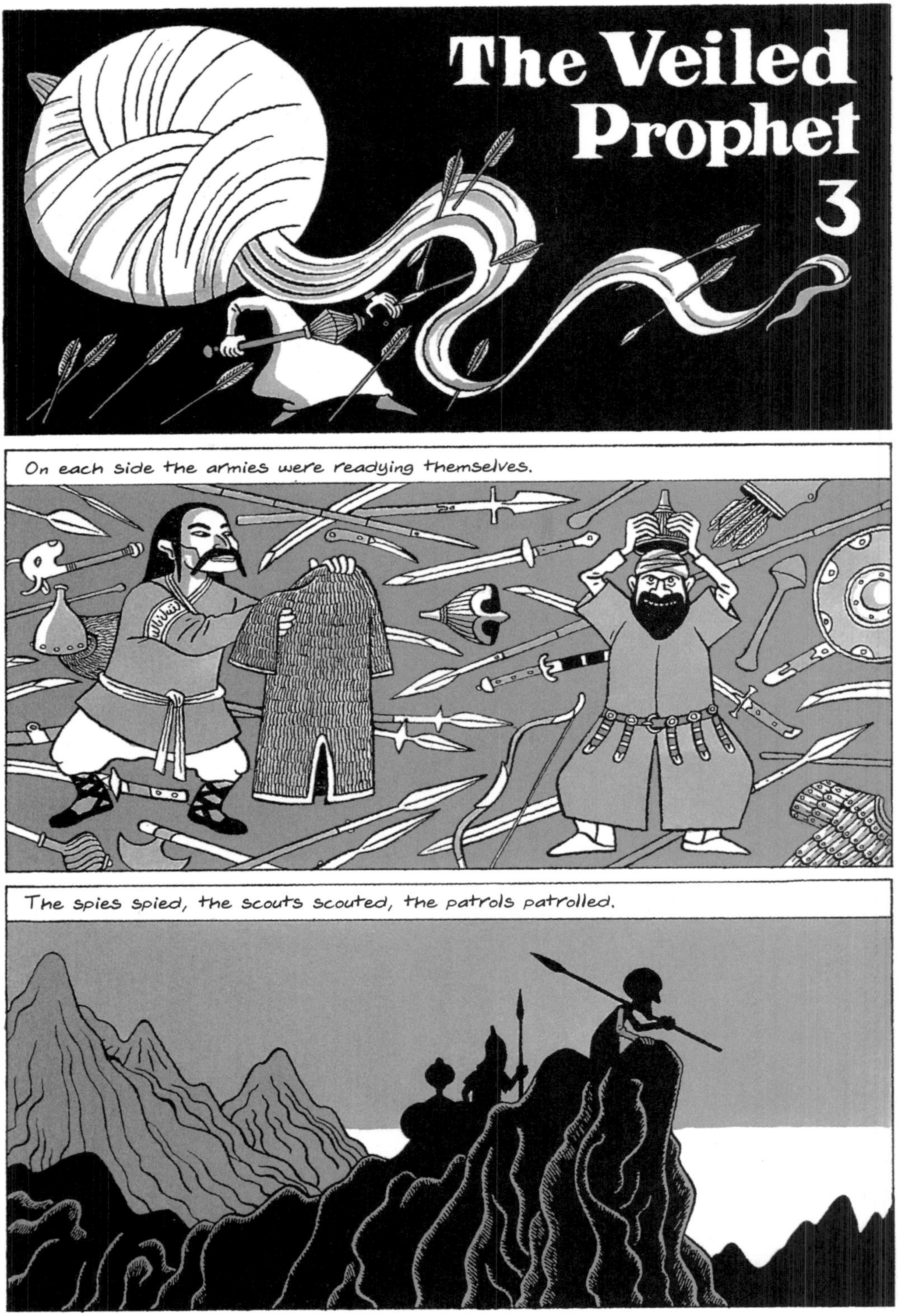
The Veiled Prophet
3
On each side the armies were readying themselves.
The spies spied, the scouts scouted, the patrols patrolled.

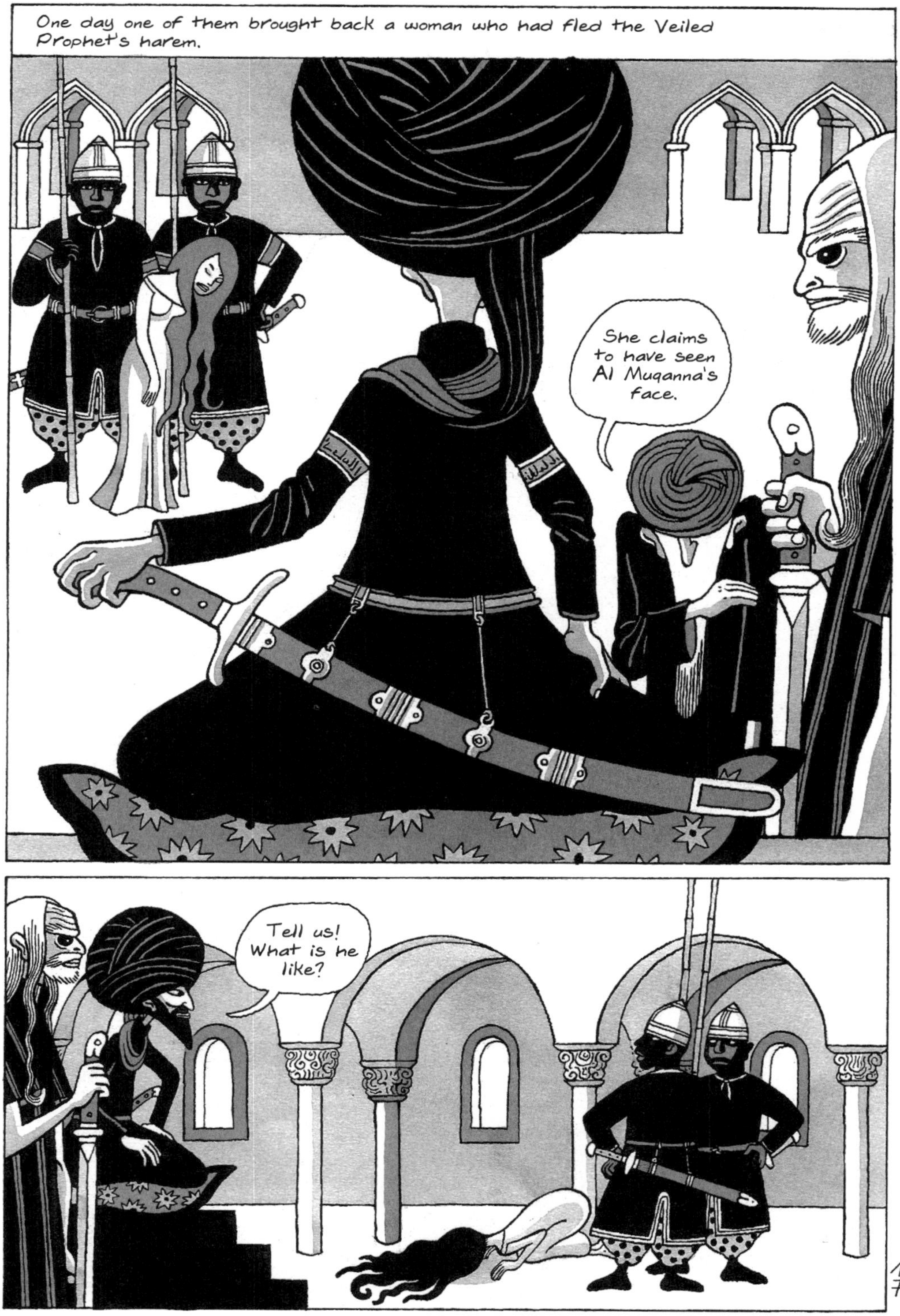
One day one of them brought back a woman who had fled the Veiled Prophet's harem.
She claims to have seen Al Muqanna's face.
Tell us! What is he like?

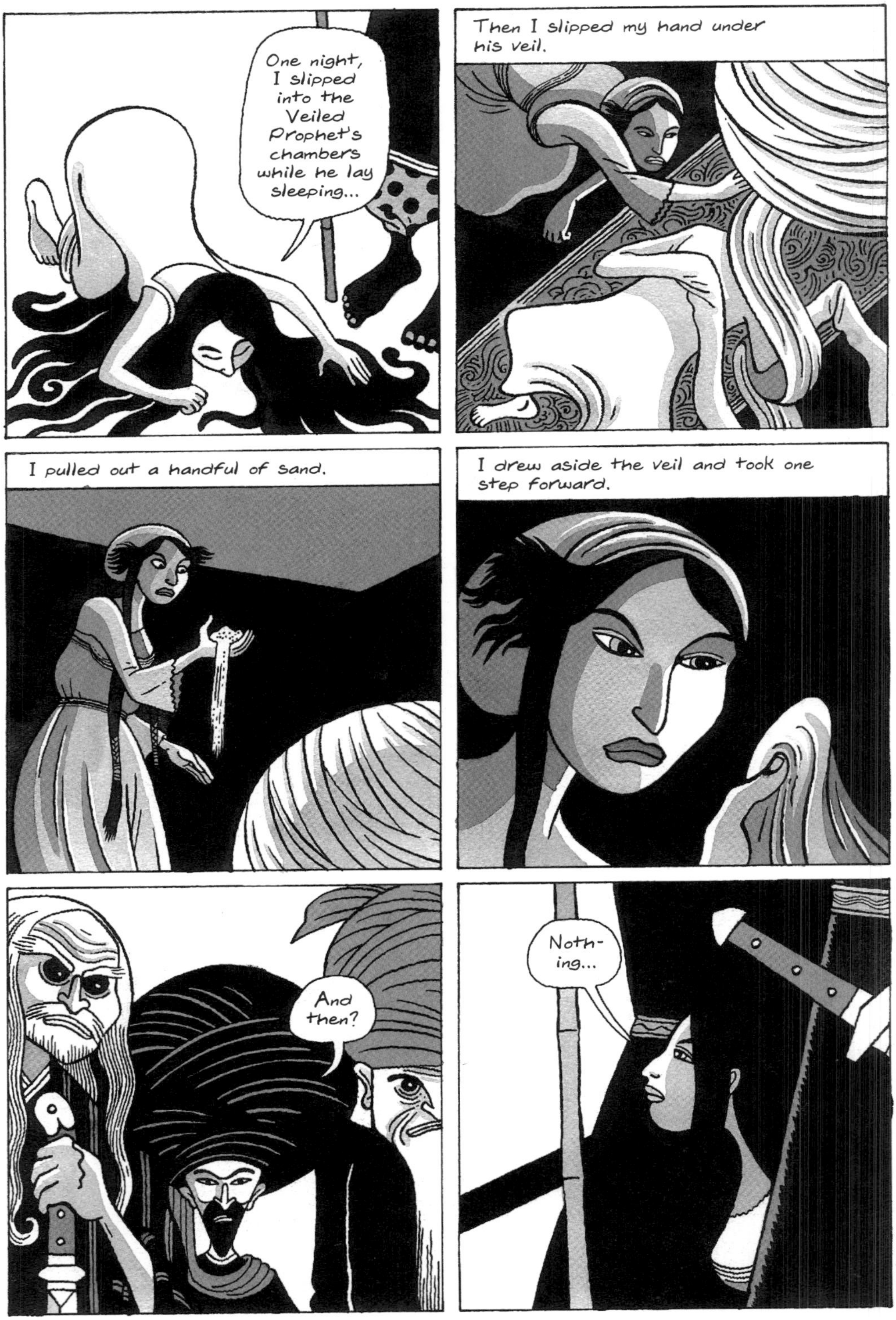

One night, I slipped into the Veiled Prophet's chambers while he lay sleeping...
Then I slipped my hand under his veil.
I pulled out a handful of sand.
I drew aside the veil and took one step forward.
And then?
Noth- ing...

I found myself in the desert. At my feet was a well. It looked like a decapitated neck.

At the bottom of the well, my face was reflected in water dark as blood.

Above the well, a giant moon crushed the desert.

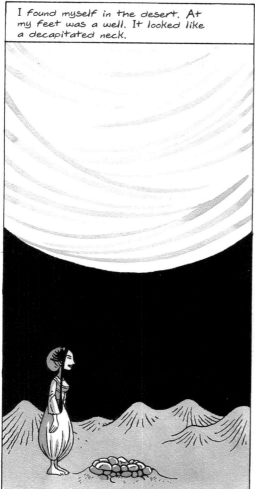

I took one step back and I found myself back in the Veiled Prophet's chambers. I fled that very night.

19

A desert... a well...

It is from this well that will emerge the rain of corpses announced by al-Muqanna!

?

How can one battle an army of the dead?

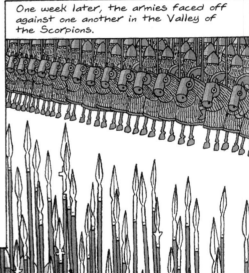

One week later, the armies faced off against one another in the Valley of the Scorpions.

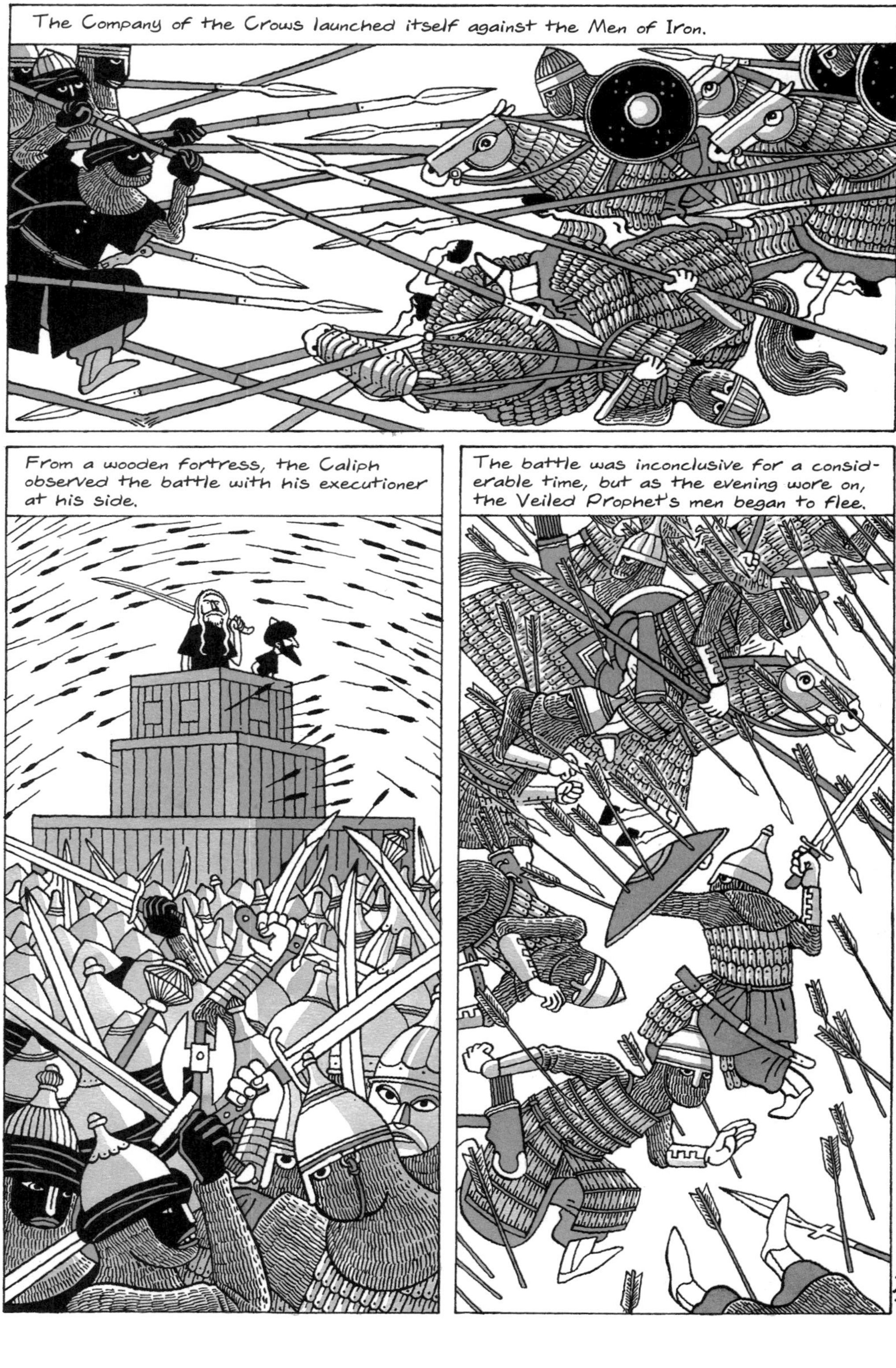
The Company of the Crows launched itself against the Men of Iron.
From a wooden fortress, the Caliph observed the battle with his executioner at his side.
The battle was inconclusive for a considerable time, but as the evening wore on, the Veiled Prophet's men began to flee.

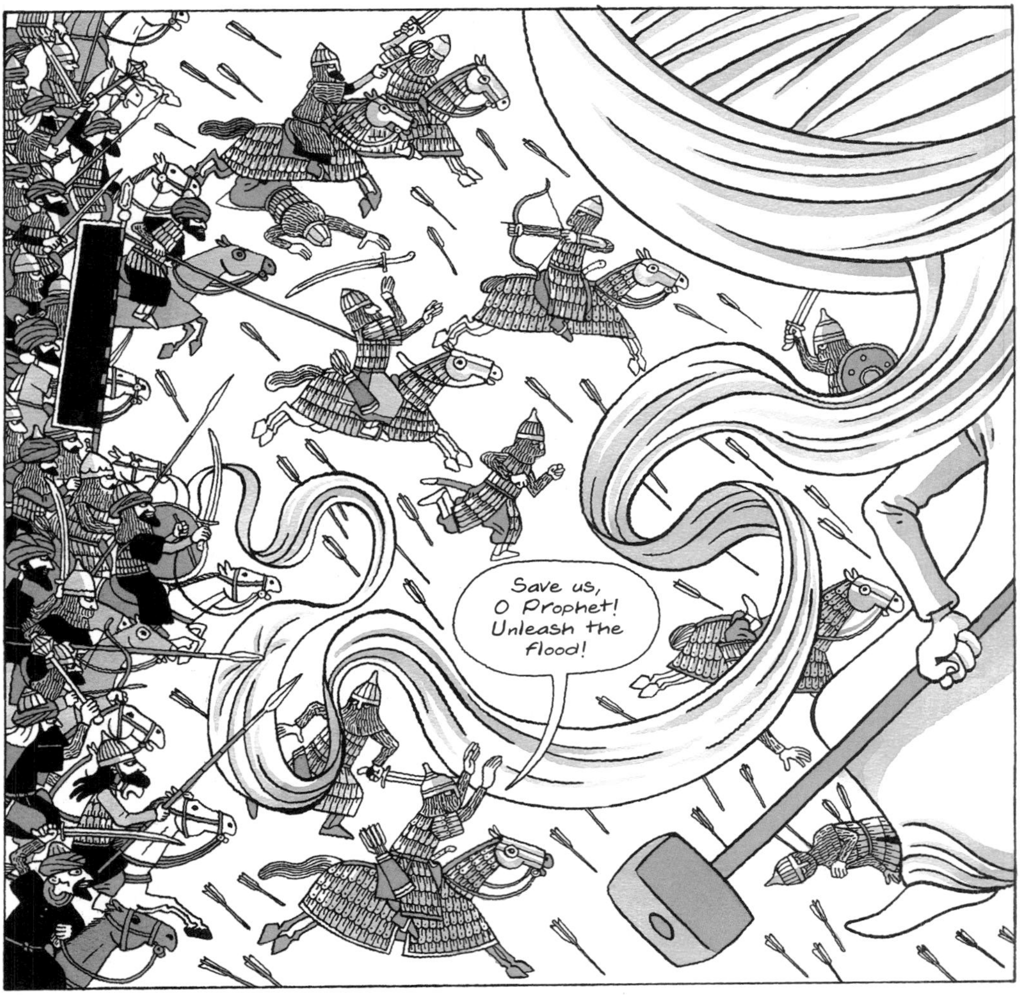
Save us, O Prophet! Unleash the flood!

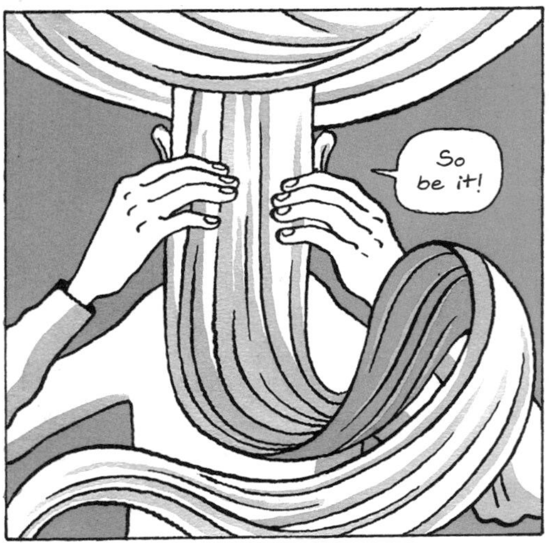
So be it!

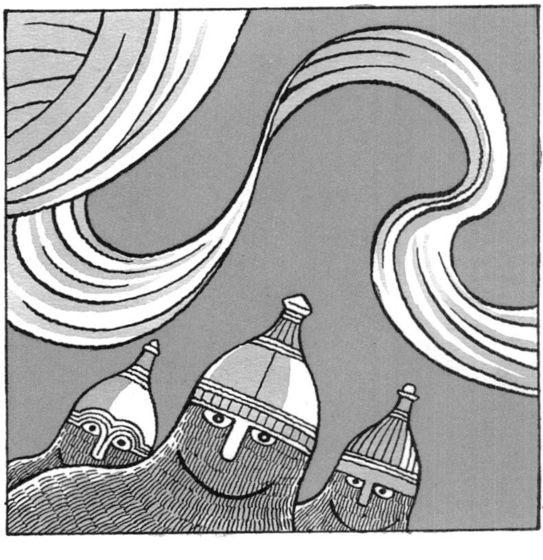

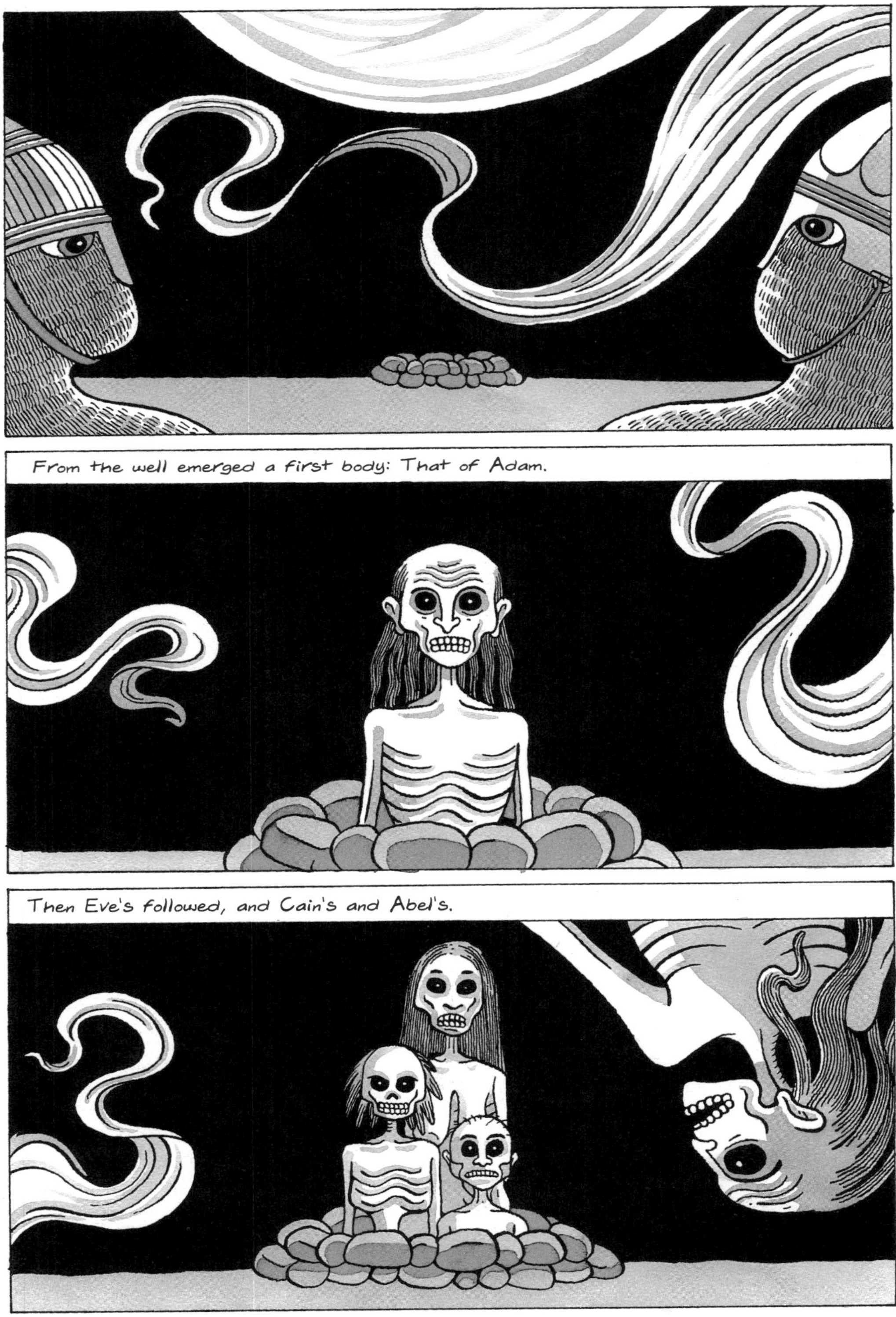
From the well emerged a first body: That of Adam.
Then Eve's followed, and Cain's and Abel's.

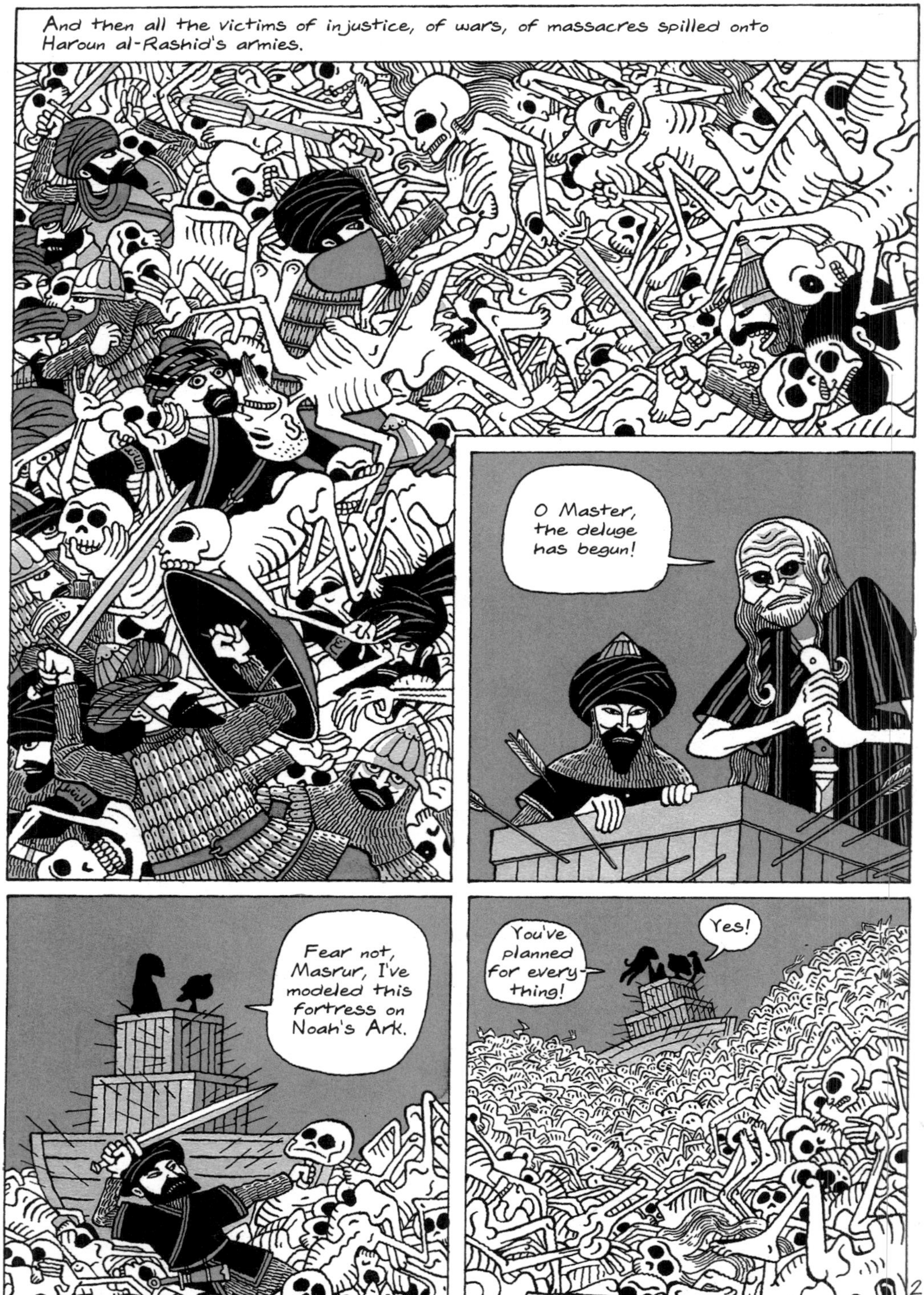
And then all the victims of injustice, of wars, of massacres spilled onto Haroun al-Rashid's armies.
O Master, the deluge has begun!
Fear not, Masrur, I've modeled this fortress on Noah's Ark.
You've planned for every-thing!
Yes!

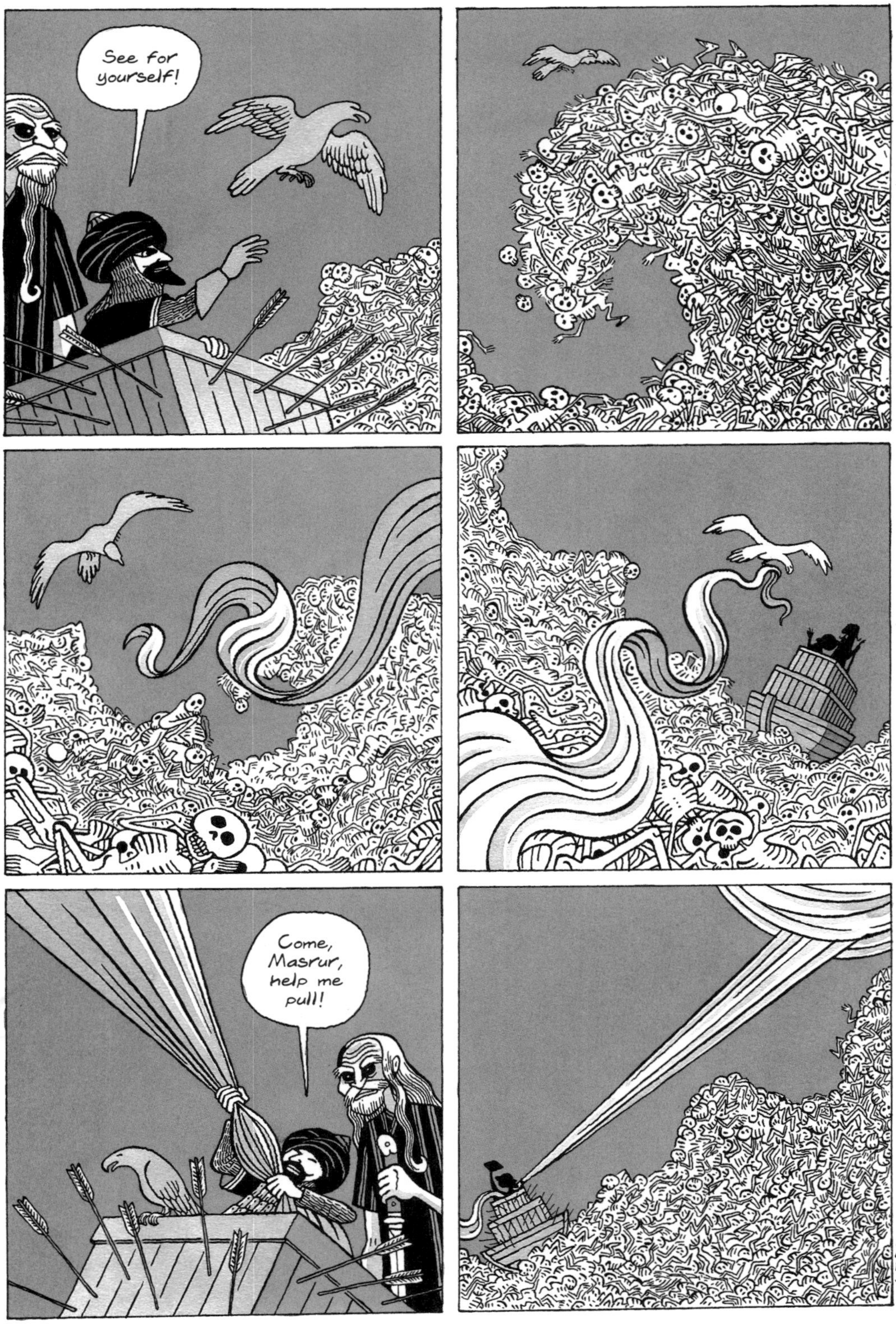

See for yourself!
Come, Masrur, help me pull!

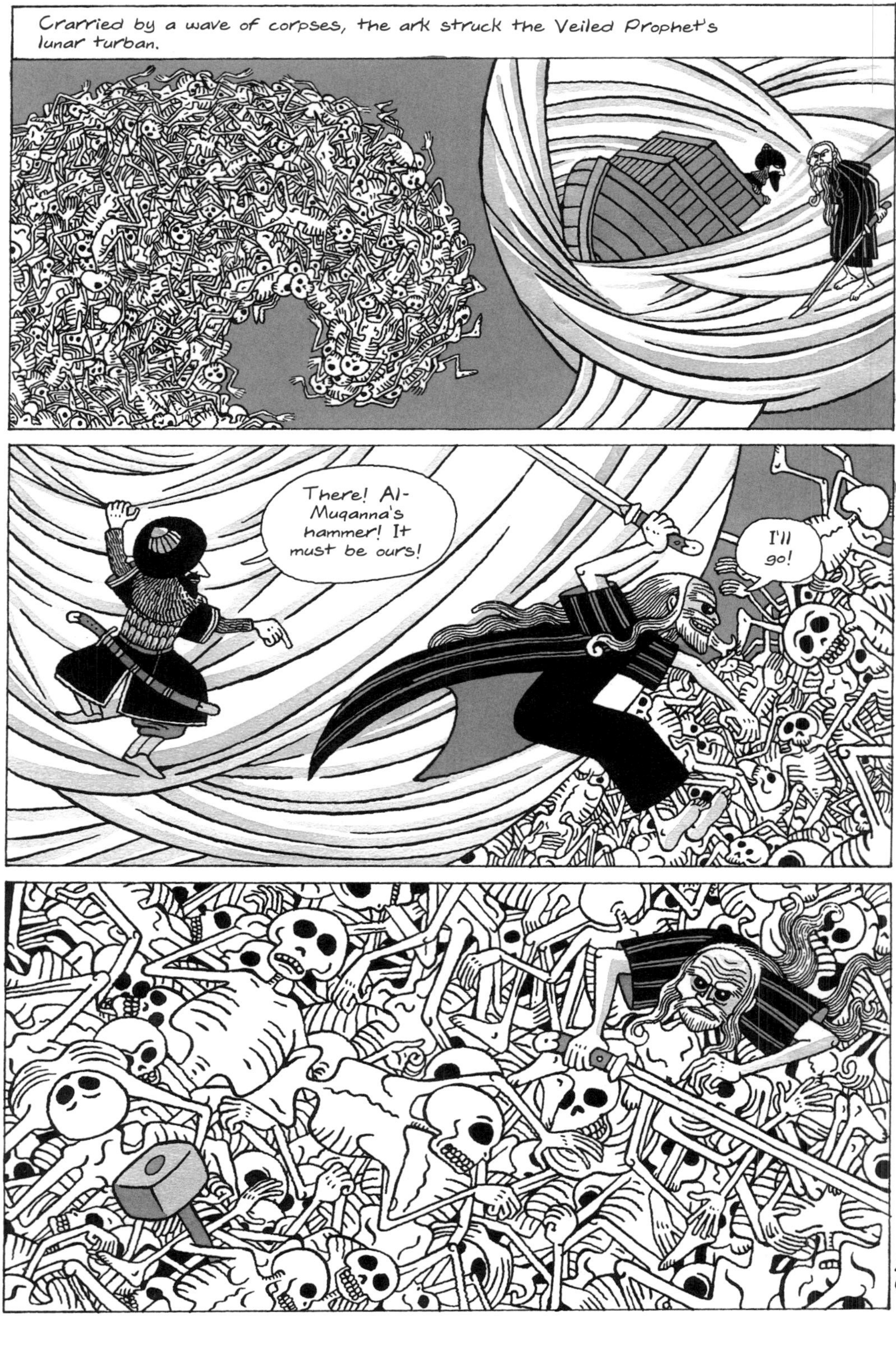
Crarried by a wave of corpses, the ark struck the Veiled Prophet's lunar turban.
There! Al-Muqanna's hammer! It must be ours!
I'll go!

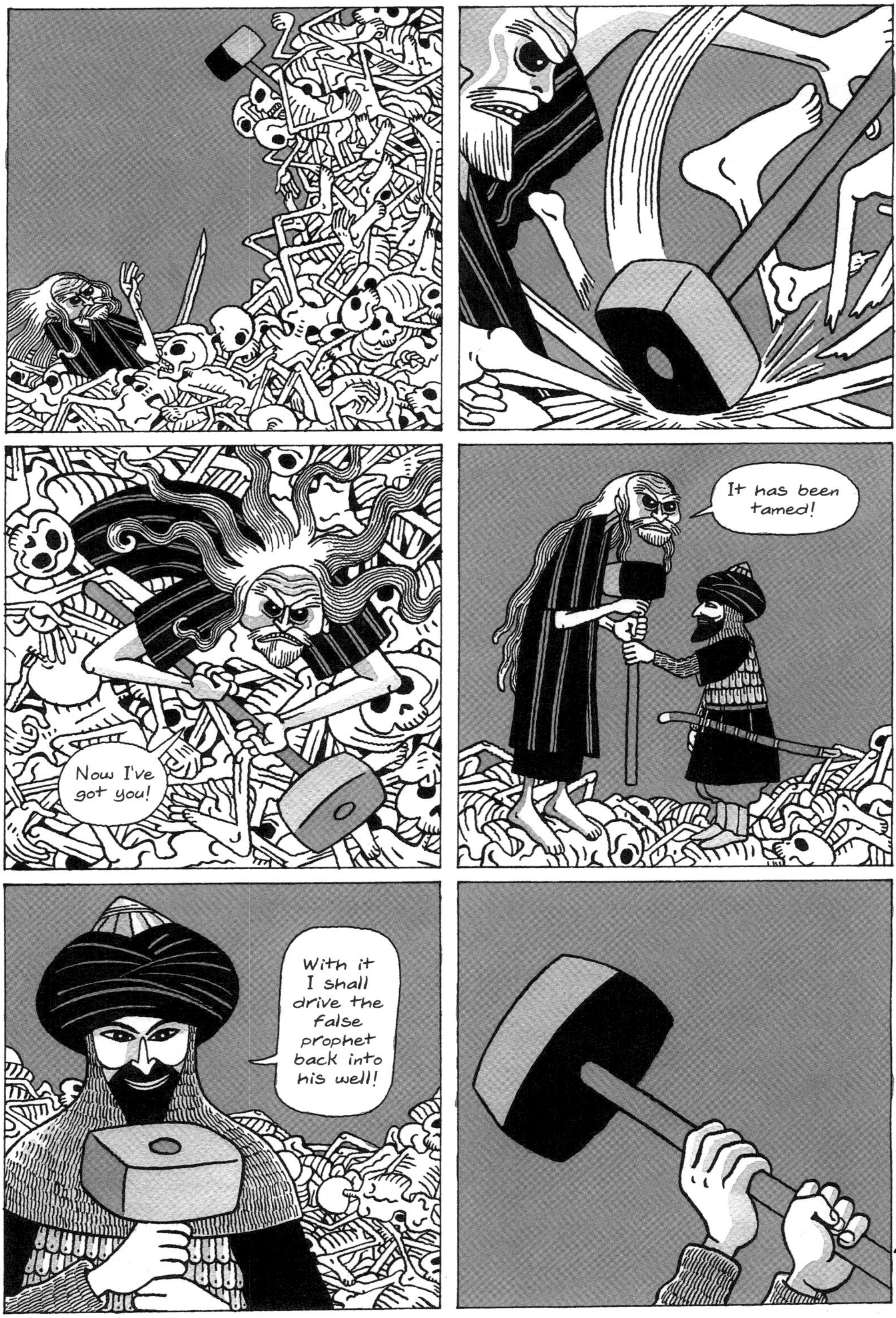
Now I've got you!
It has been tamed!
With it I shall drive the false prophet back into his well!

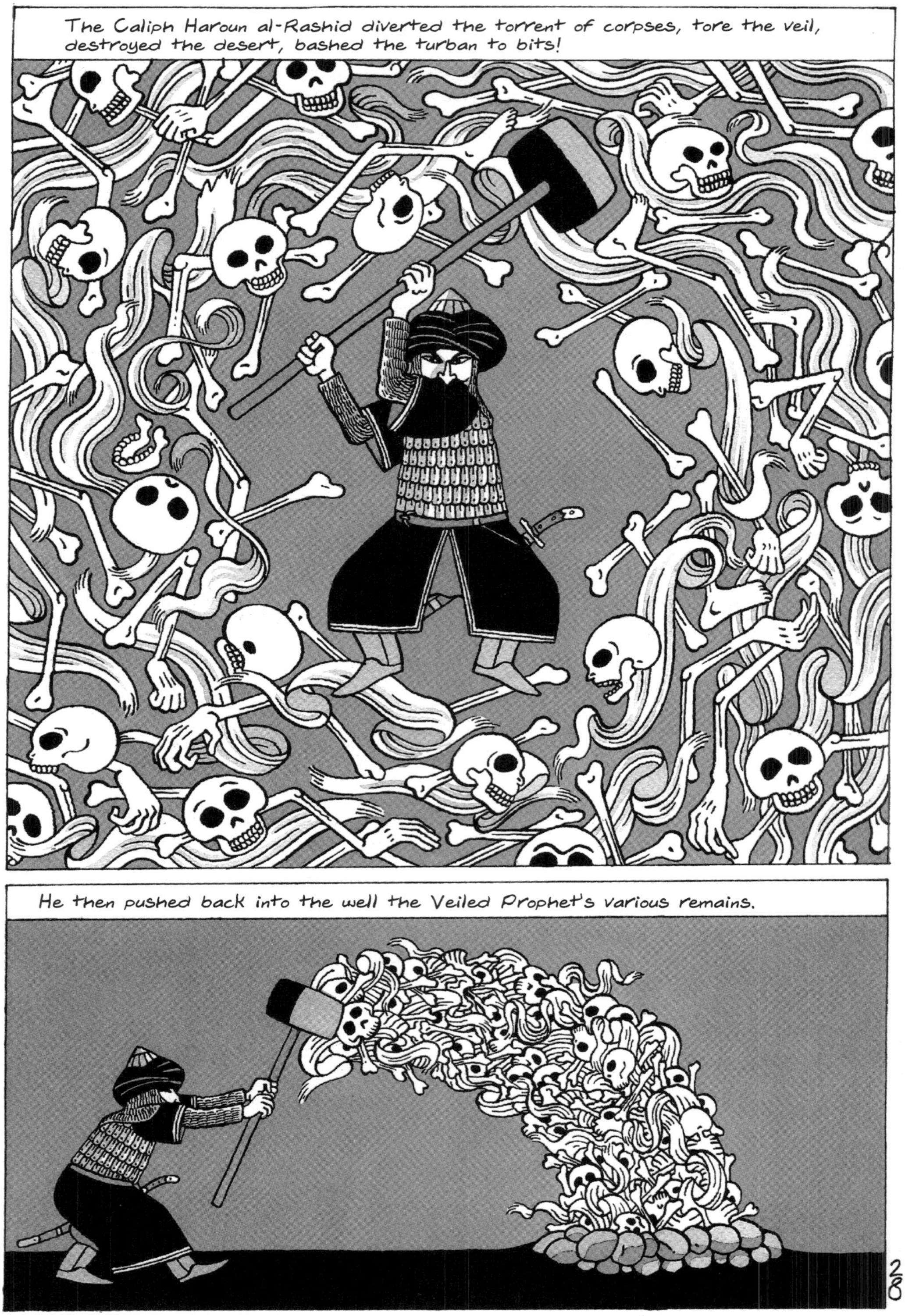
The Caliph Haroun al-Rashid diverted the torrent of corpses, tore the veil, destroyed the desert, bashed the turban to bits!
He then pushed back into the well the Veiled Prophet's various remains.

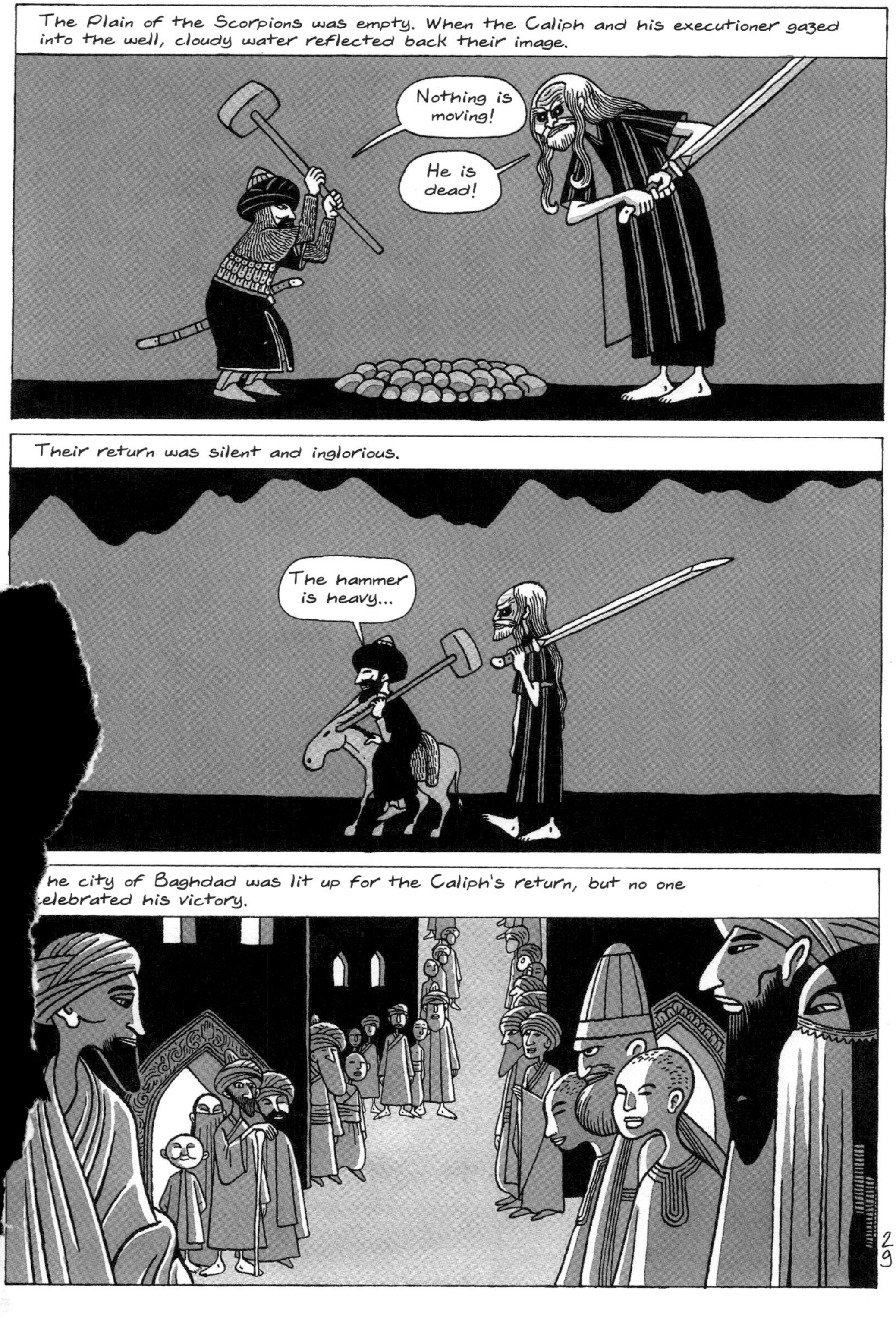
The Plain of the Scorpions was empty. When the Caliph and his executioner gazed into the well, cloudy water reflected back their image.
Nothing is moving!
He is dead!
Their return was silent and inglorious.
The hammer is heavy...
he city of Baghdad was lit up for the Caliph's return, but no one
elebrated his victory.

Without knowing exactly why, he sensed his victory to be illusory. One night, the answer came to him.

The sky was black as the walls of a well. The moon, minuscule, appeared to be a distant aperture!

Suddenly the Veiled Prophet was framed by the aperture.

And then the Caliph realized that he was nothing but a dead man, scrabbling amidst the others, at the bottom of the well.

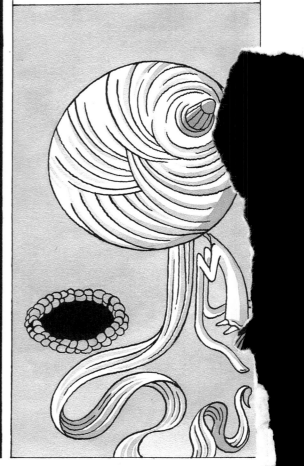